SMART CONTRACTS

This book brings together a series of contributions by leading scholars and practitioners to examine the main features of smart contracts, as well as the responses of key stakeholders in technology, business, government and the law.

It explores how this new technology interfaces with the goals and content of contract law, introducing and evaluating several mechanisms to improve the 'observability' and reduce the costs of verifying contractual obligations and performance. It also outlines various 'design patterns' that ensure that end users are protected from themselves, prevent cognitive accidents, and translate expectations and values into more user-oriented agreements.

Furthermore, the chapters map the new risks associated with smart contracts, particularly for consumers, and consider how they might be alleviated. The book also discusses the challenge of integrating data protection and privacy concerns into the design of these agreements and the broad range of legal knowledge and skills required.

The case for using smart contracts goes beyond 'contracts' narrowly defined, and they are increasingly used to disrupt traditional models of business organisation. The book discusses so-called decentralised autonomous organisations and decentralised finance as illustrations of this trend.

Smart Contracts is designed for those interested in looking to deepen their understanding of this game-changing new legal technology.

Smart Contracts

Technological, Business and Legal Perspectives

Edited by
Marcelo Corrales Compagnucci
Mark Fenwick
and
Stefan Wrbka

• HART •
OXFORD • LONDON • NEW YORK • NEW DELHI • SYDNEY

HART PUBLISHING
Bloomsbury Publishing Plc
Kemp House, Chawley Park, Cumnor Hill, Oxford, OX2 9PH, UK
1385 Broadway, New York, NY 10018, USA
29 Earlsfort Terrace, Dublin 2, Ireland

HART PUBLISHING, the Hart/Stag logo, BLOOMSBURY and the Diana logo are trademarks of Bloomsbury Publishing Plc

First published in Great Britain 2021

A catalogue record for this book is available from the British Library.

Library of Congress Cataloging-in-Publication data

Names: Corrales Compagnucci, Marcelo, 1978- editor. | Fenwick, Mark (Law teacher), editor. | Wrbka, Stefan, 1976- editor.

Title: Smart contracts : technological, business and legal perspectives / edited by Marcelo Corrales Compagnucci, Mark Fenwick and Stefan Wrbka.

Description: Oxford, UK ; New York, NY : Hart Publishing, an imprint of Bloomsbury Publishing, 2021. | Includes bibliographical references and index.

Identifiers: LCCN 2021004221 (print) | LCCN 2021004222 (ebook) | ISBN 9781509937028 (hardback) | ISBN 9781509948253 (paperback) | ISBN 9781509937035 (pdf) | ISBN 9781509937042 (Epub)

Subjects: LCSH: Smart contracts. | Contracts—Data processing. | Artificial intelligence—Law and legislation. | Blockchains (Databases)—Law and legislation.

Classification: LCC K845.E44 S63 2021 (print) | LCC K845.E44 (ebook) | DDC 346.02/20285—dc23

LC record available at https://lccn.loc.gov/2021004221

LC ebook record available at https://lccn.loc.gov/2021004222

ISBN: HB: 978-1-50993-702-8
ePDF: 978-1-50993-703-5
ePub: 978-1-50993-704-2

Typeset by Compuscript Ltd, Shannon

TABLE OF CONTENTS

LIST OF CONTRIBUTORS

Nicolas Cornell is Assistant Professor of Law at the University of Michigan Law School.

Marcelo Corrales Compagnucci is Associate Professor at the Centre for Advanced Studies in Biomedical Innovation Law (CeBIL), Faculty of Law, University of Copenhagen.

Alan Dahi Data Protection & Privacy Counsel.

Mark Fenwick is Professor of International Business Law at the Faculty of Law, Kyushu University.

Joshua S Gans holds the Jeffrey S Skoll Chair in Technical Innovation and Entrepreneurship and is a Professor at Rotman School of Management, University of Toronto.

Helena Haapio is Associate Professor of Business Law at the School of Accounting and Finance, University of Vaasa and a Contract Strategist at Lexpert Ltd.

George Kousiouris is Assistant Professor at the Department of Informatics and Telematics, Harokopio University of Athens.

Arianna Rossi is a Research Associate at the Interdisciplinary Centre for Security, Reliability and Trust (SnT), University of Luxembourg.

Matti Rudanko is Professor of Private Law at the School of Business, Aalto University.

Stylianos Tsarsitalidis is a Researcher at the Department of Informatics and Telematics, Harokopio University of Athens.

Erik PM Vermeulen is Professor of Business and Financial Law at the Department of Business Law, Tilburg University and Senior Legal Counsel at Signify (formerly Philips Lighting).

W Gregory Voss is Associate Professor of Business Law at TBS Business School.

Kevin Werbach is Professor of Legal Studies and Business Ethics at the Wharton School, University of Pennsylvania.

Stefan Wrbka is Unit Head and Academic Coordinator for Business Law at the University of Applied Sciences for Management and Communication, Vienna.

Introduction: The Technology, Use-Cases and Law of Smart Contracts

MARCELO CORRALES COMPAGNUCCI, MARK FENWICK AND STEFAN WRBKA

Smart contracts – self-executed, autonomous agreements in the form of computer code hosted on a blockchain – are, according to many observers, poised to disrupt the theory and practice of contracting. The perceived advantages of smart contracts are manifold. They can facilitate the performance and execution of agreements without the necessity of intermediaries and are said to provide better security, enforcement and verification systems than traditional contracts. Moreover, they seem to be immutable, irrevocable and cost-efficient. This makes smart contracts an attractive and convenient option for many different types of agreement, particularly in a business context.

A smart contract is a tamper-proof, digital agreement that runs on a decentralised blockchain. As such, smart contracts have two obvious advantages over traditional arrangements. First, smart contracts are shared records, meaning that the parties do not need to keep a personal copy. This is a significant advantage, especially for modern companies where departments operating as silos may have conflicting working procedures resulting in no single or reliable record of truth.

Second, smart contracts are reliable, and execution can be relied upon to a greater degree than in the past. In traditional agreements, the deal might not be implemented as initially agreed by the parties, either due to a choice or mistake. Smart contracts operate in the blockchain environment where they are executed exactly as written and do not require any approval at each step. If the predetermined conditions are fulfilled, then the agreement is performed automatically.

Today, many transactions include a third party to handle the counterparty risk that another party defaults on their obligations. The parties may be reluctant to perform their obligations if there is no guarantee that the counterparty will reciprocate. One way to think about the emergence of platforms, such as Uber or Airbnb, is that they provide structural mechanism to solve this problem of counterparty risk.

Blockchain's decentralised infrastructure, however, generates and guarantees trust without the need for intermediaries. According to advocates of these technologies, blockchain replaces trusted third parties with an open and secure protocol that all parties can trust. And, crucially, neither party can control or change the contents of the blockchain ledger as it is decentralised. Central servers are replaced with a decentralised network of computers that record all transactions in the shared ledger. In this way, distributed computing ensures the ledger is always accurate, and the decentralised network keeps the ledger secure.

As such, smart contracts are a scripting language overlaid on the blockchain that enables transactions on a blockchain that mirror 'real life' contracts by defining if/then conditions. For example, *if* an asset hits a certain price on a specific date, *then* a payout should be made to the other party (or parties) to the contract. A smart contract developer could programme the contract conditions according to any specifications. The if/then parameters are then tied to inputs and outputs of the smart contract. To take a simple example, consider a smart contract in the case of a car loan. If the borrower misses a payment (tracked via a blockchain-like technology) then the contract/code would not allow the use and operation of the car, ie, the contract would be automatically 'enforced' via network technologies that disable the vehicle, rather than through the use of a third party. Such contracts may produce efficiency, timing and performance improvements as a result of the automation of the contract's terms. This automation is achieved by computer code, which controls the automated performance in the context of an Internet of Things environment where digital devices are interconnected.

As this simple example shows, a smart contract utilises code to execute an agreement. In addition, the term 'smart contract' is also often used to refer to traditional text-based contracts in which the ordinary language text references the use of such a 'code-only contract' to effect some (but not necessarily all) of the provisions.

While smart contracts can be applied in many different situations, they are still in an early phase of development – they are a relatively new and untested technology and the range of possible and effective use cases is still being worked out. At present, the actual tasks that smart contracts can perform are relatively basic and straightforward. However, as the adoption of blockchain-based platforms and applications accelerates, the expectation is that smart contracts will become increasingly sophisticated and capable of handling more complex and diverse transactions.

However, the deployment of smart contracts in the real world still needs further testing. The relative immaturity of the technology makes them potentially vulnerable to hacking. The lack of regulation is also a bottleneck for the development of more sophisticated forms of contract. This means that we need a more integrated or interdisciplinary approach to such contracts. There are still multiple concerns to be resolved relating to the technology, business models, appropriate markets, consumers and the law. Moreover, such contracts inevitably raise regulatory issues that need to be addressed by policymakers. Several countries have already started to develop new regulatory approaches, as legal commentators identify issues with such agreements.

Addressing the many challenges created by smart contracts requires going beyond a single disciplinary perspective or frame of reference. In particular, the integration of technological, business and legal issues is crucial. This edited volume brings together a series of contributions by leading scholars and practitioners currently working in this space to examine the main issues that are driving the development of smart contracts, as well as the current response of key stakeholders in technology, business, government and the law. As such, the book explores the critical technical, business and legal challenges created by these potentially game-changing technologies and attempts to devise sound practical solutions in a broader scope regarding the functional and non-functional requirements of such contracts.

* * *

In exploring these themes, this book comprises eight substantive chapters and some concluding reflections on the future.

By way of an overview of critical themes and debates, in chapter one Kevin Werbach and Nicolas Cornell provide a general introduction to smart contracts and the technologies underlying them. Such contracts were first theorised more than 20 years ago, but the recent development of Bitcoin and blockchain technologies rekindled excitement about their potential among technologists and industry. Start-up companies and major enterprises alike are now developing smart contract solutions for an array of markets, purporting to offer a digital 'bypass' around traditional contract law.

For lawyers, smart contracts pose an important and challenging question: Do smart contracts offer a superior solution to the problems that contract law addresses? This chapter aims to understand the potential and limitations of smart contracts from the perspective of this question. It concludes that smart contracts offer novel possibilities, may significantly alter the commercial world and will, over time, demand new and innovative legal responses. But smart contracts will not displace contract law. Understanding why can bring into focus the essential role of contract law as a remedial institution. In this way, smart contracts help illuminate the central role of contract law more than they obviate it.

Joshua S Gans (chapter two) proceeds from the observation that smart contracts stored on a blockchain are potentially self-executing, but this ultimately depends on the state of information recorded on the blockchain ledger itself. His chapter demonstrates that by improving the 'observability' of smart contracts and reducing the costs of verifying contractual obligations and performance, the use cases of feasible contracts can be significantly enlarged. Moreover, by providing commitments to various monetary payments, a blockchain can potentially create a foundation for mechanisms that have been shown to overcome the traditional difficulties of contractual incompleteness. This claim is demonstrated using an international trade environment example, but the implications of this argument are far-reaching. Thus, even though smart contracts must respect the incentives of decision-makers in their obligations, they can use easily verifiable elements and create incentives to reduce hold-up and other commonly experienced contractual difficulties.

Matti Rudanko (chapter three) explores self-enforcing and tamper-proof smart contracts from the perspective of contract law, particularly the variety of liability based contractual remedies and the adaptiveness of contracts to shifting real-life circumstances. Moreover, the possibilities of linguistic analysis and computer sciences are considered in the research on coded languages in their relationship with natural languages, including questions of (oftentimes intentional) ambiguity and the flexibleness of language. This connects with the implementation of traditional contract law principles in the context of smart contracts, eg, the protection of the weaker party, by the use of indeterminate legal concepts such as good faith and equity that are, based on contract law-specific reasoning. Special attention is drawn to the contract law analysis of the intention of parties to conclude a contract. A novel approach to regulating smart contracts is developed by seeking models from securities markets, which also involve anonymous contracting. The chapter concludes with some reflections on smart contracts from the broader perspective of the principle of the rule of law and legal certainty.

W Gregory Voss (chapter four) begins with the observation that, despite the apparent potential of smart contracts to streamline transactions in many areas of business and government, they may also be subject to the provisions of data protection and privacy laws since personal data is often going to be processed. The chapter focuses on the European Union's General Data Protection Regulation (GDPR) as the most significant and influential data protection legislation, given its omnibus nature and extraterritorial scope.

By their nature, smart contracts raise difficulties for the classification of the various actors involved, which will have an impact on their responsibilities under the law and their potential liability for any violations. The analysis focuses primarily on the role of the data controller in the context of blockchain technology used in smart contracts. In doing so, the significance of classification is highlighted in the context of the GDPR.

Furthermore, certain rights granted to data subjects under the GDPR may be difficult to guarantee in smart contracts, such as the right to rectification and the right to erasure – the so-called 'right to be forgotten'. The chapter addresses these issues, along with the relevant advisory guidance and recommendations, such as the use of encryption to make data inaccessible, and the storage of data off-chain. The critical distinction between anonymised data and personal data is explained, together with its practical implications in smart contract settings. Finally, the GDPR requirements of data minimisation, data security ('integrity and confidentiality') and 'privacy by design' are discussed. These requirements highlight how data protection and privacy must be considered when smart contracts are designed and implemented, adding to the costs of utilising such agreements.

Arianna Rossi and Helena Haapio (chapter five) approach smart contracts from the perspective of legal design. Legal design is an emerging interdisciplinary approach that merges proactive legal thinking with design thinking. Together, they place the end-user and user experience (UX) at the centre of the discussion and apply human-centred design principles to prevent or, at least, mitigate real-world problems experienced by many users. The approach is increasingly used in fields such as contracting and privacy. This chapter introduces legal design in the context of health data sharing based on smart contracts. In particular, the chapter explores the opportunities that design patterns offer to respond to recurring challenges, to protect people from themselves, prevent cognitive accidents and translate expectations and values into design-oriented requirements. The user interface layer (UI), when properly designed and built, allows users to translate their intentions into a form that meets their objectives and is legally sound. The chapter explores these issues in the context of healthcare contracts. The goal? Promoting transparency and trust in smart contracts.

Stefan Wrbka (chapter six) discusses smart contracts in the context of unfair contract terms. Twenty-five years ago, the European Economic Community responded to the increased use of standard form contracts with the adoption of the Unfair Contract Terms Directive (UCTD). The goal was to lay down minimum protective standards to ensure that consumers would not be deprived of their statutory rights in B2C transactions by lopsided, business-friendly crafted standardised contract regimes. The UCTD did not intend to stop the use of standard form contracts. Instead, it primarily aimed to strike a balance between the business-side interests in utilising contractual templates to save time and transaction costs and the consumer-side interest in enjoying mandatory protective standards. With the rise of smart contracts, the idea to save both time and money has reached the next level. Advancements in digital technology (paired with legal expertise) are often deemed to increase contractual certainty, speed up contractual negotiation, conclusion and execution phases, and lower transaction costs. These perceived advantages do not come risk-free, however. Smart contracts can be understood as a development of standard form contracts in the sense that they are designed and crafted by their primary users – professional sellers and service providers – with the help of IT experts. Consumers have little influence on this process. The chapter argues that the likely risk that results from this unilateral making of smart contracts needs to be considered in regulatory efforts to guarantee a similar degree of balance of interests as the UCTD envisaged concerning ordinary standard form contracts. This becomes even more obvious when one thinks of the automatic enforcement mechanisms embedded in smart contract regimes.

Stylianos Tsarsitalidis, Marcelo Corrales Compagnucci, George Kousiouris and Alan Dahi (chapter seven) investigate the broad range of real-world applications of smart contracts and relevant rules associated with them by examining the requirements coming from supply chain management and the current technology landscape. Issues such as copyright protection, product delivery, etc, have been enforced through various technological means. However, more dynamic means are now needed. The modern supply chain is a complex network of suppliers and creators. It has become increasingly difficult to control and track abnormal conditions occurring during manufacturing, delivery, sale and management. The chapter uses the AffectUs:TagItSmart semantic and event detection framework as a use case example to demonstrate how the aforementioned concepts could be implemented. The basic idea is that relevant pseudo-code can be used as triggering logic or core rules in potential smart contracts for supply chains. The transformation of these rules and the use of semantics will provide a more effective and multilayered end-to-end supply chain solution that can aid in the integration with a smart contract rationale.

Mark Fenwick and Erik PM Vermeulen (chapter eight) locate the emergence of smart contracts and blockchain, more generally, in the context of ongoing technology-driven changes in the organisation and governance of business, in particular, a trend towards more decentralised business models and organisational forms. The closed, hierarchical modern corporation, which was so successful in an earlier phase of industrial capitalism, is less suited to the demands of an innovation-driven economy. In the context of the digital transformation, flatter, more open and distributed forms of operating and governing business have emerged. This chapter argues that, in order to understand their historical significance, the emergence and proliferation of smart contracts need to be located in this broader narrative. The chapter considers more recent use cases of smart contracts to highlight the diversity and disruptive potential of these technologies. In particular, the chapter discusses recent developments in decentralised autonomous organisations (DAOs) and decentralised finance (DeFi).

Chapter nine concludes with some reflections by the editors on the current situation and prospects of smart contracts. Various ongoing uncertainties – technological, business and legal – are described. In particular, as a blockchain-based technology, many of the challenges of developing and deploying smart contracts are the same as blockchain and need to be considered together. Nevertheless, in spite of these remaining and significant uncertainties, there is widespread interest in blockchain and business-related initiatives considering blockchain. The fact that so many 'old world' organisations, as well as younger start-ups, are exploring possible uses of blockchain, as well as smart contracts is, at least, suggestive that it is not all just hype and that something significant is happening.

1

Contracts: Ex Machina*

KEVIN WERBACH AND NICOLAS CORNELL

I. Introduction

Technological advancements hold the potential to alter our very conception of the law. It is already common to suggest that technologies can operate as a kind of law, regulating the behaviour of users.[1] But, thus far, traditional legal enforcement has generally remained available as a backstop. Is it possible for emerging technologies to displace the law even for enforcement, law's historically essential province? In this chapter, we examine a significant contemporary example: digitally enforced smart contracts based on the distributed cryptocurrency technology of Bitcoin and the blockchain that facilitates it. Enthusiasts of various stripes believe that smart contracts offer the potential to displace the legal system's core function of enforcing agreements.[2]

It has traditionally been assumed that enforceable agreements – the lifeblood of the modern economic and social world – require the backing of a legal system. Nearly four centuries ago, Thomas Hobbes described the impossibility of binding agreements without the law:

> If a covenant be made, wherein either of the parties perform presently, but trust one another; in the condition of mere nature (which is a condition of war of every man against every man,) upon any reasonable suspicion, it is void: but if there be a common power set over them both, with right and force sufficient to compel performance, it is not void. For he that performeth first, has no assurance the other will perform after, because the bonds of words are too weak to bridle men's ambition, avarice, anger, and other passions, without the fear of some coercive power .... But in a civil estate, where there a power set up to constrain those that would otherwise violate their faith ... he which by the covenant is to perform first, is obliged so to do.[3]

* Adapted from K Werbach and N Cornell, 'Contracts Ex Machina' (2017) 67 *Duke Law Journal* 313.

[1] See generally L Lessig, Code and Other Laws of Cyberspace (New York, Basic Books, 1999).

[2] See M Byrne, 'Do Lawyers Have a Future?' (20 September 2016) *The Lawyer*, available at www.thelawyer.com/issues/online-september-2016/do-lawyers-have-a-future-2; A Cunningham, 'Decentralisation, Distrust & Fear of the Body – The Worrying Rise of Crypto-Law' (December 2016) 13 *Scripted* 237, available at perma.cc/PAP2-VWVA.

[3] T Hobbes, *Leviathan* (Oxford, Oxford University Press, 1996) 91 (originally published in 1651). See generally AT Kronman, 'Contract Law and the State of Nature' (1985) 1 *Journal of Law, Economics & Organization* 5.

Hobbes's basic idea – that binding agreements require a system to ensure that counterparties can trust one another to perform – is an intuitive and powerful argument for the essential role of the law.[4]

Yet recent technological advances have led to speculation that smart contracts might largely, or entirely, displace the apparatus of contract law.[5] As one commentator succinctly puts this radical claim, 'Smart contracts don't [need] a legal system to exist: they may operate without any overarching legal framework. De facto, they represent a technological alternative to the whole legal system'.[6] Mainstream legal trade journals wonder whether 'innovations offered by the Bitcoin 2.0 generation of technology may create a world where … technology renders some contract causes of action obsolete'.[7] Even world leaders have taken notice: Russian Prime Minister Dmitry Medvedev declared that 'Smart [c]ontracts represent [a] new challenge to legal regulation. Systems creating such contracts live by their own rules, beyond the boundaries of law'.[8] In short, smart contracts may offer the hope – or possibly the threat – of circumventing Hobbes's age-old essential role for the law.

The reaction to these new possibilities runs the gamut, from gleeful triumph to killjoy scepticism. Supporters claim smart contracts will obviate the need for contract law, revolutionise business arrangements, and restructure property ownership.[9] Sceptics see the blockchain foundation as little more than a Ponzi scheme. Some technologists argue that, despite their name, smart contracts have nothing to do with contracts.[10] One group conspicuously absent from the debate over smart contracts is contract law scholars.

Upon inspection, the story is complex. Smart contracts may or may not transform the world, but they provide real benefits and seem likely to enjoy significant adoption over time. They represent the mature end of the evolution of electronic agreements over several decades. Firms can achieve significant cost savings and efficiency gains when using computers to automate contracting. Smart contracts could greatly extend those benefits, by taking advantage of Bitcoin and the blockchain as open platforms for secure exchange of value without mutual trust.[11] As they are adopted, or used in lieu of traditional contracting, smart contracts will

[4] cf A Ripstein, 'Private Order and Public Justice: Kant and Rawls' (2006) 92 *Virginia Law Review* 1391, 1418.

[5] See D Tapscott and A Tapscott, *Blockchain Revolution: How the Technology Behind Bitcoin Is Changing Money, Business, and the World* 47 (New York, Portfolio, 2016).

[6] A Savelyev, 'Contract Law 2.0: "Smart" Contracts as the Beginning of the End of Classic Contract Law' (2016) National Research University Higher School of Economics Working Paper No. BRP 71/ LAW/2016 21, available at papers.ssrn.com/sol3/papers.cfm?abstract_id=2885241.

[7] A Hinkes, 'Blockchains, Smart Contracts, and the Death of Specific Performance' *Inside Counsel* (29 July 2014), available at https://perma.cc/6FSQ-TT47.

[8] Savelyev, 'Contract Law 2.0' (2016) 15.

[9] See, eg Norton Rose Fulbright LLP, Can Smart Contracts Be Legally Binding Contracts? (2016) 2, available at perma. cc/SKV7-Z8P8.

[10] See, eg 'Explainer: Smart Contracts', *Monax*, available at perma.cc/45AT-KUEF.

[11] See generally K Werbach, 'Trust, But Verify: Why the Blockchain Needs the Law' (2018) 32 *Berkeley Technology Law Journal* 489.

force courts, legislatures and other legal actors to confront difficult questions about the application of basic contract doctrines.

They will not, however, replace contract law. While smart contracts can meet the doctrinal requirements of contract law, they serve a fundamentally different purpose. Contract law is a remedial institution. Its aim is not to ensure performance *ex ante*, but to adjudicate the grievances that may arise *ex post*. Smart contracts bring this core function of contract law into sharper relief, as they eliminate the act of remediation by admitting no possibility of breach. But, the needs that gave rise to contract law do not disappear. If the parties do not or cannot represent all possible outcomes of the smart contract arrangement *ex ante*, the results may diverge from their mutual intent. The parties' expression may also not produce legally sanctioned outcomes, as in the case of duress, unconscionability and illegality. Promise-oriented disputes and grievances will not disappear, but their complexions will shift. In such scenarios, either the parties or the state will seek to reintroduce the machinery of contractual adjudication. Once one properly appreciates what is – and what is not – the function of contract law, it becomes evident that the reports of its death are greatly exaggerated.

The remainder of this chapter unfolds as follows. In section II, we evaluate smart contracts, which have been undertheorised so far, by asking how existing legal categories might apply to smart contracts. In section III, we consider whether smart contracts can serve as a substitute for contract law. We answer this question in the negative, by analysing the larger question of what contract law is for. In section IV, we consider likely responses to the practical and doctrinal questions we raise. Section V concludes.

II. Conceptualising Smart Contracts

A. Are Smart Contracts Contracts?

The first important question that smart contracts pose is: Are they actually contracts? Ultimately, we think the answer is 'yes'. But this question turns out to be ambiguous, requiring the answer to another question first: What do we mean by a 'contract'? Different ways of defining contracts, in terms of legal enforceability, intent of the parties, or an exchange of promises, all complicate the analysis of whether smart contracts are contracts at all. After considering such standard definitions, we will suggest that smart contracts should nonetheless be considered contracts because they are agent-generated mechanisms to shift rights and obligations.

According to the standard legal definition, a contract is a promise or an agreement that is legally enforceable.[12] This definition, though widely accepted, has

[12] eg, American Law Institute, *Restatement (second) of Contracts* (Philadelphia, American Law Institute, 1981) § 1 ('A contract is a promise or a set of promises for the breach of which the law gives a remedy, or the performance of which the law in some way recognizes as a duty').

the unfortunate linguistic consequence of implying that agreements that turn out to be unenforceable were not contracts to begin with. Terms like 'unconscionable contract', 'fraudulent contract' and 'illegal contract' all become something like oxymorons. Even commonplace judicial iterations of this standard, like 'To be legally enforceable, a contract must be supported by consideration',[13] become essentially redundant.

We care about whether smart contracts should be understood to be contracts in the ordinary sense, whether they are enforceable or not. So it seems that we need a different definition of 'contract' for these purposes. One way to understand the question would be: Do smart contracts constitute promises or agreements that are *intended* to be legally enforceable? Corresponding to this formulation of the question, another definition of a contract is an agreement intended to be legally enforceable, whether it turns out to be or not. This definition has the advantage of avoiding the issues raised above, because it leaves open the question of enforceability. The unenforceable contract is still, conceptually, a contract as long as the parties thought that it would be enforceable, wrong though they may have been.

Of course, the intent that matters here is objective, not subjective, intent as it is manifested by the actions of the parties. As Judge Hand famously explained:

> A contract has, strictly speaking, nothing to do with the personal, or individual, intent of the parties. A contract is an obligation attached by the mere force of law to certain acts of the parties, usually words, which ordinarily accompany and represent a known intent.[14]

Still, according to this understanding, a contract exists if and only if the actions of the parties, judged objectively, manifest an intention that an agreement is to be legally enforceable.

When applied to smart contracts, this definition raises a serious issue. Smart contracts are designed to eliminate the need for legal enforcement. The central feature of a smart contract – what supposedly makes them smart – is that legal enforcement will not be necessary, or even possible. In a very real way, smart contracts are *not* intended to be legally enforceable. This is not to suggest that they are intended to be legally invalid; rather, the question of legal enforcement should never arise. In this sense, smart contracts are *not* intended to be enforced in a legal proceeding. This lack of intent may lead to the conclusion that, even conceptually, smart contracts are not truly contracts at all. They may look more like so-called gentlemen's agreements intended to be carried out, but never intended to reach a courtroom.

This appearance would be misleading, however, because it is quite different to intend that a solution will not be needed than to intend that it will be unavailable. I do not intend that my car will be needed as a vehicle for escaping the zombie

[13] See, eg *Hartbarger v Frank Paxton Co*, 857 P.2d 776, 780 (N.M. 1993).

[14] *Hotchkiss v. Nat'l City Bank*, 200 F. 287, 293 (S.D.N.Y. 1911); see also *Lucy v Zehmer*, 84 S.E.2d 516, 522 (Va 1954) ('If his words and acts, judged by a reasonable standard, manifest an intention to agree, it is immaterial what may be the real but unexpressed state of his mind.'); Restatement (Second) or Contracts (1981) §17 cmt. c ('[I]t is clear that a mental reservation of a party to a bargain does not impair the obligation he purports to undertake.').

apocalypse, but if the zombie apocalypse comes, I do not intend to abandon my car and traverse the wasteland on foot. By the same token, smart contracts are not intended to be enforced by a court, but that's not to say that, if they end up in court, the parties intend them to be unenforceable.

It is better to think of a contract as any agreement that is meant to have practical consequences on the rights and duties of the parties – that is, is not merely aspirational.[15] This avoids the above difficulty, because whether legal enforcement was anticipated is irrelevant.[16] Smart contracts would be contracts as long as they manifest an exchange of concrete obligations. They would be contracts as long as they are meant to alter concretely the normative relation between the parties.

Yet there is still some difficulty with this definition, because this understanding of a contract requires an exchange of promises or obligations. Do smart contracts involve promises or obligations? In a significant sense, no. The smart contract sets in motion machinery that the parties cannot subsequently prevent. The smart contract is not fulfilled by some further action of a contracting party, but rather by the completion of this mechanical process. As an analogy, if Bob balances a pail of water on top of a door, he does not promise to drop water on whoever next opens the door. Rather, he has merely set up the mechanical process by which that will inevitably happen. In a similar way, a smart contract to transfer one bitcoin upon such-and-such event occurring is not really a promise at all. A smart contract would not say, 'I will pay you one bitcoin if such-and-such happens', but rather, 'You will be paid one bitcoin if such-and-such happens'.

Some of the computer scientists working on smart contracts appear to be vaguely aware of this point. For example, Ethereum's White Paper states that its contracts 'should not be seen as something that should be "fulfilled" or "complied with"; rather, they are more like "autonomous agents" that live inside of the Ethereum execution environment'.[17] As this suggests, the language of 'contracts' is a poor fit, because this sort of smart contract is not an exchange of promises or commitments. Creation of a smart contract – while setting certain events in motion – does not commit any party to do anything or make any prospective promise.

Nevertheless, we believe that smart contracts are, at the conceptual level, still contracts. Though they might not constitute promises per se, smart contracts are voluntary mechanisms that purport to alter the rights and duties of the parties. After all, not all traditional contracts are executory, either. A deal may still count as a contract even though it leaves nothing open to be done or performed. A conveyance, for example, is a contract that alters rights presently, and does not involve any further, open promises. Smart contracts similarly constitute present agreements without further promises to perform. The simple Bitcoin smart contract

[15] See, eg WD Rankin, 'Concerning an Expectancy Based Remedial Theory of Promissory Estoppel' (2011) 69 *University of Toronto Faculty of Law Review* 116, 142.

[16] See G Klass, 'Intent to Contract' (2009) 95 *Virginia Law Review* 1437, 1460.

[17] Leithaus, 'Comment to "Isn't Ethereum Just a DSL for the Blockchain?"' REDDIT.COM, available at perma.cc/44DG-ZV54 ('I now regret calling the objects in Ethereum 'contracts', [*sic*] as you're meant to think of them as arbitrary programs and not smart contracts specifically').

just imagined is more like a present but contingent conveyance than it is like an executory promise to pay.

Thus, the smart contract somewhat breaks down the traditional line between executory and executed contracts. Like the conveyance, there is no promise left to be performed. Unlike the conveyance, though, the smart contract does not transfer property at the time. It is neither executory, insofar as there is no action left to be performed, nor is it executed, insofar as the result is yet to be accomplished. This causes conceptual difficulty. Smart contracts are both committing to something in the future, but not exactly making a promise. As we discuss below, this hybrid between *ex ante* commitment and *ex post* enforcement is novel.

In the end, though, this complication raises more questions about the conventional definitions of contracts than it does about whether smart contracts are contracts. There can be little doubt that smart contracts purport to alter the rights of the parties. The smart contract can explain, normatively as well as descriptively, why the bitcoin belongs to one party and not the other. It constitutes an agreement between the parties, and not an idle one. That, we believe, is the essence of a contract. But it is an interesting conceptual observation – illuminated by the smart contract – that even yet-to-be-executed contracts need not create promissory obligations.

There is one final difficulty to overcome. Are smart contracts really agreements? After all, they are simply a chunk of code. Superficially, they may look nothing like a set of declarations in the form 'Party X agrees to do such-and-such'. In general, a legal contract requires mutual assent, a 'meeting of the minds' – meaning that both parties must have expressed assent to the contract. That is, contracts require overt acts of assent.[18] Parties must engage in some expression that displays a shared understanding of the agreement, and a shared intent to bind themselves by its terms. Can smart contracts, simply a chunk of code in a blockchain, constitute such shared expression?

Nothing, so far as we can tell, prevents an expression of mutual assent from being formulated in code. In general, mutual assent can take many forms, so long as it clearly implies agreement. As Surden puts it, 'At a minimum, contract laws do not explicitly prohibit expressing contractual obligations in terms of data. More affirmatively, basic contracting principles actively accommodate data-oriented representation'.[19] In the present context, such data-oriented representations could easily include a blockchain. Where one party puts on the blockchain that assets of theirs will transfer to another party if some condition is satisfied, that seems to easily satisfy the requirement of an expression of assent.

This description in terms of a party putting the code on the blockchain does point to a wrinkle. Smart contracts, on Ethereum and presumably on other platforms, are by default unilateral, because only one party places them on the

[18] See, eg *Kitzke v Turnidge*, 307 P.2d 522, 527 (Or. 1957).
[19] H Surden, 'Computable Contracts' (2012) 46 *UC Davis Law Review* 629, 656.

blockchain. That is, the default involves one party specifying a transfer to another if certain conditions are met. Out of this default, one could approximate a bilateral or multilateral contract through the creation of two or more interrelated unilateral contracts. But two unilateral contracts are not precisely the same as a bilateral contract.[20] Fashioning interdependent conditions in a way that would emulate a bilateral contract might be a challenge for smart contracts. But for the purposes of this chapter, we will leave this issue aside and generally focus on unilateral contracts, because we think the same basic analysis would apply to bilateral contracts as they might be formulated as smart contracts.

To sum up, smart contracts are contracts. They are agreements to shift legal rights and responsibilities, no less than an agreement between two parties physically exchanging goods for payment over a counter. Their status as contracts might be obscured by the fact that the parties intend litigation to be impossible, may not make any promise, and may be expressed only in code. We suggest that these details do not alter the fact that smart contracts are, indeed, contracts in the important sense.

B. What's New Here?

Is a smart contract really any different than an ordinary one? The fact that smart contracts manifest agreements in machine-readable code is not novel, and neither is the possibility of automated performance based on rules-based judgments by computers. Both are features of data-oriented and computable contracts, which have been around for some time. And just because smart contracts are being implemented today on the exotic technology of the blockchain does not mean they raise novel or interesting legal issues. As Judge Frank Easterbrook has argued, new technologies do not necessarily call for new legal doctrines, when fact patterns are fundamentally unchanged.[21]

We consider below two perspectives suggesting that smart contracts are just technological manifestations of familiar contractual processes: escrow and self-help. One perspective focuses on the mechanism smart contracts use to ensure the execution of agreements, and the other focuses on the way smart contracts employ technology to impose a remedy outside of the court system. Each perspective sheds light on the nature of smart contracts. However, neither perspective fully captures the way smart contracts operate. Smart contracts are distinct from pre-existing forms because the digital code is not just a representation of the agreement; it is the agreement.

[20] See F Parisi, B Luppi and V Fon, 'Optimal Remedies for Bilateral Contracts' (2011) 40 *Journal of Legal Studies* 245, 247.

[21] See FH Easterbrook, 'Cyberspace and the Law of the Horse' (1996) *University of Chicago Legal Forum* 207, 208.

i. Smart Contracts as Escrow

One could view smart contracts as simple escrow arrangements with a digital veneer. In a typical escrow agreement, such as a house purchase, the buyer places funds in a special account. The escrow agent can only withdraw and disburse these funds to the seller after successful inspection and resolution of any other prepurchase issues. More generally, escrow suspends execution of a valid contract, and empowers a trusted third party to complete the process. Among other attributes, this approach overcomes the possibility of a prisoner's dilemma when the parties do not fully trust one another; otherwise, whichever one acted first would be vulnerable. The escrow arrangement substitutes mutual trust in the escrow agent for bilateral trust between the parties.

Smart contracts mimic the functionality of escrow. The smart contract code can place bitcoins or other cryptocurrency tokens in a suspended state on the blockchain, where they cannot be spent until performance of the contract. The execution step may be fully automated, or it may be implemented through multiple-signature verification, known as multisig.[22] In order for a multisig smart contract to execute, more than one party must provide its private encryption keys, indicating approval to execute the previously agreed-upon transaction. If Abby wishes to purchase digital goods from Bob using a smart contract, the parties can use a multisig smart contract, for which the ultimate execution requires the digital signatures of two out of three parties, typically the buyer, the seller and a trusted third party, such as an arbitrator. If the contract is satisfactory, the buyer and seller sign, executing the terms of the contract. If either party refuses, claiming breach, the arbitrator's signature decides the outcome.

Start-ups are already using the sophisticated capabilities of smart contracts to apply escrow in new ways. For example, CryptoCorp uses multisig for preclearance checks on Bitcoin transactions, similar to the way credit card companies decline transactions if the card has been subject to fraud or the payment exceeds preset limits.[23] BitHalo has implemented an escrow system for e-commerce transactions that avoids the participation of third parties entirely, by requiring collateral to be stored on the blockchain.[24]

The fact that smart contracts can implement escrow agreements does not make them identical to escrow. Conventional escrow depends upon a trusted firm or third party, because the parties themselves cannot serve as the escrow agents. A smart contract reliant on an arbitrator gives up the decentralised trust that the blockchain makes possible. Smart contracts performing only escrow-like functions are therefore more like standard data-oriented contracts. A true smart contract may employ the escrow-like mechanism of holding bitcoins temporarily,

[22] See B Davenport, 'What Is Multi-Sig, and What Can It Do?' Coin Center (1 January 2015), available at perma.cc/W4VN-HTQT.

[23] See J Villasenor, 'Could 'Multisig' Help Bring Consumer Protection to Bitcoin Transactions?' *Forbes* (28 March 2014), available at perma.cc/QGG8-LAXB.

[24] See D Ngo, 'BitHalo Releases Decentralized Escrow Client v2.1 to Rival PayPal, Western Union' *Cointelegraph* (12 January 2015), available at perma.cc/JY2K-CVCB.

but it does so through automated execution of scripts running on the network of computers maintaining the blockchain, without an escrow agent equivalent.

ii. Smart Contracts as Self-Help

Researcher Max Raskin provides a different interpretation of smart contracts. He views them not as legal enforcement at all, but as a form of self-help.[25] To Raskin, 'Automated execution of a contract is a pre-emptive form of self-help because no recourse to a court is needed for the machine to execute the agreement'.[26] He draws an analogy to starter interrupters, which are remote-controlled devices installed in cars to prevent them from operating. A creditor can invoke the starter interrupter if the lessee of the car fails to pay. As Raskin notes, such devices are likely to be legal in most states, under the self-help repossession provisions for secured creditors at Section 9-609 of the UCC.[27] A smart contract could serve the same function, by refusing to authorise operation of the car unless the creditor receives payment.

Viewing smart contracts as self-help mechanisms accurately places the emphasis on the *ex post* enforcement function.[28] The blockchain can be used to record contractual provisions, execute contractual obligations, and perform intermediary functions like escrow, but so can garden-variety digital contracts. It is only when disputes arise, or when the remedies provided in the contract must be invoked, that smart contracts do something special. The algorithmic enforcement mechanisms, running automatically on the blockchain computing fabric, replace judicial enforcement.

Self-help, traditionally, is a judicially supervised process. Courts may restrain creditors from 'disturbing the peace' to enforce their self-help rights, for example, or if a creditor's rights are inferior to other legal obligations, such as those of bankruptcy. With a smart contract, there is no one to restrain, because the smart contract code is immutable once embedded in the blockchain. A smart contract could even include terms that are illegal, unconscionable or otherwise legally unenforceable.

More deeply, the self-help model focuses on what smart contracts *do* to the exclusion of what they *say*. Functionally, the primary distinction between smart contracts and more limited data-oriented or computable contracts lies in enforcement. The smart contract, as we have explained, fully executes the agreement. It addresses the possibility of breach, not through the deterrent potential of judicial remedies, but by making breach practically impossible. The smart contract is not merely an accessory added to the end of the contractual process to mitigate the risk of breach.

Raskin's analogy between smart contracts and starter interrupters breaks down on closer examination. The starter interrupter is a mechanism introduced, after an

[25] M Raskin, 'The Law and Legality of Smart Contracts' (2017) 1 *Georgetown Law Technology Review* 305, 306.
[26] ibid 333.
[27] See ibid 332.
[28] See Z Sinel, 'De-Ciphering Self-Help' (2017) 67 *University of Toronto Law Journal* 31, 58–65.

agreement is reached, to enforce its terms; but, unlike smart contracts, this mechanism has nothing to do with the substance of the agreement. By contrast, a smart contract literally contains the terms of the agreement, transformed into machine-readable scripting code. The fact that the agreement is enforceable algorithmically, without the participation of legal institutions, is a commitment represented in the smart contract. Thus, the self-help model paints too limited a picture of smart contracts.

At the same time, the self-help model is too expansive. This analogy attributes functions to smart contracts that they do not actually perform; the smart contract itself does not perform the breach-limiting action, the blockchain and its computing nodes do. In the self-help model, by contrast, one party enforces the agreement consistent with, but *outside* the legal machinery of contract law. The smart contract is a component of a larger smart contract system, which ensures that, for example, the cryptocurrency tokens are transferred according to the contractual terms. Just as the state's *ex post* remediation role distinguishes a legal contract from an informal exchange of promises, the integration of specific contractual terms and a general enforcement infrastructure makes a smart contract smart. The distributed ledger software both instantiates the contractual terms and enforces the contractual obligations. These functions are distinguishable, but necessarily connected.

iii. Smart Contracts as Entire Agreements

Both the escrow model and the self-help model explain smart contracts as technical mechanisms overlaid on the basic contractual process. Escrow does so to facilitate performance, while self-help provides a remedy for non-performance. These tools may reduce transaction costs and thereby make contracting more efficient. They are not, however, strictly necessary to the outcome. Neither fully captures the essence of smart contracts, because both treat smart contracts as external enhancements to the contractual process. The distinctive aspect of smart contracts is not that they make enforcement easier; it is that they make enforcement unavoidable. In order to do so, they change the nature of the contract itself.

Nick Szabo, who named the concept of smart contracts back in the late 1990s, analogised them to vending machines, which take money and dispense products automatically.[29] In Szabo's example, the physical security of the device is sufficient to make breach less attractive than compliance. But alongside physical security, another element is at work. The vending machine takes cash, which is a bearer instrument. Once the coins or bills are in belly of the machine, value has been transferred. No third parties need to be brought into the process to facilitate or secure the exchange. Szabo's example does not easily translate to other payment mechanisms, like cheques or credit cards, which require a bank to validate the transaction. This step introduces transaction costs and delay, and it means

[29] See N Szabo, 'Formalizing and Securing Relationships on Public Networks' *First Monday* (1 September 1997).

the contracting process is no longer contained within the hardware and software of the vending machine. And, intermediary validation potentially changes the performance equation. The consumer can breach the agreement by instructing the bank to reverse the charge, even after receiving the product. At that point, the smart contract would no longer govern the relationship between the parties.

Cash works for a vending machine, but not for complex financial derivatives transactions, international supply chains or major crowdfunding initiatives. Only a limited subset of transactions are sufficiently localised, low value and low velocity for cash to be a viable option.[30] For this reason, Bitcoin and other cryptocurrencies are very important for the growth of smart contracts. Bitcoin tokens are digital bearer instruments, functionally equivalent to cash, yet flexible and scalable in the manner of credit cards. A blockchain-based smart contract, like a cash transaction, therefore involves the complete exchange of value.

If I buy an ebook for my Kindle on Amazon.com, a complete transfer of value does not occur immediately. When I click the 'buy' button, the company's computers transfer the ebook to my device, with associated digital rights to prevent additional copying, and they also process my credit card and debit my account. Yet, I am in a position to prevent a complete transfer of value, because I can still ask Amazon for a refund, or dispute the charge with the credit card company. This is possible because my contract with Amazon is executory – I have traded the ebook for the promise to pay my credit card issuer. Imagining the same exchange with a smart contract, by contrast, it is as though when I click the buy button, a drone picks up a stack of one-dollar bills from my house and flies them to Amazon. The contract fully executes with no human intervention. I can still dispute the transaction with Amazon, but now the contract is fully executed. Amazon has the cash; I am now asking them to return the money, rather than preventing them from receiving it.

Because the exchange of value is entirely contained in the smart contract environment, there is no need to look anywhere else. In other words, the contract *is* the scripting code that tells the network what to transfer and when. In the Amazon example, the site's computer system transfers the ebook and processes my credit card. Those machine instructions, however, are separate from my contract with Amazon, agreeing to exchange my payment information for a particular ebook. If Amazon's programmers make an error and send me an entirely different ebook, there is no question that my contract with Amazon controls, rather than the software code the computer system uses to effectuate the contract.

For the smart contract, in contrast, everything beyond the code is just commentary. The code is a necessary part of the agreement itself, whereas Amazon's software code is just a tool to execute the human-made contract. For example, imagine that at the same time I place my order for the ebook on Amazon's website, I type up a written agreement for a different book and send it to an Amazon customer service

[30] See J Bearman, 'The Rise and Fall of Silk Road: Part II' *Wired* (May 2015), available at perma.cc/4BCZ-LTBG (recounting the story of a Bitcoin exchange commonly used for drug sales and other illegal activity).

agent, who countersigns it. In the event of a dispute, there would be an evidentiary question as to which version of the agreement controlled. In the smart contract context, such an inquiry would be meaningless. The smart contract has the entire life of the contract immutably embedded into its code, which leaves no room for a separate written agreement to specify the parties' intent. If a court concludes that some writing better reflects the parties' meeting of the minds, it would be powerless to invalidate the smart contract; it would have to find some way to reverse the transfer of value *ex post*.

The notion that smart contracts can supersede legal enforcement has been tested in the real world. A group of developers associated with Ethereum created a distributed crowdfunding system in 2016 called The DAO.[31] It was designed to implement the concept of DAO, in which corporate governance and operations are conducted automatically through smart contracts. Users pledged Ether (the Ethereum cryptocurrency) in return for tokens that gave them authority to vote on projects to fund. Organisations seeking funding would sign up through another interface and collect Ether if they received sufficient votes. Despite the novelty of the arrangement, Ethereum users pledged over $150 million in Ether in a matter of weeks after The DAO launched.

Users signed up to participate in The DAO on a website that stated explicitly, in its terms of service, that the smart contract on the Ethereum blockchain was the controlling legal authority. Any human-readable documents or explanations, including those on the website, were 'merely offered for educational purposes and do not supercede [*sic*] or modify the express terms of The DAO's code set forth on the blockchain'.[32]

Within weeks of launch, something went wrong. A hacker took advantage of a bug in The DAO's code to siphon off over $60 million-worth of Ether. Although clearly an attempt at theft, the hack was executed through a series of smart contracts that were formally valid within the rules of The DAO. Even though the stolen funds were temporarily quarantined in an account, and not immediately disbursed, from the perspective of the smart contracting system, the transactions were perfectly legitimate. Even if a court ordered the funds returned, there was no one to carry out that order. Thus, there was no legal or technical way to recover them without undermining the entire system. Ultimately, the leaders of Ethereum project had to convince a majority of mining nodes to implement a 'hard fork', which split the entire Ethereum blockchain into two incompatible paths. Only through this dramatic step, which effectively killed off The DAO and undermined confidence in the Ethereum platform, could the stolen funds be returned.[33]

The DAO example shows the power of smart contracts, and also their limitations. Smart contracts seemed to be able to replace the legal system as an enforcement mechanism for The DAO users' contractual relationship with the

[31] C Jentzsch, 'Decentralized Autonomous Organization to Automate Governance' (unpublished manuscript), available at perma.cc/SE35-Y8CC.

[32] J Ditz, 'DAOs, Hacks and the Law' *Medium* (17 June 2016), available at perma.cc/N9M5-F2GT.

[33] See F Coppola, 'A Painful Lesson for the Ethereum Community' *Forbes* (21 July 2016), available at perma.cc/FRP2-7TDR.

crowdfunding system. However, doing so came at a significant cost. Because the only enforcement mechanism was the Ethereum network's computers executing the terms of The DAO software code, there was no way to distinguish between a legitimate string of transactions and one with malicious intent.

III. What Smart Contracts Teach us about Contract Law

As we have discussed, there are reasons to be sceptical about whether smart contracts can deliver all the hoped-for gains in efficiency and flexibility. But there is a much deeper, more theoretical reason to be sceptical of smart contracts. Even if the technology could deliver all that its proponents promise, it is not clear whether its implementation would be an improvement over courts, or simply orthogonal. Put simply, the question is whether smart contracts could do what courts do, only better. We think not. Although we can see why some conclude otherwise, we think that contract litigation plays a role in our social system that smart contracts do not even purport to replicate.

Ostensibly, smart contracts remove the role of courts as enforcement agents. One might say that the contract enforces itself, or that the code itself enforces it. This means that parties no longer have the escape hatch of litigation. Once the smart contract is made, the machinery for its execution is unavoidably set in motion, ending the parties' opportunity to affect the transaction *ex post*. This may be a bit of an overstatement. Parties can use multisig, for example, to maintain some control over the execution of the contract. And in extreme cases such as The DAO hack, the entire blockchain could conceivably be forked if enough network nodes agreed. Still, if smart contracts are to be a disruptive force in contracting, this potential turns on the ability to eliminate the possibility of breach and the resultant litigation to enforce.

Does this mean that smart contracts can replace courts in the adjudication of contract cases? Courts, it might be argued, serve the function of enforcing contractual obligations. But, because courts serve this function in a costly and time-consuming way, technological advancement offers the possibility of making courts obsolete; surpassed by mechanisms that can enforce obligations, and serve the same function, with greater efficiency and customisation.

Smart contracts thus offer a window into thinking about contract law at a theoretical level. Even if one were uninterested in the technology, smart contracts could illuminate foundational issues in the theory of contract. Their theoretical possibility, whether the technology can deliver or not, raises a pointed question about what function courts play when they adjudicate a contract case. Put another way, the basic question about whether smart contracts do what courts do, only better, introduces a reciprocal question about contract law more generally: Does contract law do what smart contracts aim to do? Taking smart contracts seriously is therefore a fruitful way to examine the function of courts and contract law.

In order to answer the question whether smart contracts can do what courts do, this section describes three competing conceptions of what role courts play – or ought to play – in contract cases. Each view informs how its proponents think that smart contracts might interact with contract law. Ultimately, we argue that through the correct understanding of contract law, it is clear that smart contracts cannot supplant the role that courts play. Smart contracts are not, even conceptually, a replacement for judicial contract adjudication.

Our argument in this section is bidirectional. Insofar as many readers may already intuitively grasp that smart contracts can, at best, avoid courts but cannot substitute for them, this section provides the argument and reasoning to support that understanding.

A. Contract Law as Enforcing Promises

According to one view, contract law provides legal enforcement for promises. When a promisor makes a commitment to a promisee, this commitment – the promise – generates an obligation to do the thing promised. Even without contract law, a moral obligation is created when one party makes a promise to another. While the exact source of this moral obligation is subject of philosophical dispute, there is little doubt that promises generate obligations. Contract law, the argument goes, serves to strengthen and support these moral obligations by creating corresponding legal obligations. At its core, contract law binds promisors, not simply morally, but also legally.

The paradigmatic articulation of the view that contract law enforces promises is Charles Fried's 1981 book, *Contract as Promise*.[34] For Fried, the capacity to make promises is a form of freedom, allowing parties to bind themselves and thus shape their obligations. By enforcing such voluntarily assumed obligations, the state supports the freedom of contracting parties. The core idea is that contracts are binding, as the self-imposed obligations of contracting parties. Contracts, like promises, are the result of voluntary acts performed with the intent to place the actor under an obligation. The ability to bind oneself in this way – to assume an obligation voluntarily – is itself a form of freedom. But one need not share Fried's account of promissory obligations in order to think that contract law's purpose is to provide legal obligations that correspond to the moral obligations of promises.[35]

The essential idea is that promises are an important part of human life, and that contract law supports promising by offering legal recognition and enforcement. Contract law layers legal obligation on top of our moral obligations in order to bolster them. By making it the case that a party must, legally, do what it has promised, we affirm that people ought to do what they promise, and we thereby affirm

[34] See generally C Fried, *Contract as Promise: A Theory of Contractual Obligation* (Oxford, Oxford University Press, 1981).

[35] See generally, eg, TM Scanlon, 'Promises and Contracts' in P Benson (ed), *The Theory of Contract Law* (Cambridge, Cambridge University Press, 2001) 86.

the institution of promising. The point of contract law, then, is to help ensure that people are truly bound by their promissory commitments.

From this perspective, contract law might appear incrementally more successful the more it affirms that promisors must do as they have promised. In this light, elements of contract law that diverge from ensuring that parties keep their promises may seem troubling.[36] Particularly, it may appear problematic that contract law generally imposes only expectation damages, rather than specific performance. Specific performance more closely matches our moral obligation to do the thing promised. Insofar as the point of contract law is to strengthen and affirm our moral obligations, and insofar as our moral obligations are to do as we have promised, then contract law should aim to align morality and legal obligation.

If one holds this conception of contract law's function, then smart contracts may seem like an appealing alternative to court-based contract law. Courts exert legal force upon us to do as we have promised, thus strengthening our voluntarily assumed commitments. But legal force is a relatively clumsy mechanism. If we want people to do as they have promised, then a mechanism that automatically and completely ensures performance may look like a triumph, at least to the extent that it does not come at the expense of other freedoms.

Smart contracts, according to this line of thought, are like specific performance on steroids and without the state's coercive machinery. Smart contracts make it the case that promisors will do precisely what they promise, radically strengthening promises. If this is the point of judicial contract enforcement, then it looks like smart contracts offer a superior technology, and smart contracts would leave judicial enforcement essentially obsolete.

Of course, there is room for concern within this picture of contract law as enforcing promises. First, one might suggest that smart contracts, by making performance inevitable, are no longer promises at all. If so, smart contracts would not reinforce the practice of promising. Whereas contract law supports promising by giving promisors legal reasons to perform, smart contracts do away with the need for reasons altogether, and fail to support the moral agency involved in promising. Pragmatically, it may not be obvious why we should value promising, apart from the reliable commitments that promising enables. But, assuming we should value promising for other reasons, then smart contracts highlight the fact that contract law is about creating or supporting reasons to fulfil our moral obligations, and not only about creating reliable consequences.

Second, one might think that contract law is not only about supporting promises, but about the community or state being the entity lending support. On this view, it is essential that contract law strengthens promising through a political medium. In a contract case, we collectively express our affirmation of an obligation and lend our resources to enforcing that obligation. Smart contracts, by contrast, would strengthen promissory obligations without this state involvement.

[36] See, eg SV Shiffrin, 'The Divergence of Contract and Promise' (2007) 120 *Harvard Law Review* 708, 749.

Of course, to their proponents, this is a key feature of smart contracts. But, to others, this might be a bug. Even though smart contracts would strengthen promises, it would be problematic that this strength fails to come from the political community. Smart contracts would thus raise worries similar to those expressed toward private arbitration or penalty clauses.[37] That is, one might worry that something is lost simply by transferring the power away from the political community.

Leaving aside worries like these, the general point is that if the function of contract law is to strengthen moral obligations to keep promises by adding legal coercion, then smart contracts seem well suited to supplant this function. In short, if contract law is about making people keep their promises, then smart contracts look like they can do that job even better than courts.

B. Contract Law as Voluntary Liability

A second view of contract law conceives it as a method to create legal liability voluntarily, in a way that is not necessarily connected to morality or promising. According to this view, contractual obligations need not correspond to moral obligations.[38] Instead, contractual obligations can be fashioned where it is in the interest of parties to create them. By creating legal liability, parties can create a distinctive obligation that can serve any number of purposes, from enhancing agency[39] to facilitating efficient transactions.[40]

There are three key elements in this second view. First, contracts – as opposed to promises – involve parties agreeing to legal liability if they fail to perform. The crucial element of contract law is that certain agreements are legally binding; that is, they are subject to agreed-upon legal sanctions for breach. But whether and how any agreement is legally binding is ultimately up to the parties.[41] Rather than understanding legal liability as parasitic on existing moral obligations, this view sees legal liability as the elective creation of the parties involved.

Second, the legal obligations of contract reflect parties opting into liability. Insofar as parties opt into a system of legal penalties, the legal obligations describe those actions to which a legal sanction will attach. Thus, by making it the case that a party will face a sanction for failing to perform, that party thereby generates its own obligation to perform.

Third, because contracting is about parties choosing to attach legal consequences to future actions, questions of contract law should address how to determine what the parties intended, or would have chosen, *ex ante*. The basic question is what

[37] See, eg, OM Fiss, 'Against Settlement' (1984) 93 *Yale Law Journal* 1073, 1075.

[38] See JS Kraus, 'The Correspondence of Contract and Promise' (2009) 109 *Columbia Law Review* 1603, 1617.

[39] See, eg, R Kar, 'Contract as Empowerment' (2016) 83 *University of Chicago Law Review* 759, 761.

[40] See, eg, CJ Goetz and RE Scott, 'Enforcing Promises: An Examination of the Basis of Contract' (1980) 89 *Yale Law Journal* 1261, 1266.

[41] See, eg, R Barnett, 'A Consent Theory of Contract' (1986) 86 *Columbia Law Review* 269, 319.

the parties would want, perhaps subject to certain additional nuances.[42] A range of contract doctrines can then be explained as default rules, presumed to be what most parties would want unless they explicitly indicate otherwise. Contract law, then, is fundamentally about enabling transactional activity, by creating a system in which one can voluntarily bind oneself through opting into flexible and predictable consequences for breach.

If this is what contract law does, then smart contracting again looks like it could supplant it. According to this second view, the fundamental purpose of contract law is allowing people to create reliable consequences, enabling them to shape their behaviour. The essential feature of contracts is the communication of information about what will happen in the future. Efficient or agency-enhancing transactions can only take place if such communication is intelligible and trusted.

Smart contracts offer the possibility of highly reliable communication about future outcomes. This is true in two ways. First, because the agreed-upon result occurs automatically, uncertainty about performance, and about judicial recognition, disappears. A promisee no longer needs to wonder whether the promise will be kept, or whether a court will recognise the breach. Second, because the code is itself the contract, provisions are laid out in precise, operational terms by definition, to a heightened degree as compared to traditional contract language.

In a well-functioning smart contract, the contract necessarily answers interpretive questions in determinative ways. In short, if contract law exists to facilitate reliance through the ability to opt into predictable future consequences, then smart contracts seem to serve this function even more seamlessly. If contract law is a commitment mechanism, then smart contracts seem to be a superior commitment mechanism.

Again, there is room for concern. Specifically, one might worry that the *ex ante* information costs to determine all contingencies could make smart contracting overly costly. While this is undoubtedly a significant concern, it is ultimately a practical rather than theoretical objection. If smart contracts came with an array of well-understood default rules, that could mitigate the *ex ante* information costs. To the extent that they persist, it would be a contingent matter to decide in what situations the information costs outweigh the gains in certainty. Smart contracts would, at least some of the time, be a better technology than *ex post* contract litigation. And this reflects the fact that, on this view, smart contracts and contract law serve the same underlying function.

C. Contract Law as *Ex Post* Adjudication

We believe that smart contracts are not, even theoretically, a substitute for contract law. Consequently, we believe that the above views about contract law's function,

[42] cf I Ayres and R Gertner, 'Filling Gaps in Incomplete Contracts: An Economic Theory of Default Rules' (1989) 99 *Yale Law Journal* 87, 91.

which appear to suggest that smart contracts could replace contract law, are unsatisfactory. These two arguments are mutually reinforcing: one can see the incommensurability of smart contracts and contract litigation by attending to the true function of contract law; and one can see the inadequacy of the above views about contract law by attending to the way in which smart contracts cannot serve the same function as contract law.

Both views of contract law described thus far assume an *ex ante* perspective that focuses on how contract law shapes our deliberations and motivations. That is, for both views, contract law is about giving us reasons to act. On the first view, contract law shapes our deliberation by supplementing our moral obligations with corresponding legal obligations. As such, contract law gives us an additional legal consideration in favour of keeping our promises. On the second view, contract law allows us to generate obligations that will shape our deliberations going forward, by electing to impose liability for some actions. As such, contract law creates motivations to comply, which need not correspond with our moral reasons, through the imposition of potential legal liability.

If one holds the second, motivation-creating view of contract law, then it is natural to see smart contracts as supplanting contract law. After all, why create motives for action when one can ensure the action itself? If contract law is about facilitating our actions going forward, then the smart contract seems like an appealing innovation.

But that is not what contract law is about. Contract law does not exist to alter our reasons going forward – though it surely does that. Rather, it exists to adjudicate the justice of a situation *ex post*. It is backward-looking. Its basic function is to decide whether one party has wronged another party by failing to perform a promised action. That is, contract law is a fundamentally remedial institution, not aimed at creating new reasons to perform, but aimed at resolving disputes, taking those reasons as already given. One can see this backward-looking, remedial character in the way that contract law waits for breach, waits for an aggrieved party to bring forward a complaint, and even then rarely orders conduct. We suggest that contract law is not about creating forward-looking reasons, because other mechanisms might serve that purpose equally or better.

A simple example can illustrate the differences between the three views. Suppose Abby promises Bob that she will pay him back the money that he is considering lending to her. By promising, Abby creates a moral obligation. She now has a special sort of reason to pay the money back. These points about obligation and reasons are true independent of the law. What might contract law add? On one view, it might add an additional obligation – a legal obligation – that corresponds with the moral obligation. So, Abby's moral reasons to pay the money back would now be bolstered by parallel legal reasons or legal motivations. On another view, contract law might add an option for an additional liability. By promising, Abby has subjected herself to moral responsibility, and in doing so, she has created reasons to perform by opening herself up to moral sanctions. In addition, contract law allows her, if she would like, to subject herself to even more accountability – legal accountability. Thus, she could create more, or different, motivations to perform by opening herself up to a new set of sanctions. The difference between these two views is that on the first, but not the second, the legal obligations correspond with the moral obligations. But, according to both answers, contract law adds further obligations and thus additional motivation to pay Bob back.

But an altogether different answer about what contract law adds is the view that contract law creates a forum to determine what happens if Abby does not perform.[43] On this view, contract law does not change anything about Abby's obligations. Those were complete the moment that she promised – she has reason to pay the money back because she promised to pay the money back.[44] Contract law did not make it that case that Abby *had to* do anything; Abby herself made it the case that she *had to* do something. Contract law adds something *ex post* to deal with failure. It is not about ensuring that she performs, but about responding if she does not. Contract law enables an avenue for Bob to complain if Abby does not fulfil her obligations.

One might think that this avenue for complaint feeds back into the reasons that Abby has to perform. And, in a way, that is true. Abby does get a reason to perform from contract law – specifically, she will be liable to a complaint from Bob if she does not. But that is an indirect, independently empty reason, because it is a new reflection of the reason that she already had. It would be almost absurdly circuitous to think that contract law's primary function was about shaping reasons in such a redundant way. It is much more straightforward to see contract law as fundamentally about adjudicating the wrongs of broken agreements, and the function of creating reason or motivation as incidental.

When one views contract law in this way, it is apparent that smart contracting does not even purport to do what contract law does. The two have fundamentally different objectives. Smart contracting functions to ensure action. Contract law functions to recognise and remedy grievances. Smart contracts could not – even in theory – replace contract law. At best, smart contracts might reduce the need for contract litigation. But that would not mean that smart contracts serve the same function in a superior fashion. Rather, shifting to smart contracts would mean a shift to an altogether different mode of interaction, and one not clearly superior.

IV. Smart Contracts in Practice

If smart contracts do something fundamentally different than contract law, does that mean legal scholars can safely ignore them? Perhaps it was all just a misunderstanding, borne out of Szabo's unfortunate choice of terminology two decades ago.

[43] See generally NB Oman, 'Consent to Retaliation: A Civil Recourse Theory of Contractual Liability' (2011) 96 *Iowa Law Review* 529.

[44] See J Raz, Morality of Freedom (Oxford, Clarendon Press, 1986) 35.

If he had called his idea 'intelligent agents' or 'virtual vending machines', perhaps there would be no reason to examine the legal implications further, but we believe there are still reasons. Our conclusion – that smart contracts are orthogonal to contract law – does not end the inquiry. Smart contracts will be used in situations otherwise subject to contract, and will still be nominally subject to contract law. Problems are likely to arise. These in turn will produce responses with real consequences, both for the parties involved, and for the development of contract law.

Proponents of smart contracts argue they will eliminate the friction of legal disputes. This view is overly optimistic. While the potential benefits of smart contracts are substantial, the potential problems are significant as well. There is a Frankenstein dimension to a smart contract: an instrument that fuses something innately human, entering into and enforcing agreements, with something mechanical, derived from scientific experiments. Science fiction authors since Mary Shelley have warned of the consequences of such cyborgs. Perhaps the benefits of smart contracts will exceed the costs. Perhaps the benefits can be magnified, or the costs minimised. We should, nonetheless, carefully assess both sides of the ledger.

Contract law is, of course, far from perfect. Yet by switching from the *ex post* adjudication of contract to the *ex ante* reduction of agreements to software code, smart contracts will in some cases merely shift problems rather than eliminate them. Smart contracts are likely to face two kinds of problems, practical and doctrinal. These difficulties will create pressure for responses. Some traditional solutions can be grafted onto the technical apparatus with limited disruption. Others, however, will involve reintroduction of law. They may even lead to greater regulatory involvement in contract.

A. Imperfections of Algorithmic Enforcement

There are significant practical limitations in replacing human enforcement of agreements with software running on the blockchain. Things simply do not always go according to plan. Anyone who has seen an error code on their computer screen knows that sophisticated software-based systems are imperfect. Even if the underlying blockchain consensus mechanisms are reliable, the smart contract applications running on top of them may not be. The failure of The DAO should be a cautionary note for smart contract developers.

Even without bugs, there are reasons to doubt smart contracts will always operate as desired. First, they require reduction of human-readable language to machine-readable code. This limits their scope to those subjects and activities that can readily be specified. For example, a contract to unlock my connected car upon presentation of a certain cryptographic key can easily be encoded through a programming language such as Ethereum's Solidity. The network address for the car lock, the desired key, and the action to be taken, are all subject to precise definition. At the other extreme, some contractual terms simply cannot be expressed through formal logic, because they imply human judgement. A machine has no precise way to assess whether a party used 'best efforts', for example.

Building a computerised system able to interpret smart contracts like humans can is effectively a challenge for artificial intelligence.[45] And that challenge is unlikely to be solved any time soon. Despite great advances in machine learning, computers do not have the degree of contextual, domain-specific, subtle understanding required to resolve contractual ambiguity. In this regard, smart contract platforms like Ethereum are also vastly less sophisticated than state-of-the-art artificial intelligence systems like IBM's Watson.

Even if the smart contract operates exactly as designed, it may produce suboptimal results, either in the minds of one or both parties, or as a matter of economic efficiency, because it is fixed. Sometimes, for example, non-performance is the desirable outcome. Much has been made of the idea of efficient breach.[46] If a builder contracts with a carpenter to make custom woodwork for a new home, but notifies the carpenter that the home will not be built before initiation of that work, non-performance and compensation to the carpenter may be the best result. One interpretation is that contract law is designed to facilitate such non-performance, assuming the legal default rules for contractual remedies stood behind the parties' negotiation.[47] But, one need not accept the theory that the law sanctions efficient breach to appreciate that the law does not lock parties into performance.

The general lesson is that facts may change between the *ex ante* specification of contract rights and the *ex post* adjudication of legal effects. Parties to smart contracts can try to hedge against such changes by incorporating qualifying language or *force majeure* clauses, but those kinds of imprecise terms are difficult to specify in computer code. In other cases, parties may wish to advantageously alter a contract prior to performance. Under standard contract law, such modifications are unproblematic.[227] For smart contracts, such modifications pose a difficulty. Upon agreement, a smart contract is locked in place and secured by pledged cryptocurrency. To enable an intermediate step before execution, the smart contract code would need to incorporate the possibility of modification explicitly. As a technical matter, this would increase the complexity of the process. It would also introduce the kinds of difficulties already described about how to express complex ideas in code, like when and how parties can modify the set terms of a smart contract.

As the literature on relational contracts recognises, contracts are often more than a one-time interaction between parties, followed by performance or judicial

[45] S Omohundro, 'Cryptocurrencies, Smart Contracts, and Artificial Intelligence' (2014) 1 *AI Matters* 19, 20, available at perma.cc/T46Y-QCKH.

[46] See, eg RA Posner, *Economic Analysis of Law*, 5th edn (New York, Aspen, 1998) 13–14; RL Birmingham, 'Breach of Contract, Damage Measures, and Economic Efficiency' (1970) 24 *Rutgers University Law Review* 273, 284.

[47] See S Shavell, 'Is Breach of Contract Immoral?' (2006) 56 *Emory Law Journal* 439, 452.

resolution of a dispute. Instead, contracts are elements of ongoing relationships. Both the parties and the courts view the contract in light of social and relational norms. *Ex ante*, parties to a relational contract must anticipate later renegotiation, and *ex post*, courts must determine how to fill gaps in the agreed-upon contract. Smart contracts attempt to atomize the contractual process. They formally strip away the time dimension of interactions between the parties, and the uncertainties of future judicial resolution. Yet, smart contracts bind real people, who have real relationships, and their performance unfolds over time. This makes it impossible to avoid some of the messiness that attends traditional contracts.

B. Doctrinal Concerns

Contract law developed over centuries to account for situations that arise in the execution of agreements. Through the inductive process of the common law, courts evolved solutions to novel problems. Upon closer examination, many of these rules are in tension with smart contracts' mechanism of automatic, irrevocable enforcement.

At a basic level, a smart contract can meet the legal requirements for a valid and enforceable common law contract: offer, acceptance, consideration, capacity and legality. But a host of potential problems lurk beneath the surface. At virtually every turn, smart contracts might operate in ways contrary to legal contracts. That is, although smart contracts may be legal contracts, they may also fall victim to almost every legal deficiency. Nothing in a smart contract ensures a true meeting of the minds; nothing ensures consideration; and so on. Below, we describe a number of ways that smart contracts might operate problematically, and contrary to the law of contracts.

i. Problems with Meeting of the Minds

A smart contract is computer code representing an agreement between two or more parties, so one question might be whether it truly represents a meeting of the minds. Computers, after all, do not have minds, at least not outside the realm of science fiction. But this objection is quickly overcome. In modern contract law, offer and acceptance are evaluated objectively; that is, we allow evidence that both parties intend to be bound, and discard evidence about indicia of internal mental states. The fact that parties submit their cryptographic private keys to commit their resources to the smart contract is proof of such an intent.

The parties' mutual intent to be bound does not, however, prove a meeting of the minds about the specific contractual provisions. The doctrine of mutual mistake excuses performance when both parties were mistaken about an essential fact. If the smart contract refers to cotton delivered by the ship *Peerless*, but there are two – or 17 – ships of that name, standard contract law can hold the agreement unenforceable.[48] But the smart contract would go ahead and execute. In a unilateral contract, the mistake might not even need to be mutual for a court to rescind it. In other words, there might be an executable smart contract that does not satisfy the legal conditions for mutual assent. This is because even seemingly *ex ante* elements of contract law, like assent, actually turn on how matters look *ex post*.

The basic problem here is that smart contracts are not really smart, at least not in the way that contract law is smart. Smart contracts are not smart enough to adjust as events unfold. Even beyond mistakes, parties may not anticipate the exact scenario that arises at the time of performance. Most contracts are incomplete, in the sense that they do not specify an outcome for every possible state of the world.[49] Courts can fill in the blanks when the contractual expression of the parties' intent is unclear. With a smart contract, this approach is foreclosed.

A second problem related to meeting of the minds arises when the contract itself is clear, but does not represent the intent of the parties, for example, if a party enters into an agreement due to fraud or duress. In such a situation, performance may be excused. The contract itself is valid; it is simply not enforceable. Yet, the distinction between validity and enforceability is precisely the one that smart contracts elide.

A smart contract is valid if it is accepted as part of the consensus process on the blockchain ledger. Once that happens, it is ineluctably enforced, even if fraudulently induced. The blockchain does not have any context regarding *why* parties provide private keys to authorise a smart contract, only that they did. And no one can ask an arbiter to excuse performance because she signed with a gun to her head, because there is no arbiter. The arbiters are the computers operating the blockchain, and they only listen to the code of the smart contracts themselves.

As a practical matter, furthermore, the plaintiff in such a scenario would have difficulty asserting an affirmative cause of action. Duress itself is not a tort. And fraud is significantly different as a cause of action than as an affirmative defence. The most effective recourse for someone improperly induced to enter in a smart contract would likely be to sue for restitution of the ill-gotten gains, after the smart contract executes.

ii. Problems with Consideration

Similar problems arise with consideration, another basic requirement for an enforceable contract. Consideration distinguishes contracts from unenforceable gifts.[50] All promises may create moral duties, but not all promises create legal

[48] See AWB Simpson, 'Contracts for Cotton to Arrive: The Case of the Two Ships Peerless' (1989) 11 *Cardozo Law Review* 287, 295.

[49] See OD Hart, 'Incomplete Contracts and the Theory of the Firm' (1998) 4 *Journal of Law, Economics, & Organization* 119, 123.

[50] See JM Perillo and JD Calamari, *Calamari and Perillo on Contracts*, 6th edn (St Paul, West Law Publishing, 2009) § 4.1.

obligations. For smart contracts, there is no test for consideration. A typical smart contract involves some consideration that induces the reciprocal promise. However, there is nothing stopping someone from encoding a gift promise to the blockchain. Such a promise would execute irrevocably, in the same manner as any other smart contract. The rest of consideration doctrine, like the distinction between adequacy and sufficiency, similarly goes by the wayside when there is no way to test enforceability before execution.

The absence of consideration from smart contracts sheds further light on how they differ from legal contracts. Consideration doctrine supports the view that contract law exists to provide remedies for breach, and not to generate *ex ante* obligations. If the point of contract were to enforce promises, or to allow parties to advert to liability voluntarily, contract law ought to allow them to make binding gift promises. But from its *ex post* vantage point, contract law can distinguish unenforceable gifts and mutual legal obligations. By contrast, smart contracts load all the effort into the *ex ante* specification of contractual terms.

iii. Problems with Capacity

The issues with legal capacity are somewhat different. Here, the question is not what the contract includes, but who it binds. Those without legal capacity, including children, people with significant mental impairments, and the excessively intoxicated, are excused from contractual performance. As with consideration, smart contracts have no means to test for capacity. There is no legal limitation on minors having private encryption keys or owning bitcoins, as they are currently restricted from having credit cards or accounts on payment services like PayPal.[51] And if someone digitally signs a smart contract while dead drunk, or another person exploits those circumstances to get them that person do so, there is no future opportunity for subjective evaluation by the other party.

The absence of a capacity test raises a deeper set of issues for smart contracts. The parties to a smart contract, at a technical level, are not people. They are cryptographic private keys. The secret private key represents the individual, based on a mathematical relationship with the associated public key. It is virtually impossible for someone who does not possess the private key to generate a valid digital signature that matches a given public key. This allows cryptographic keys to form the basis for digital identity systems.[52] Identity, however, is a rich concept, and requires layering various capabilities for authentication, access, and more. Moreover, even if a key uniquely belongs to an individual, the person and the key are not the same. An individual may possess many digital identities, backed by different private keys. The key may be linked to personally identifiable information that points to the specific individual. On the other hand, the key may designate a persistent

[51] See S Williams, 'Americans' Average Credit Score Is Rising – How Does Yours Compare?' *Newsweek* (4 December 2016), available at perma.cc/3AVE-HBEU.

[52] See LJ Camp, 'Digital Identity' (Fall 2004) *IEEE Technology and Society Magazine* 34, 40.

digital identity hiding the associated real-world person (pseudonymity) or, it may give no information at all about identity (anonymity).

It may not be right, then, to say that smart contracts are agreements between people. In the case of the computable or data-oriented contract, the negotiation and specification of an agreement may be left entirely to machines. But there, it is generally easy to view the computers as agents for their human programmers, who specify the conditions under which the computers can contract. The relevant practical difficulties are not so different from those which agency law has addressed for centuries. With a smart contract, however, the connection between the humans and the agreement becomes more attenuated. The power of execution and enforcement is given over entirely to machines. The humans no longer have the capacity, in the colloquial sense, to avoid performance of the agreement. Perhaps they likewise do not have the capacity, in the legal sense, to perform it.

This analysis connects with the conclusion above that smart contracts are not promises, even if they are contracts. That may be easy to accept conceptually, but as the foregoing discussion shows, things start to unravel when viewed doctrinally. Law bakes in assumptions about the human nature of contract. It may not be difficult as a thought experiment to imagine a contract that does not meet contract law's doctrinal specifications. However, once one dives into the analytical problems of contract law, the difficulties quickly multiply. This illustrates why smart contracts could not supplant contract law.

iv. Problems with Legality

Perhaps tautologically, a legally enforceable contract cannot effectuate an illegal purpose. Smart contracts, however, are not enforced by the legal system. Imagine, for example, a price-fixing conspiracy implemented through a series of smart contracts that adjust prices in lockstep. The participants could be prosecuted under antitrust law, but the smart contracts would continue to operate. Further, there is no mechanism to stop a smart contract from implementing an unconscionable term, or a term that incorporates liquidated damages amounting to a penalty. Because the smart contract is self-executing, an action in court finding the terms unenforceable may have no practical effect; the contract will be performed regardless.

The legality test and various public policy rules hint that contract, generally considered a bastion of private law, retains a penumbra of public law. Again, this reinforces the view that contract law is an adjudicative mechanism and is not principally concerned with reasons and obligations. Legal adjudication is a public function, drawing on the coercive power of the state. Individuals acting together may have no problem effectuating a scheme in derogation of public policy, but as Thomas Hobbes argued, the state is granted an extraordinary monopoly on violence for the very purpose of preventing the war of all against all.

These arguments of political theorists imagining a hypothetical state of nature become tangible with smart contracts. The hacking of The DAO illustrated the problem with contracts that have no opportunity for public oversight. The hack was simultaneously valid as an enforceable smart contract within the software system, yet demonstrably invalid as theft in the minds of the contracting parties. If the perpetrator had exploited a bug in a conventional crowdfunding service such as Kickstarter to siphon off investors' funds, there would be no practical or legal difficulty in cancelling the suspect transactions and returning the funds. Ethereum, in contrast, had no alternative to the nuclear option of the hard fork. While that may have fixed the immediate problem, the solution used a bazooka to shoot a mouse and caused significant collateral damage.

Even if a hard fork is effective, it transfers final adjudication from the institution of the courts to the polity of validation nodes. A hard fork stands or falls on whether a majority of the mining power in the blockchain network adopts it. This is not how contracts work. We do not adjudicate disputes through opinion polls or the ballot box. We grant the judge or jury authority to decide, constrained by the procedures of the legal system, the traditions of the common law, and the opportunity for legislative modification going forward. The limitations of direct democracy are familiar to anyone who has read the *Federalist Papers*. Miners' interests may be even further removed from those of the community as a whole than 'factions' in a democracy.

This is not to say that smart contracts are a threat to democratic values. One can imagine many scenarios in a world where smart contracts are prevalent, but legal analysis cannot rest entirely on imagined scenarios. We have no way of knowing how popular smart contracts will become, let alone how frequently controversies like The DAO hack will arise. What matters is that the seemingly abstract conflicts between smart contracts and basic doctrines of contract law touch deeper nerves, with potentially significant consequences. And, as in section III, we investigate smart contracts for what they illuminate about conventional contracts.

C. Looking Forward

Having established that smart contracts both clarify the purpose of contract law in theory and challenge its application in practice, we conclude with a sketch about what happens next. Any recommendations at this time are necessarily provisional. Smart contracts are so new, and their prospects are so uncertain, that firm predictions are unwise, let alone normative judgments from those predictions. However, that is no reason to ignore potential consequences while there is still time to avoid them. And given the various considerations we have discussed, it is unreasonable to assume smart contracts will be implemented seamlessly.

i. Best Practices

The parties entering into smart contracts are not powerless to avoid their shortcomings. Knowing they cannot rely on the judicial decision-makers to fill gaps, one can expect parties to put more effort into contract design and drafting.[53] Additionally, just as transactional lawyers provide expertise in the construction of business agreements, a new class of 'legal engineers' may arise to aid in the creation of smart contracts. Parties can also employ technical mechanisms to lessen the rigidity of smart contracts. For example, giving authority to human oracles who decide whether the factual basis for performance has been met, or employing arbitrators who resolve disputes through a multisig arrangements, may avoid some of the draconian implications of fully self-enforcing agreements.

Already, organsations involved in the development of smart contract platforms are starting to create templates that embody best practices for smart contract drafting.[54] Using these templates, parties could avoid repeating mistakes in prior smart contracts, and they could draw on the expertise of industry groups carefully thinking about potential pitfalls. Smart contracting systems or, 'contractware' to use Raskin's term,[55] could be programmed to offer templates automatically based on the desired agreement. Default terms, for example, requiring an opportunity for mutual modification prior to execution, could be mandatory to issue a smart contract on a particular platform. Parties could consult technical auditing firms to certify the integrity of smart contract code. Even if the platforms are not subject to any legal duties regarding the contracts they enable, they still may care about avoiding harmful outcomes due to either ignorance or malfeasance by parties.

We cannot predict how well this optimistic story will play out. Surely, technical mechanisms for improving the quality of smart contracts will not eliminate the potential problems, any more than the ready availability of skilled lawyers prevents disputes over legal contracts.

ii. Restitution

It would be a grave mistake to think that smart contracts will eliminate litigation. Litigation – like nature – will find a way. Parties will inevitably feel they were treated unfairly at times, and they will inevitably bring those complaints to court. The difference, however, will be the posture of the litigation. Rather than complaining parties seeking fulfilment of alleged promissory obligations, complaining parties will seek to undo or reverse completed transactions. Litigation will persist, but it will shift from claims of breach, to claims of restitution.

One might think that this effectively shifts contracts from liability rules to property rules.[56] That's not quite right, because one could have a smart contract that

[53] See EA Posner, K Eggleston and R Zeckhauser, 'The Design and Interpretation of Contracts: Why Complexity Matters' (2000) 95 *Northwestern University Law Review* 91, 120.

[54] See CD Clack, VA Bakshi and L Braine, 'Smart Contract Templates: foundations, design landscape and research directions' (2016), available at perma.cc/6FZR-NGPW.

[55] See Raskin, 'Law and Legality' (2017) 307.

[56] See G Calabresi and AD Melamed, 'Property Rules, Liability Rules, and Inalienability: One View of the Cathedral' (1972) 85 *Harvard Law Review* 1089, 1106–10.

awards liability damages in a self-executing way. Rather, the difference is between *ex ante* enforcement and *ex post* adjudication. We have tried to illustrate that it is a mistake to conceive of these as simply two different forms of 'enforcement'.

An effort to recover already-transferred resources is different than an effort to enforce an agreement. Thus, an action for restitution is very different than an action for breach of contract. At a minimum, the roles of the parties are reversed. In an action for breach, the non-performing party seeks to enforce a transaction; whereas, in an action for restitution, the performing party seeks to reverse the transaction. Reversing who stands as plaintiff shifts the burdens of proof and litigation. In situations such as mutual mistake, there may be no a priori reason to favour one side. But when actions arise from claims of fraud, repugnance to public policy, or gifts without consideration, the balance of equities may shift in undesirable ways.

Those seeking redress for injuries suffered due to smart contracts may be forced to plead actions beyond quasi contract. To take an example highlighted earlier, both the plaintiff and the defendant can raise a claim of fraud, but the legal context is quite different. The plaintiff's claim is a tort, the defendant's claim is an affirmative defence in contract, and the legal requirements are different. Moreover, in practice, such litigation may unfold quite differently if the focus shifts from the contract to the technical structures associated with it. Because the transfer of value associated with the smart contract is tied to the parties' cryptographic private keys, the plaintiff may need to sue to force the defendant to give up that key, or perhaps computer passwords protecting it. Law enforcement agencies have done just that, when pursuing proprietors of Bitcoin exchanges promoting illegal activity like drug trafficking.[57] If that is the model, however, we have strayed quite far from the private law domain of contract.

iii. Regulation

Indeed, the paradoxical result of smart contracts may be to expand the scope of government intervention into technological advancements, which has traditionally been a paradigmatic environment of private ordering. Once again, the shift from *ex post* adjudication to *ex ante* enforcement creates an inversion. Contracts free individuals to trust each others' commitments because they can rely on the power of the state to enforce them in cases of breach. Smart contracts remove the state from adjudication, but in so doing, they create pressure to reintroduce the state at the front end of the process. The only way to prevent smart contracts from facilitating illegal or disfavoured conduct is to regulate them.

It is a myth that the blockchain is inherently incompatible with regulation. Any distributed ledger system may be more or less decentralised, and more or less

[57] See J Matonis, 'Key Disclosure Laws Can Be Used to Confiscate Bitcoin Assets' *Forbes* (12 September 2012), available at perma.cc/3JS9-L9GE.

anonymous, based on its technical design. Bitcoin and Ethereum are examples of 'permissionless' systems that have no supervisory entity authorised to accept or reject participation in the mining network. Other smart contract platforms, such as the Corda system for interbank transactions, only recognise trusted nodes, such as member banks. This makes them less resistant to government intervention or private domination. A Corda smart contract could easily be subject to regulatory oversight, like the Anti-Money Laundering and Know Your Customer regulations that mandate identification of bank customers.[58] Even for a permissionless system, centralised intervention is not impossible; it is just very difficult and costly, as shown by the Ethereum hard fork to resolve The DAO hack.

Perhaps a more apt parallel is the regulation of digital signatures. With the rise of e-commerce in the 1990s, it quickly became clear that digital signatures based on public-key cryptography could solidify commitments in the same manner as conventional signatures on traditional contracts. A digital signature, however, is not really a signature at all. It is a private key that generates an associated public key. Ultimately, the E-SIGN Act pre-empted contrary state law, and ensured that rules requiring signatures could be satisfied with their digital analogues. The legal effects and limitations of digital signatures were therefore not defined by handwriting specialists, but by government.

Under many scenarios, regulators might interpose themselves into the workings of smart contracts. Generally speaking, these will involve regulation of the contracting software platforms or blockchain validation nodes, rather than the parties themselves. Someone knowingly entering into an illegal smart contract has still violated the law, but it will likely be easier to police the enabling systems. The kinds of smart contracts parties can form will depend on the functionality and interfaces of the available tools. This recalls the fate of P2P file-sharing systems like Napster, which facilitated widespread copyright infringement. The Supreme Court eventually concluded that even when P2P services had no specific knowledge of or ability to prevent infringing transfers, the services were still liable if set up to induce them. A smart contract system that facilitated copyright infringement, for example, by granting users digital rights to content without proper licences, would likely suffer the same fate.

As noted earlier, nothing technically prevents execution of an illegal smart contract. The infamous Silk Road online marketplace used Bitcoin payments to facilitate sales of illegal goods, but the transactions themselves used the same electronic contracting mechanisms as legitimate sites like Amazon.com or Ebay. If smart contracts can further automate such activities, or financial crimes like money laundering, there will be pressure to prohibit intermediaries from enabling or processing them. Moreover, legal requirements, like the automatic stay in

[58] See I Allison, 'R3 Develops Proof-of-Concept for Shared KYC Service with 10 Global Banks' *International Business Times* (10 November 2016), available at perma.cc/7AM7-7TPP; A Begum, 'R3's Corda Uncovered: It's Not Blockchain' *Global Trade Review* (1 October 2017), available at perma.cc/LZ7K-HMZ9.

bankruptcy law, can supersede contractual obligations. Courts and legislatures may attempt to require smart contracting systems to incorporate exceptions for such contexts. Administrative regulation of smart contracts is also a possibility.

Various agencies, including the Federal Trade Commission (FTC), the Securities and Exchange Commission, and the Consumer Financial Protection Board, have authority to prevent unfair or deceptive practices. This extends to situations where companies do not intend consumer harms, but fail to take sufficient precautions against them. For example, the FTC successfully brought an enforcement action against Wyndham Hotels for inadequate information security practices, which led to losses of customer data. One could imagine a similar action against the developers of The DAO, the Ethereum Foundation, or miners who processes its transactions, based on their failure to offer adequate safeguards for funds pledged to the crowdfunding system. It is difficult to evaluate what this would mean in practice. The Ethereum Foundation is a Swiss non-profit, The DAO software is an open-source project, and the miners are a changing collection of voluntary participants around the world. Imposing regulatory obligations on any of them would be problematic. Yet if significant consumer harms materialise, regulators are unlikely to walk away.

An analogous situation occurred in the early days of the commercial Internet. The Digital Millennium Copyright Act of 1998 gave intermediaries immunity from liability for copyright infringement, but only if they complied with notice-and-takedown procedures when notified of infringing material. Congress or a state legislature concerned about smart contracts running amok might grant a safe harbour to software creators, application providers and validation node operators, but condition that safe harbour on the adoption of templates, functional limitations, and audits for executable smart contracts. Such rules could be vague or overbroad, chilling the adoption of smart contracts, or they might provide security for parties who otherwise would be disinclined to use smart contracts. At this point, the specifics are too difficult to predict with any confidence.

To some degree, this is a familiar story. Where freedom of contract stands in the way of important public policy objectives, it must give ground. That occurred most famously when the New Deal eventually broke through the *Lochner* court's resistance to economic regulation.[59] Smart contracting systems offer a kind of technical due process protection from legislative or judicial interference. While they may hold the state at bay to an extent, they will not eliminate it from the picture.

V. Conclusion

Our goal has been to analyse smart contracts from the perspective of law – and vice versa. Though there is significant evidence that smart contracts will eventually

[59] See, eg, *Nebbia v New York*, 291 U.S. 502, 523 (1934).

enjoy widespread adoption, we make no assumptions about their technical and business trajectory. Even if smart contracts turn out to be a fad, they can help us better understand legal contracts. And if blockchain-based smart contracts fail, another technology will inevitably arise to achieve the same objectives. The very act of unpacking smart contracts may help to anticipate – and thus, to mitigate – potential difficulties.

Smart contracts are just one part of the larger trend of computerised technologies purporting to displace or replace human decision-making. In areas like hiring, finance and copyright enforcement, algorithmic systems are touted for their speed, efficiency and reliability, unlike error-prone and potentially biased humans. Indeed, the benefits are considerable. But it quickly becomes clear that machines are prone to their own errors and biases. Additionally, the introduction of algorithmic systems into historically judgement-laden fields creates challenges for legal and practical accountability. As a result, both legal scholars and computer scientists are developing techniques to promote fairness and transparency in these decisions. A similar dynamic can be expected for smart contracts.

Contract law is nothing if not resilient. We have little doubt it will survive the onslaught from smart contracts, if indeed that is what is happening. However, contract law may learn something about itself from its new challenger.

2

The Fine Print in Smart Contracts

JOSHUA S GANS

I. Introduction

Beyond its initial application in creating digital tokens (aka Bitcoin), one of the more intriguing possibilities from blockchain technologies is that they could support what have been termed 'smart contracts'. These contracts are based on an idea by Nick Szabo. 'A smart contract is a computerized transaction protocol that executes the terms of a contract.'[1] Szabo is quick to point out that automated contract execution is not new. He argues that a vending machine does just that. You indicate what you want, pay the price and, following that, the machine dispenses the product. What is new is the idea that the contract involved could be both purely digital (the vending machine is not) and complicated in that it may involve complex calculations, multipart deals, transfer of rights and various forms of encryption.

Contracting has always been about the fine print. Contracts are a set of obligations, many of which arise in particular circumstances. To be sure, at a high level a contract is representing a transaction, trade or exchange of payment for goods and services. But things often do not go to plan and contracts anticipate these. If there is a disruption, whose responsibility is it to bear the costs? If there is a dispute, how will it be resolved? And when is it the case that it is better for everyone to walk away from their obligations?

Smart contracts promise to automate all of this. To be sure, code can capture the fine print, but what it cannot do is determine whether a particular event or state that gives rise to obligations has arisen. That relies on interfacing with the 'real' world. Moreover, it often relies on a human element to make sure the right information is injected at the right time. As with every other situation involving humans, that is a weak link in full automation. We want to have automated contracts that we can trust and rely upon, but to make them work properly there is often human choice in the fine print. Importantly, to understand fully the

[1] N Szabo, 'Smart Contracts' (1994), available at www.fon.hum.uva.nl/rob/Courses/InformationIn-Speech/CDROM/Literature/LOTwinterschool2006/szabo.best.vwh.net/smart.contracts.html.

prospects for smart contracting today we have to pay attention to that fine print. We can't leave it unread.

So how do blockchain technologies factor into this? Blockchain technologies involve a ledger of information which represents the consensus of a decentralised mechanism. In other words, the information in the ledger is not vouched for by one agent (as would be the case in a centralised system). Instead, it is vouched for by many, distributed agents who agree that the information on the blockchain today was the same as the information placed on the blockchain at an earlier time. Moreover, the information on the blockchain is *valid* in that it conforms to a set of constraints (perhaps based on what was there earlier). There is nothing that implies that the information on the blockchain is 'The Truth' but instead that, whatever it was, it was placed there at a specific time and has not been altered.[2]

It is at this point where the usefulness of the blockchain in contracting becomes apparent. A contract is an agreement between two or more parties. When such an agreement is reached, the fact of that agreement as well as the terms of it can be put on the blockchain. That way, if there is a dispute as to what was agreed to and when, it is very easy to verify that information.[3] To be sure, in the paper economy, we have relied on paper and copies to provide a similar function (usually distributing it amongst different parties so that later a consensus can be identified). But in the digital world, there is concern that such information could be easily altered. Hence, it is critical to have an immutable record.

Compared to paper, however, the blockchain offers the possibility of more. Why simply record a contract when you can code the contract? In Bitcoin, two parties agree to the transfer of bitcoins from one to another at a specific time. However, the protocol then does an extra step: it transfers the ownership of the bitcoins as specified in the agreement. To do this actually requires a number of steps. First, the payor notifies the network they wish to send bitcoin to the payee and provides their private key. Second, the network then checks that the payor does, in fact, own those bitcoin (by verifying they possess the correct private key) and that they have not already told the network of their intention to send them to someone else. Third, only then, is the intention converted into a reassignment of ownership in the next block on the blockchain. All of these steps are performed when we give cash to one another (it is more complicated for cheques and wire transfers). Having the cash in hand signifies the first two steps and then giving it to the payee completes the process. In other words, the Bitcoin protocol is able to

[2] This statement is not quite true. What the information and time on the blockchain tell us is the current consensus, which is that the information was on the blockchain at that time. In principle, the blockchain may have forked at a subsequent time with a potential rewrite of history. That said, forks are public, as are the changes they bring about. Thus, the path from the initial vouching for the information to the present can be traced.

[3] Catalini and Gans highlight that it is this potential reduction in the cost of such verification that represents the principal economic effect arising from blockchain technologies (see C Catalini and JS Gans, 'Some Simple Economics of the Blockchain' (2016), available at papers.ssrn.com/sol3/papers.cfm?abstract_id=2874598).

automate the execution of the agreement to transfer bitcoin ownership once the payor validly initiates it.

If the Bitcoin protocol can automate a digital property rights transfer, then it is not hard to imagine that an automated protocol could execute more complex contracts. One such complexity may be to include a contingency. For Bitcoin, execution takes place at the discretion of the payor. But one can also imagine that the transfer might be contingent on some event. For instance, perhaps the payment should only be made if it rains in a particular location next Thursday. That could be coded along with a data source for the event of rain (which has the property that it either does or does not occur). Then having agreed to the contract and provided the relevant signatures (ie, private keys), the process would be automated from that point forward.

The validation of an agreement and its contents is critical to being able to automate an agreement's execution. Without that validation, the parties could not be sure what was being executed was what they intended. For this reason, the blockchain provides the means to validate the code of an agreement and also to verify its performance. However, this does not necessarily imply that a blockchain can fully automate a contract perfectly. That, as we will see, depends on the nature of the agreement.

The purpose of this chapter is to consider when precisely smart contracts will be useful if hosted on a blockchain. In particular, it will highlight what I will call 'the fundamental smart contract challenge' that results because smart contracts are inherently digital but must, in order to be useful, interact with non-digital activity. This is something that has been neglected in discussions of the blockchain even if, as I will argue, economists have concentrated almost exclusively on such issues over the past two decades of contract theory. It is the fine print we cannot neglect.

In the end, a smart contract is an automated contract. They key issue will be to identify what aspect of contracting is automated. Varian noted that an increasing number of transactions were becoming computer mediated as a result of the Internet.[4] He noted that it was possible to use data to make contracts more nuanced. For instance, a car rental company could monitor the speed of driving and adjust a driver's rate accordingly. Car finance companies could put in connected sensors into cars and prevent operation if payments were missed. Online advertisers, like Google, could run auctions in real time based on the submitted bids of advertisers. In each case, data was collected after the contract was signed which then determined the payments and sometimes obligations of parties. Computer-mediation allowed these to be automatically executed.

More ambitiously, Casey and Niblett[5] see the possibility of 'self-driving contracts'. These contracts do not even go the way of computer-mediated

[4] H Varian, 'Computer-Mediated Transactions' (2010) 100 *American Economic Review* 1.
[5] AJ Casey and A Niblett, 'Self-Driving Contracts' (2017) 42 *Journal of Corporation Law* 101.

transactions in specifying the full details and contingencies of the contract. Instead, they see a future where parties could specify intentions or goals and then an artificial intelligence will fill the gaps in the contract in line with these goals as more is learned about the environment the parties are operating in. The way they see this as working is that artificial agents can fill in contractual gaps in the way a court or a mediator might do today. However, while those gaps may be filled in requires explicit judicial enforcement. They see this as requiring various changes in how contract law operates today.

Such contracts do not necessarily require a blockchain and, as such, are not really part of the scope of smart contracting as it is postulated. That said, they do involve the notion of automation which is a key part of smart contracting.

II. Obligations and Trust

Contracts are made up of obligations. For instance, a buyer and seller may strike an agreement whereby the buyer is obliged to pay the seller some money while the seller is obliged to supply a good or service to the buyer. An agreement will facilitate trade or other valuable interactions when an agent can be reasonably certain that an obligation on another party will be met.

Trust is a means of creating reasonable expectations that obligations will be met when the performance of obligations is separated in time. To see this, trustless performance of obligations can occur when exchange is simultaneous. For instance, a buyer and seller meet and, at the same moment, fulfil payment and product supply obligations; hostages might be exchanged on a bridge to allow the obligations to be fulfilled simultaneously; the first experiments in kidney exchanges worked with donors having operations simultaneously. If trust is present, then simultaneity is not required and obligations can be performed at different times.

There are, of course, social mechanisms that allow trust to arise so that obligations can be time-separated. Some people might be considered trustworthy, and others can assess this via social cues. In other situations, parties have an ongoing relationship and the prospect of repeated interactions causes them to honour and expect to have honoured obligations.

Beyond such social forces, there have been institutional mechanisms that have developed to allow obligations to be performed sequentially. The most ubiquitous of these is contract law. Contract law bundles obligations together and then sets forth conditions under which the performance of those obligations will be required. To ensure performance, an independent third party – usually a court – will assess obligation performance and impose penalties or other requirements if obligations are not met. The expectation of such verification and sanction serves to cause agents to meet their obligations. In the process, the obligations become trusted.

Another critical institution that allows trust to develop is reputation. Reputation allows a relationship to extend beyond the parties that can directly observe the performance of past obligations. By having a means of communicating that performance in a public manner, an agent can have an incentive to perform obligations in order to preserve their reputation and enhance opportunities for future dealings. As an institution, reputations require a means of accounting for past performance in a manner that can be verified, be secure and be communicated widely.

In order for a blockchain to have value it must work to enhance trust in situations where neither current social nor institutional mechanisms are present. Blockchains are sometimes held to be trustless technologies, but this refers to their potential ability to work independently of social mechanisms for trust. In order to fulfil an economic function, they need to substitute for technologies – both legal and other – that provide institutional bases for trust. In this regard, smart contracts that are supported by the blockchain will still be measured by their ability to enhance trust in terms of the set of obligations that comprise those contracts.

III. The Contract Workflow

In order to understand the potential value of the blockchain in facilitating smart contracts it is useful to explore, in somewhat laborious detail, the workflow associated with contract performance, execution and verification. Much legal and economic work on contracts focuses on the contract formation process – its terms, whether an agreement is possible, etc. Here, instead, I focus on what happens after a contract and its terms have been agreed upon.

Consider two parties to a contract – the erstwhile Alice and Bob. Each has obligations – x_A and x_B – that they have agreed to perform. If this occurs, Alice receives $v_A(x_B) - c_A(x_A)$ while Bob receives $v_B(x_A) - c_B(x_B)$. The values and costs may include some form of payment between them. In each case, if an obligation is not performed, it costs the performer nothing and reduces the value received by the other to zero.

It is useful to note at this stage that most contractual obligations are created by an event – or what I will term a *state*. The most obvious state is a signature on an agreement. However, some states may be that an obligation to ship a good will only be created once payment is received or, alternatively, a payment will only be made once a good is received. In other situations, the state may represent an external event, eg, an insurance payout only arises in the case of an accident. In other words, it is a state that triggers the creation of an obligation even within an agreed-upon contract. Thus, one common form of conflict is a dispute over whether the relevant state underlying an obligation has occurred. If it has, then a party will expect an obligation to be performed. If not, then no such expectation is warranted. Thus, if there is uncertainty or misunderstanding over whether an underlying state has arisen, this can cause a discord in expectations regarding the performance of an obligation.

For this reason, a party will likely have to monitor whether the underlying state triggering an obligation owed to them has arisen. In some situations, that state may be the performance of an obligation themselves. This may involve checking on a delivery, examining work quality or ensuring a payment has reached an account. For each state, suppose that it costs the monitoring party, m, to confirm with certainty whether a state has occurred or not. In some situations, this may be a cost to confirm whether an obligation itself has been performed. A party may want to incur this cost in order to know whether they should challenge performance or not.

In addition to monitoring underlying states and performance between the parties, obligation performance will often be verified by a third party (such as a court). This is distinct from monitoring as that third party requires what is termed 'hard evidence' that performance has taken place. This may be some form of validated receipt or the results of a trusted audit. This too is costly and, critically, involves the cooperation of the party performing the obligation. That party can, at cost z, provide hard evidence if it exists.

It is useful to note here that digitisation provides potential costs and benefits with regard to this workflow. Digital technologies often imply a reduction in m – in that it is easier for a party receiving an obligation to check the underlying state or performance to their own satisfaction. By contrast, a purely digital indication of a state or performance may not be sufficient to verify performance to third parties. This is because digital assets can typically be easier to manipulate, tamper with or misrepresent. Thus, when there is a digital workflow, this means that the verification cost, z, may be higher.

To see the roles these costs play in contractual performance, let's focus on Alice and her incentives to undertake her contractual obligations. If Alice chooses to perform her obligations, then Bob faces a choice as to whether to confirm that performance or not. As Bob does not know whether Alice has chosen to perform or not, this is a difficult choice. Importantly, expending those costs allows Bob to challenge Alice's performance and require her to produce hard evidence. If she has performed, that is possible and she incurs z, and the matter is settled. If not, then some dispute resolution process would arise. Note that if there is no dispute resolution process, Alice has no incentive to produce hard evidence, Bob has no incentive to confirm performance and Alice has no incentive to perform her obligations. Thus, the contract agreement would be infeasible.

On the other hand, suppose that if Bob is successful in his dispute, he receives d while Alice pays d. In this case, so long as $z < d$, Alice will want to produce hard evidence if she has it, and so long as $c_A(x_A) + z < d$, Alice will want to perform her obligations. In addition, Bob will gain $d - m$ if he confirms non-performance and $- m$ if he confirms performance. This means that Bob will play a mixed strategy at this node in any equilibrium. He will want the probability that he monitors, p, to be such that Alice has an incentive to perform: that is, so that $c_A(x_A) < p(d - z)$. Thus, Bob's expected costs of monitoring would be pm which is at least $mc_A(x_A)/(d - z)$. These costs represent a weight reducing the set of contracts that would otherwise be feasible. Notice that the higher is d, the lower are these expected costs, but that if z is too high, then regardless of other factors, the contract will not be feasible.

Given this analysis we can prove the following:

Proposition 1. The contract will only be feasible if $d > z$ and

$$v_A(x_B) + v_B(x_A) > (c_A(x_A) + c_B(x_B))(d - z + m)/(d - z)$$

What this analysis shows is that to improve the scope for contracting, it is important to both reduce the costs of observability (m) as well as the costs of verification (z). Moreover, these have to be reduced for each obligation.

IV. Impact of Blockchain Technology

With this model in place, we can now turn to consider the impact of blockchain technology. Blockchain technology involves three elements. First, and at the core of the technology, is a *distributed ledger*. While some argue that blockchain technologies are, at essence, a database that records the timing and nature of states when a ledger is distributed, it has a significant security advantage over centralised databases. Typically, a centralised database has a single point of attack for access to all of its entries while a distributed ledger's entries must be individually attacked in order to be altered. The trade-off for this security is that centralised databases are more adaptable and easier to scale than distributed ledgers.[6]

What this means is that the distributed ledger – that is, the blockchain itself – is a place where states can be recorded. Their security means that they can then be relied upon to create obligations. In effect, this means that these represent a reduction in the monitoring costs (m) that might otherwise be necessary. Moreover, to the extent that states are used to create obligations outside of any particular set of parties, say, for instance, a regulatory reporting requirement or tax liability, when a state is securely recorded on the distributed ledger, it obviates the need for human auditors to confirm those states. This is especially so when the entries on two or more secure ledgers can be read to confirm one another.[7]

The second element of blockchain technologies is a *virtual machine*. All blockchains have a codebase that indicates the actions that can be coded with respect to both ledger entries and token assignment. Bitcoin's is fairly limited, allowing

[6] See J Abadi and M Brunnermeier, 'Blockchain Economics' (2018), available at papers.ssrn.com/sol3/papers.cfm?abstract_id=3310346; and B Arrunada and L Garicano, 'Blockchain: The Birth of Decentralized Governance' (2018), available at papers.ssrn.com/sol3/papers.cfm?abstract_id=3160070.

[7] S Cao, LW Cong and B Yang, 'Financial Reporting and Blockchains: Audit Pricing, Misstatements, and Regulation' (2018), available at papers.ssrn.com/sol3/papers.cfm?abstract_id=3248002.

for token transfer and some other simple functions. By contrast, Ethereum has a virtual machine that is Turing complete – meaning that it is rich enough to perform the functions of any classical computer. This, of course, allows the creation of obligations to be automated and so has a role in reducing monitoring costs (m), but critically, the fact that contracts are coded allows them to adhere to standards of clarity and compliance that, say, a lawyer would otherwise provide, and also to allow interdependency – eg, by allowing obligations in different contracts with a different set of parties to also be created. In other words, a common code can reduce the costs of sharing state information more widely.

The final element of blockchain technologies is a *token*. Tokens are a digital asset that can only appear in one entry in the ledger at a time. In this respect, they are capable of being made rival even though they are purely digital. Obviously, this provides a means of creating a currency that can be used for payments (as in Bitcoin) including to those that provide resources to the blockchain infrastructure. However, such tokens may also be used to underpin measures of the performance of obligations (such as a reputation score) and also as a means of communicating the performance of obligations themselves.[8] In this regard, they provide a means of commitment – the possession of a token can generate certain decision and control rights. Such rights can, in turn, assist in creating favourable incentives for obligations to be performed. However, we leave the details of this to a discussion below and turn next to consider why such incentives are a challenge for smart contracts. In particular, you will note that while blockchain technologies can potentially reduce m, there is nothing inherent in these elements that reduces verification costs (z). That is, unless you can find a way to use the blockchain to obviate the need for a human third party that undertakes verification functions.

V. The Fundamental Smart Contract Challenge

Recall that a smart contract is not necessarily a legal agreement – the parties may have an underlying contract which is legally binding. Instead, the smart contract is the code for the contract's execution. It is a means by which obligations can be recorded, triggering certain other obligations that may operate in an automated way.

As already noted, one way in which smart contracts can improve contracting opportunities is by making the performance of obligations more easily confirmed. In the context of our model this would allow a reduction in m – the costs to any party of monitoring contractual states. This is most obviously useful with regard to payments, but one can imagine situations where important information is digitised – such as the delivery of a product – and this could be recorded and made

[8] The seminal work in this regard is NR Kocherlakota, 'Money is Memory' (1998) 81 *Journal of Economic Theory* 232.

known at a low cost. Of course, digitisation has generated the opportunities for such transmission of information. Blockchain technologies may facilitate these, but because the information required only has to be confirmed by the parties to the contract and not outside of the relationship, it is not clear whether such technologies add additional value.

The challenge for smart contracts comes with regard to performance obligations that need to be verified – that is, to provide hard evidence that an outside party would be able to use to confirm contract performance. In some situations, hard evidence – or its equivalent – can come when the party receiving the obligation confirms that the obligation has been performed. But for the most part the challenge arises because a party performing an obligation has an incentive to claim an obligation has been performed while those receiving it may have an incentive to claim it has not been performed; this is especially the case if their own obligations (eg, making a payment) is contingent upon the obligation being reported as performed. Importantly, with transparency (low or incurred m) the parties themselves have common knowledge of obligation performance or non-performance.

To emphasise this further, note that hard evidence only exists if an obligation has actually been performed, but either party can possess that quality. Following Bull and Watson,[9] suppose that Alice is able to produce a document in the event that Bob performs his obligation, but not otherwise. Then that document is positive evidence of performance while its absence is negative evidence of non-performance. Suppose, in a smart contract, there will be a payment from Alice to Bob if Bob performs his obligation, but not otherwise. The question is: will Alice disclose the document to trigger the smart contract payment? If that payment is positive, it is easy to see that she will not. If Bob performs his obligation, Alice will receive the benefit of that and not have to pay if the document is not disclosed. Of course, if Alice were to be paid if Bob performs his obligation, then the incentives would be aligned. More generally, a party should receive a positive payment if state 1 arises rather than state 2, if that party has positive evidence of state 1 or other parties have positive evidence of state 2. In our case, if the smart contract is going to trigger a payment from Alice, then either Alice needs to have a document that proves non-performance or Bob needs to have a document that proves performance. Without either of these, there is no hard evidence that can support the smart contract envisaged here.

Note that this places a lot of weight on the technical environment that exists. Not only must hard evidence of obligation performance exist, that evidence must be in the hands of the 'right' agent. Moreover, that agent is a different agent depending upon whether the obligation is been performed or not. In other words, for a smart contract to work and reduce the costs associated with verification, it must be

[9] J Bull and J Watson, 'Evidence Disclosure and Verifiability' (2004) 118 *Journal of Economic Theory* 1.

the case that the costs of verifying the right evidence at the right time by the right person must be reduced. For purely digital documents this may be a challenge as digital documents may be easier to fabricate than other documents – that is, technically, a digital document might be able to be produced by both performance and non-performance, in which case it is cheap talk rather than hard evidence.

The ability to generate hard evidence is the fundamental smart contract challenge. To the extent that contract obligations rely on evidence to be provided outside of a purely digital realm where evidence may be hard-coded, any smart contract needs to create incentives for disclosure of the truth of contract performance. The remainder of this chapter will examine candidates for this that might arise from blockchain technologies, including security that allows sensors to be embedded in smart contracts, machines learning predictions as a substitute for hard evidence, and mechanisms to elicit truth-telling.

VI. Working through the Fine Print

Given this discussion, I now turn to work through the fine print of a particular contractual situation that might be assisted with the support of smart contracts. It has the quality of being difficult to achieve as well as having human elements that underpin that difficulty. In doing this, I will show how innovations in economics – particularly, mechanism design – might enable the performance of smart contracts.

A. Simple International Trade Example

To ground this discussion of smart contracting and what it can do, consider the following, very simple, example of international trade. A buyer (B) in one country wants to purchase a product from a seller (S) in another country. We assume that the buyer has a value (V) on the product while the seller has costs (C) of producing the product and shipping it to the buyer. They agree on a price (P) for the buyer to pay the seller in return for shipping the product. This price is less than the buyer's value and higher than the seller's cost; that is $V > P > C$. Thus, both the buyer and seller are better off from the deal.

If their contract was easily enforceable, all would be well. However, let's assume that this is not the case. For instance, suppose that if the seller ships the product to the buyer but the buyer does not pay, the seller ends up with $-C$ rather than $P - C$ while the buyer gets V rather than $V - P$. Thus, if the buyer does not have to pay before the product is delivered, they have an incentive to not pay. On the other hand, suppose that payment is required upfront. That mitigates the seller's risk, but there may be a new risk for the buyer. For instance, suppose the seller can ship an inferior product (worth $v < V$ to the buyer) for a smaller cost ($c < C$). In this case, if the buyer has already paid, the seller earns $P - c$ rather than $P - C$ by shipping the inferior product. This results in the buyer getting $v - P$ rather than $V - P$. If $v < P$, the buyer would not want to take that risk. They would return rather than keep the inferior product for that price.

What this demonstrates is that regardless of the order in which obligations (payment or shipping as the case may be) are performed, one side finds entering the arrangement too risky. Thus, absent some other mechanism, valuable international trade will not take place.

It is useful to reflect on why this international trade example results in transactional failure whereas many similar transactions take place within economies every day. The key assumption here is that while the performance of the contract is readily observable to both parties (ie, m is low or 0), because of a high verification cost (z), it is not possible to rely on a court in either location or somewhere in between to enforce the contract. In other words, transactional failure arises because of *costly verification*. To be sure, social trust could substitute for this lack of verification. While the absence of trust is assumed here, it is also a realistic assumption given that this is a one-shot transaction where neither party has information regarding the past history of the other.[10]

B. The Simplest Smart Contract

Blockchain has proven that it can hold digitised tokens in a ledger and transfer them between different accounts/owners with the permission of the token-holder. In other words, it is a form of purely digitised payments. This is not to say that such payments do not exist elsewhere; it is just that they are the blockchain's proven application.

Proponents of the blockchain realised early on that payment movements could be easily programmable. It is this aspect that caused those proponents to see blockchain technologies as particularly suited to smart contracts. The 'smart' pertained to an agreement that would be executed on the recording of other events on the blockchain.

The simplest smart contract is capable of solving one type of risk in our international trade example: the risk of buyer non-payment. Without a smart contract, the only way a seller can mitigate that risk is asking for payment upfront. However, for a buyer that creates the risk that the seller might not ship the item at all. A smart contract can resolve this issue, and it does this by way of an escrow arrangement.

Suppose that the contract asks the buyer to place tokens in a holding (or escrow) account to cover P. The seller cannot immediately access those tokens.

[10] Interestingly, this situation has been at the heart of issues to do with trading on platforms such as eBay. eBay's solution was to improve procedures that potentially lowered z, but z remained positive nonetheless. (See AJ Schmitz and C Rule, *The New Handshake: Online Dispute Resolution the Future of Consumer Protection* (Chicago, American Bar Association, 2017)).

Instead, the contract specifies an event or state – recorded on the blockchain – that will trigger the transfer of those tokens to the seller. If that state does not occur within a certain period of time, the tokens revert back to the buyer. In this way, the escrow arrangement can be automated.

The key to this happening is for the state to be capable to blockchain verification. One form of an event may be that the buyer simply acknowledges receipt of the goods. The idea here is that the buyer would not do so if they had not, in fact, received the product. Another event could be for the seller to send evidence that the product had been shipped and received to a third party who was trusted to review these and that third party, upon confirmation, would trigger the event. The problem here is that not much is being saved beyond a normal escrow service where the third party did the entire job. The idea of a smart contract is that such processes would be automated.

There is a way such automation could happen. Shipping companies today send shippers receipts that record various events. One could imagine a smart contract plugging directly into the information posted by shippers. Once the product has been acknowledged to them as received, then the event would be triggered and the payment made. It would save the buyer having to take the additional step of acknowledging receipt and it would not require a separate step of having a third party verify this information.

To be sure, these services exist and it is not our task here to work out if the blockchain saves on the broad costs associated with escrow services. It just should be noted that the blockchain could enable that service and it could operate entirely on the blockchain given the appropriate connections with other services – notably shipping company systems.

C. The Sensor Solution

While a simple smart contract might resolve one risk – buyer non-payment – the other risk – the seller sending a poor quality product – remains. At a first pass, the verification of product quality lies outside of the digital realm and so cannot be automated.

Nonetheless, there are situations were hardware in the form of sensors can measure the quality of certain products. If this hardware can be directly and securely linked to the blockchain, they could form part of the event that would trigger a payment in a smart contract.

The challenge here is that such technologies require a careful reworking of the supply chain. At the moment, this is the purview of larger companies that design supply chains for quality assurance. It is far from clear that there exist areas of international trade where sensor verification could open up what is, in effect, new and distinct supply chains.

Thus, while sensors may improve supply chains, it is not clear they have a distinct role in verification. It may be that because the blockchain is regarded as more secure, sensor information may be more readily accessible for use in contract performance verification. Nonetheless, there are simply limits as to how far into the real-world digitisation can progress. While sensors may be incorporated into smart contracts, they are far from a general purpose solution.

D. The Machine Learning Solution

One possible way a smart contract could open up new possibilities is if it executes contractual performance based on the outcomes of machine learning algorithms. Such algorithms would take data from sensors and other digital evidence and then be able to predict the likelihood that performance took place based on that data. In this way, if the likelihood of performance was sufficiently high, then contract could automatically execute.

In this way, what artificial intelligence methods combined with a blockchain housing a smart contract could do is mimic a court's procedure in verifying contract performance. In other words, the court itself could be automated and the potential dispute process could be so cheap that it could just run on each contractual obligation rather than being triggered by one of the parties.

E. The Mechanism Design Solution

We have seen that the key contracting challenge is not the verification of payments – the blockchain and other solutions help there. In addition, when all the relevant parts of a contract can be digitised, verification using the blockchain becomes possible. The question we now turn to ask is: can the blockchain help with verification that is not digitised?

Let us return to the international trade example. Recall that if payments are capable of verification, the primary risk is the buyer receiving a product that is inferior to what was promised; that is, it has a value to them, v, that is less than the expected v. Moreover, this poses a risk to trade if $P > v$ in which the buyer would not want to take the risk. Finally, the buyer could hold up payment to the seller if the product is of low quality; however, the buyer could also do that if the product is as expected. Thus, not only do buyers face risks of receiving inferior products, but sellers who supply the right product face risk of payment not being made.

This is a problem for which there are no easy solutions. For instance, we have already noted that one potentially easy verifiable process that can be integrated into smart contracts is the shipment and receipt of goods. This would work to ensure the buyer received the product. However, it could also work in terms of ensuring that the seller received a returned product. In this case, suppose that a buyer received a product that was of low quality. The buyer could simply return it and once that return was received by the seller, the funds in escrow would be paid back to the buyer.

However, there are risks here as well. First of all, the seller, who knowingly sent a poorer quality product to the buyer may encourage the buyer to accept a lower price rather than a return. If the buyer has their own costs in trying to return a product, they might accept this. But, taken as a whole, the buyer does not have the product they wanted and, instead, has ended up with something that, while they were willing to pay for it rather than return it, is ultimately worse off than expected. Such issues cause people to avoid entering into such transactions in the first place.

Second, one way out of this would be for the seller to commit to compensating the buyer should the buyer want to return the product. Smart contracts could help facilitate this by requiring the seller to place tokens in escrow, being paid only if it is required. The seller would thus have incentives to send the expected product to the buyer. But even here there are risks. Unscrupulous buyers who face low costs in trying to return a product may take advantage of sellers in order to receive the compensation for returns. In other words, a seller who ships a good quality product may find themselves having to pay for a return regardless.

All this means that a simple 'return it if you do not like it and we will cover the cost' contract will not overcome the challenges in ensuring the product of the expected quality is shipped and then accepted by the buyer.

To resolve this, we want to find a mechanism that gives sellers the incentives to send the right product and buyers the incentive to only complain and withhold payment if they receive the wrong product. The good news is that both the buyer and seller actually know the truth – whether the good or bad product has been shipped and received. The bad news is that, by assumption, no one else knows this information.

There is, however, an economic mechanism that can work to resolve this. It is based on the mechanisms studied by Moore and Repullo[11] and Maskin and Tirole.[12] In particular, it is a 'simple sequential mechanism'.[13] What these mechanisms involve is a set of rewards/punishments to each party based on the 'messages' or claims they make regarding what is going on. Ideally, the rewards are designed so that if one party tells the truth, they earn more than if they lie.

[11] J Moore and R Repullo, 'Subgame perfect implementation' (1988) 56 *Econometrica* 1191.

[12] E Maskin and J Tirole, 'Unforeseen contingencies and incomplete contracts' (1999) 66 *Review of Economic Studies* 83.

[13] J Moore, 'Implementation, contracts, and renegotiation in environments with complete information' (1992) 1 *Advances in Economic Theory* 182.

Before introducing the mechanism, it is worth noting that I am not the first to propose this nor to highlight the notion that blockchain technologies might enable it. Holden and Malani[14] examine the 'hold-up' problem whereby choices that cannot be contracted upon (that is, verified by a third party) could be resolved by a simple sequential mechanism. They are not thinking about the more pedestrian international trade-type issues but, instead, the broader issue of incentives for cost reduction and quality in higher stakes business arrangements. They argue that what has limited such mechanisms is the possibility that parties to a contract may renegotiate outcomes. They then explore whether a blockchain could commit the parties not to engage in such renegotiations that can undermine mechanisms by denying them commitment power to shape incentives. It is not clear whether a blockchain could engage in a commitment against renegotiation when the stakes are high (so high that parties would be happy to bear the costs of court adjudication). However, I should note that this is not what is at the heart of my discussion here. In particular, as the costs of verification are otherwise prohibitively high in the international trade example this also implies that renegotiation is infeasible. Instead, here I rely on the feature of smart contracting to make payments triggered by states and obligations.

Here is a mechanism that can achieve a truth-telling outcome in the international trade example. It focusses on the buyer's incentive to report the truth.

(1) (Announcement) The buyer announces the quality of the good (V or v)

- If the quality announced is V, the contract is completed and payment is made.
- If the quality announced is v, the seller can challenge the claim.
- If there is no challenge, no payment is made to the seller and the product is returned with the buyer receiving compensation of f.
- If there is a challenge, we move the 'Challenge' stage

(2) (Challenge) The buyer is immediately fined, F, to be paid to the seller

- The seller offers the buyer the choice between:
  1. keeping the product for a price of p ($< P$); or
  2. returning the product for compensation of f.
- If the buyer chooses option 1, the new price is struck and the contract concludes with relevant payments being made.
- If the buyer chooses option 2, the product is returned, with the seller paying the buyer f and the seller paying a fine of $2F$ to a third party.

[14] R Holden and A Malani, 'Can Blockchains Solve the Holdup Problem in Contracts' (2018), available at bfi.uchicago.edu/wp-content/uploads/WP_No.2018-12.pdf.

The resulting game tree is as depicted in Figure 2.1. This mechanism has a unique equilibrium outcome whereby the seller always sends the buyer the good quality and the buyer always accepts this.

Figure 2.1 Extensive Form Game

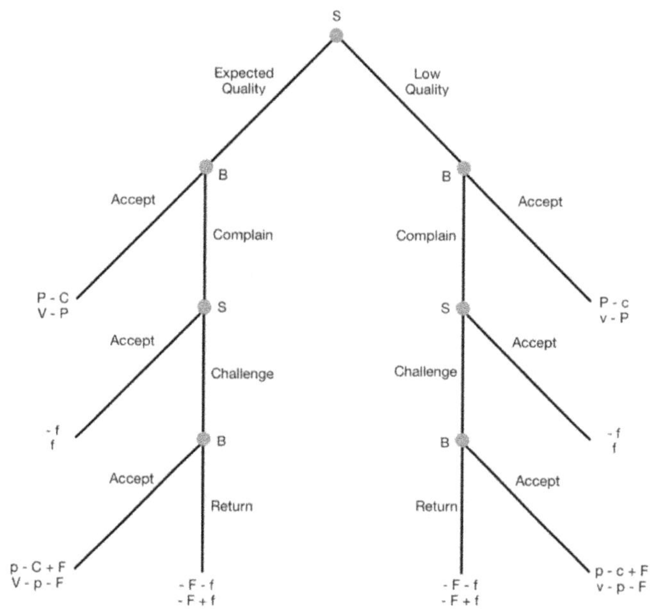

Proposition 2. Consider a contract where, if there is no seller challenge, the buyer can return the product and receive compensation of f but otherwise must pay P. If the seller challenges, the outcomes are as specified above. Suppose that: (i) $V > p + f > v$; and (ii) $P < p + F$ and (iii) $F > f$, then international trade in the good quality product takes place.

Proof: Suppose the quality of the good is V, but B claims v. Suppose S initiates the challenge. B will face a choice between $V - p$ and returning the product for f. So long as $V - p > f$ or $V > p + f$, B will keep the product. In this case, S ultimately receives a payment of $p + F$ while B ultimately pays $p + F$. It is worthwhile for S to initiate the challenge as they receive F.

Suppose the quality of the good is v and B claims this. If S initiates the challenge, B will face a choice between $v - p$ and f. B will choose to return the product if $v - p < f$. In this case, S will be fined and so ultimately receive $f - F$ while B will ultimately pay $F - f$.

First, note that if $V > p + f > v$, B will have an incentive to claim the truth about product quality (paying P for a good quality product as $V - P > f$ by (i) and asking for a return otherwise) prior to any challenge and to match any challenge from S when the product quality is v. Given this, if the product quality is v, S does not have an incentive to launch a challenge.

Second, as noted above, *S* has an incentive to initiate a challenge if the product quality is *V* (and is claimed otherwise by *B*) while *B*, because of this, does not have an incentive to claim the product quality is not *V* prior to the challenge.

Finally, *S* earns *P* – *C* by shipping the good quality product and, at most, – *f*, by shipping the bad-quality product.

Some remarks are in order. First, there is considerable leeway here in the choice of fines (*F*), compensation (*f*) and prices (*p*). Indeed, *f* might be zero or even negative while *F* could be very small. The key is that both parties want to avoid a challenge being triggered as this results in a loss to each of them.

Second, there may be concern that the challenge mechanism would not work as, once triggered, there is an incentive to limit the damage by agreeing to an alternative arrangement. Indeed, this may even happen by the seller threatening to challenge. While this might be a concern generically, in this example, we have already assumed a situation where, absent a mechanism and set of escrow payments, it is hard for the seller and buyer to contract. How then would they be able to enforce a renegotiation between them? It would seem that the incentives to adhere to the contract would be stronger than seeing if you can fix things up later on.

Third, there is a practical concern that both parties may not want to enter into an arrangement where they could end up worse off if the other party does something stupid or makes a mistake. This is the argument of Aghion et al.[15] Indeed, Aghion et al[16] test this mechanism in the lab. While they demonstrate that people may fear losses due to mistakes, the variant of their experiment that is closest to the situation modelled here where the buyer who receives a high-quality product does not face a challenge, did perform well in their experiments. Beyond the lab, only real-world adoption would constitute a practical test.

What is interesting about this mechanism is that because it requires escrow funds of *P* + *F* from the buyer and *F* from the seller, a blockchain with a smart contract is perhaps uniquely able to provide the confidence that payments will flow as intended. The contract makes all factors transparent and automates all actions. In other words, it provides a substitute for a court verification process that might otherwise be too costly.

F. Some Practicalities

It is reasonable to wonder how such a mechanism might look in practice. For instance, what is the magnitude of the escrow required of buyers and sellers as

[15] P Aghion, D Fudenberg, R Holden, T Kunimoto and O Tercieux, 'Subgame-Perfect Implementation Under Value Perturbations' (2012) 127 *Quarterly Journal of Economics* 1843.

[16] P Aghion, D Fudenberg, R Holden, T Kunimoto and O Tercieux, 'The Role of Bounded Rationality and Imperfect Information in Subgame Perfect Implementation – An Empirical Investigation' (2017) 16 *Journal of the European Economic Association* 232.

part of a transaction? To explore this, let's suppose the following: $V = \$30$, $v = \$0$, $P = \$15$, $C = \$10$ and $c = \$5$. In this case, for Proposition 2 to apply $p + f$ must be less than \$30 while $p + F$ must be greater than \$15. So let's suppose that $p = \$10$ while $F = \$6$ and $f = \$6$. Under this deal, if the expected product is shipped, then the buyer (in a challenge round) would keep it as this would get them \$14 in surplus while returning it would get them \$0. By contrast, if the poor product is shipped, then the buyer will choose to return it as it is worth nothing to them and not worth paying the discounted \$10. Notice that any positive discounted price would lead to this outcome here. Given this, the seller would accept the challenge if the low-quality product was shipped but otherwise offer the buyer a discounted price. Overall, then the buyer who receives their expected product does not challenge (as this would raise their effective price by \$1) and one who does receive a low-quality product challenges as they can get a return refunding the potential fine they would otherwise pay.

Seen in this light, the challenge mechanism here is a just a variant on a 'no questions asked' return policy. The buyer can always return the item but has to (a) put up \$6 in escrow if they do this and (b) agree to consider a counter offer from the seller. Therefore, unless the buyer wants to return the item they do not need to put more than the original price of the product in escrow. For the seller, however, to assure the buyer, they would need to keep the original price in escrow plus the difference between that price and the effective challenge price (of $P + f = \$21$). With \$21 in escrow, if there is a challenge the seller can refund P and pay the buyer f for their trouble. Thus, the buyer need not pay any money beyond the agreed price upfront and the seller need only keep that price and put in an additional amount to cover the refund amount to assure the buyer.[17]

VII. Future Directions

This chapter has looked at fine print of smart contracts. The goal was to understand where blockchain technologies – made up of a distributed ledger with a virtual machine and token layer – could enhance the possibilities for efficient contracting. That meant being explicit on where contracts work and do not work today without the assistance of such technologies. This led to a focus on security (as provided by the distributed ledger), clarity (as provided by virtual machines) and commitment (as provided by tokens).

The good news is that blockchains can make the monitoring of states (including verified obligation performance) cheaper precisely because those states can

[17] If the seller did not want even this risk, f could be set to be \$0. In this case, the buyer may be concerned about being out of pocket if a challenge needed to be mounted because this, by definition, means they pay a higher price in that eventuality. Rational economics alone cannot tell us whether these considerations would matter.

be relied upon due to security features. The bad news is that most contractual situations that struggle today do so because of issues to do with the incentives for humans to perform obligations that cannot be easily measured – either digitally or by a third party such as a court.

Nonetheless, because so much can be included in smart contracts running off the blockchain, there is potential to innovate and deploy economic mechanisms that could create incentives for humans to perform and report on obligations in a truthful manner. In other words, the commitment engendered by the blockchain could substitute for a lack of trust in the real world. Whether these mechanisms exist, are practical, can be understood by real people and yield a return are still open questions. But it should be clear that the missing fine print in smart contracting is economic innovation in mechanisms and markets.

3

Smart Contracts and Traditional Contracts: Views of Contract Law

MATTI RUDANKO

I. Introduction

A. Research Questions and Exclusions

Contracts are traditionally understood as tools of business and human beings to arrange their mutual relationships in a predictable but flexible way, adaptive to varying circumstances of real life, and offering legal protection in case of contractual disorders. Smart contracts are self-enforcing and tamper-proof contracts, based on coded algorithms.[1]

The topic of this chapter is smart contract as seen from the point of view of contract law, including issues of appropriate methods of implementing legal protection. A comparison is made between the self-enforcing and tamper-proof nature of smart contracts and the contract law approach, including a variety of liability-based contractual remedies and responsiveness of contracts to changing real-life circumstances. For this purpose, the role and possibilities of linguistic analysis and computer sciences are considered for the research of coded languages in their relationship with natural languages, including questions of (perhaps intentional) ambiguity and pragmatic flexibleness of language. This reflects also on the implementation of contract law principles, eg, protection of the weaker party, by the use of indeterminate legal concepts such as good faith and reasonableness.

In the following, usually only contract law aspects of smart contracts are included. For instance, the application of the EU General Data Protection Regulation (GDPR 2016/679), and the problem of interaction of smart contracts

[1] Szabo defined smart contracts as machine-readable transaction protocols which create a contract with predetermined terms, or a set of promises, specified in digital form, including protocols within which the parties perform on these promises'. See N Szabo, 'Formalizing and Securing Relationships on Public Networks' (1997) 2 *First Monday* 1.

with the external world entailing loss of trustlessness, disintermediation and decentralisation.[2] The chapter also excludes questions of private international law and international jurisdiction (general judicial power of courts) related to smart contracts.[3]

B. Methodological Aspects

Smart contracts as an object of research is here considered to belong to an ontological sphere that can be called 'digital law'.[4] It is located in the intersection of at least three ontologically different areas: legal science; empirical sciences; and computer science. In computer science, ontology relates to an artefact, a structure of knowledge modelling the selected application area.[5] The more legal reasoning takes the form of algorithms and other computer processes, the more relevant to law becomes also the understanding of ontology in computer science, and the more does this ontology affect the development of normative systems.

Digital law brings forth a special ontological category for norms: 'digital normative existence' (existence of norms in digital systems). It is possible that in the 'cyberspace of law', normative sciences have to be influenced by the ontology, epistemology and methodology of computer sciences.[6] This may have implications for the methodology of legal science – it is not clear that traditional ontology of norms is sufficient or even adequate for digital normative existence. Neither are norms the only beings in the cyberspace of law, but there can also be digital agents like legislators, judges and contracting parties, perhaps equipped with artificial intelligence (AI) characteristics. It is important to adopt methodological inputs of cognitive sciences in research of areas like consciousness, intelligence and neuroethics in law.

[2] For a good introduction to the extensive discussion of these questions, E Mik, 'Smart Contracts: Terminology, Technical Limitations and Real World Complexity' (2017) 9 *Law, Innovation and Technology* 269. See also J Goldenfein and A Leiter, 'Legal Engineering on the Blockchain: "Smart Contracts" as Legal Conduct' (2018) 29 *Law & Critique* 141.

[3] S Bourque and S Fung Ling Tsui, *A Lawyer's Introduction to Smart Contracts* (Warsaw, Scientia Łask, 2014) 12.

[4] Digital law is not an established and exactly defined scientific category. It is adopted here as a comprehensive concept for digitalised elements in the 'realm of law': in legislation and other norm-giving, in application of law in courts and public agencies, in the legal thinking of lawyers and other actors, in contracting practices, etc. 'Law' consists of different norms like legislative acts, lower-level official statutes, self-regulation and contract provisions.

[5] See, eg D Man, 'Ontologies in Computer Science' (2013) 31 *Didactica Mathematica* 43.

[6] See, eg DR Koepsell and WJ Rapaport, *The Ontology of Cyberspace. Questions and Comments.* This is a document consisting of two papers, originally presented at the Tri-State Philosophical Association Meeting, St Bonaventure University, 22 April 1995. This document is SUNY Buffalo Department of Computer Science Technical Report 95-25 and SUNY Buffalo Center for Cognitive Science Technical Report 95-09.

C. The Structure of the Chapter

After this introduction, section II summarises the common descriptions of smart contracts and examines the relationship between the trustlessness feature and truthfulness of transactions, the position of contractual intent in smart contracts, and smart contracts as an agent. A special proposition for regulation of smart contracts is presented with a reference to financial markets regulation. In section III possibilities of maintaining contract law reasoning, including principles of protection of the weaker party and reasonableness (adjustment of contracts) in a smart contract environment, are considered and the self-enforcement of smart contracts is compared with contract law protection based on other remedies. This view is supported in section IV by a comparative survey of contract language and code. The chapter is concluded in section V by a rule of law view on smart contracts.

II. Smart Contracts, Traditional Contracts and Contract Law

A. Smart Contract Characteristics

In smart contracts in the blockchain environment, a software code includes and comprises the contract in its entirety, defines and arranges the preconditions for the contractual performances, and also takes care of the execution of the contract without the interference of the contracting parties when predefined conditions are met.[7] Smart contracts also may collect data from the physical world environment to process it according to what is provided in the contract, and make decisions based on this information. A smart contract also is immune to unauthorised changes in its contents by a party or anybody else.[8]

The blockchain 'can be described as a decentralised, peer-validated crypto-ledger that provides a publicly visible, chronological and permanent record of all prior transactions. It resembles a spreadsheet that anybody can add a row to, but cannot otherwise update or delete anything'.[9] Smart contracts are based on databases which are geographically replicated and synchronised between users, known

[7] R Koulu, 'Blockchains and Online Dispute Resolution: Smart Contracts as an Alternative to Enforcement' (2016) 13 *ScriptEd* 53.

[8] K Lauslahti, J Mattila and T Seppälä, *Smart Contracts: How will Blockchain Technology Affect Contractual Practices?* (2017) 68 *ETLA Reports* 11, available at www.etla.fi/wp-content/uploads/ETLA-Raportit-Reports-68.pdf.

[9] Mik, 'Smart Contracts' (2017) 6.

as distributed ledger technologies (DLT). So-called permissionless ledgers, unlike permissioned blockchains, have no restrictions to access, being decentralised and visible to all.

Each 'node' – ie actor participating in the blockchain system – has to provide a 'proof-of-work', a set of data based on intense and extensive computing ('mining') to create a block and append it to the blockchain. The identity of the node and the contents of the proof-of-work is then easy for other nodes to verify.[10]

Mining means that, to ensure that the other network users accept the proposed block as part of the shared blockchain, the party must produce a solution to a complicated mathematical problem specific to each individual block. The block structure is designed so that any tampering with the data replaces the problems to be solved with other ones. When this happens, the solutions developed to previous blocks no longer apply, which results in rejection of the fraudulent block by the other nodes, which can continue to run the system with their own inputs.[11]

In smart contracts, there is no element, or even need, of trust between the parties, nor any requirement of external monitoring of contractual obligations or enforcement.[12] This is why the system is called *trustless*. Szabo's theory states that smart contracts diminish the number of frauds and other malicious phenomena while lowering transaction costs as contract terms are automatically implemented.[13]

In the following section I explore whether the verifiable nature of the set of data guarantees 'truthfulness', ie compatibility of what is appended in the blockchain with real transactions.

B. Being Trustless – Being Truthful?

Smart contracts are here considered as digital programs based on a blockchain consensus architecture that automatically implement their internal logic as certain preconditions are met, and which are also able to prevent unauthorised changes of their internal logic as a result of their decentralised nature.[14]

One of the basic elements of the blockchain system is being 'trustless'. The truthfulness of an event is not based on guarantees given by a trusted third party, but on a 'distributed consensus' of a majority of nodes. What this means in terms of truthfulness remains in many cases unclear. The system can bring about a consensus on the sufficiency of the proof-of-work, but cannot guarantee trustlessness of

[10] ibid 7.

[11] J Mattila and T Seppälä, *Blockchains as a Path to a Network of Systems: An Emerging New Trend of the Digital Platforms in Industry and Society* (2015) 45 *ETLA Reports* 7, available at www.etla.fi/wp-content/uploads/ETLA-Raportit-Reports-45.pdf.

[12] Koulu, 'Blockchains and Online Dispute Resolution' (2016) 54.

[13] Szabo, 'Formalizing and Securing Relationships' (1997).

[14] Lauslahti, Mattila and Seppälä, *Smart Contracts* (2017) 7.

anything that happens or exists outside of its cryptographically secure domain – including contractual performance. The 'blockchain itself is "trustless" because it creates and confirms a certain state of affairs and replaces the need to trust third parties with the ability to trust the technology itself'.[15]

'Mining' can result in so-called 'validation' of a transaction as a requirement of its recording in the blockchain, by a consensus of the majority of nodes. The consensus, however, only reflects the understanding of the majority that the required proof-of work was produced. This means that the transaction input exceeded the transaction output and that the conditions of the locking scripts have been fulfilled. But the validity of the transaction in the legal sense – including legal capacity or absence of vitiating factors like duress or illegality – is something different, being beyond the capabilities of the blockchain system.[16] What is included in the blockchain does not not necessarily reflect reality.[17]

In order to become a real platform (and not only a database) for any complex transactions the blockchain should be attached to an interface to the external real world. This could take the form of protocol layers or scripts on top of the blockchain. But this kind of an addition would lack the element of trustlessness (based on a distributed consensus) in the sense inherent in the original system.[18]

C. Conclusion and Essential Elements of the Contract, Especially Intent

For the legal validity of smart contracts, or even their inclusion in the category of contracts, some inherent contract law related qualifications have been considered necessary. For example, evidence of the contracting parties' intention to create legal relations, proof of the relevant contractual terms, and external enforceability have each been considered necessary elements of a contract.[19]

It is true that seen from the perspective of traditional contract law, consent, declaration of intent and the purpose of communicating it to the other party have all been considered necessary prerequisites for classification of an act as a (legally enforceable) contract. From the perspective of common law-based contract law systems, Eliza Mik reduces these prerequisites into two criteria: intention and consideration. Under common law, consideration need not be adequate; it only

[15] Mik (n 2) 7–8.

[16] If a smart contract executes an agreement that was formed under duress or as a result of an actionable misrepresentation, the smart contract will self-enforce but the underlying agreement may be set aside. See Mik (n 2) 15.

[17] Mik (n 2) 9.

[18] Mik (n 2) 8.

[19] European Union, 'Impact of Digital Innovation on the Processing of Electronic Payments and Contracting: An Overview of Legal Risks', available at op.europa.eu/en/publication-detail/-/publication/f935cf2c-04a8-11e8-b8f5-01aa75ed71a1/language-en.

needs to be sufficient in the eyes of the law.[20] Consent (which has to be in some way made known to the other party) refers to a party's free will to become bound by the contract.[21]

A contract, as a legal act, is a combination of two or more accordant expressions of will of parties. For them, the contract forms a basis of rights and obligations. but it is only the parties to the contract and not any third party (but in certain exceptions) that can base their claims on the contract.[22] In this section, the contractual characteristic, and especially the intent of parties, of smart contracts are considered more closely. The wide scale of smart contracts shows examples corresponding to a high degree of traditional contracts. In other cases, however, even the existence of parties instead of mere computer programs remains unclear.[23]

According to Finnish law, the binding force in contract law of an expression of will requires that the declaration of intent is to its contents individualised enough, containing all content elements of the contract and, in principle, being able to be accepted by a simple yes reply and thus leading to the formation of a complete contract. In addition, the offer has to be addressed to a certain other person or a limited group of persons. Public declarations of intent to completely indefinite addressees are as a rule non-binding, but if the group of addressees is somehow restricted, the declaration of intent can be valid.[24]

The element of the will of both parties to enter the agreement, as required in traditional contracts, applies as well to smart contracts as a necessary prerequisite for the contract to be valid. As in traditional contracts, the offer–acceptance mechanism, consisting of a combination of two expressions of will, is not typically the only or the best explanatory model of the conclusion of a contract.[25] Besides this model, regulated in Finland in the Contracts Act (1929), there are other contracting processes like contracts concluded through negotiation, implied contracts and tacit agreements. For example, using public transportation or parking in a paid parking lot are seen as examples of implied contracts, not concluded as a combination of explicit expressions of intent, but rather based on social norms.[26]

[20] Mik (n 2) 14. For a short introduction to the doctrine of consideration and its use in English contract law, see, eg S Wheeler and J Shaw, *Contract Law* (Oxford, Oxford University Press 1994) 317–24. For the related bargain theory analysed by tools of economics see R Cooter and T Ulen, *Law and Economics*, 2nd edn (Reading, Mass, Addison-Wesley, 1996) 162–65. See also M Eisenberg, 'The Bargain Principle and its Limits' (1982) 5 *Harvard Law Review* 741. For a more extensive presentation of the doctrine of consideration and its connections to contract law, see E McKendrick, *Contract Law*, 6th edn (New York. Palgrave Macmillan, 2005) ch 5.

[21] Lauslahti, Mattila and Seppälä (n 8) 10. See also eg, A Saarnilehto, V Annola, M Hemmo, J Karhu, L Kartio, E Tammi-Salminen, J Tolonen and J Tuomisto, *Varallisuusoikeus [Property Law]* (Helsinki, Sanoma Pro Oy, 2012) 323.

[22] O Norros, *Vastuu sopimusketjussa [Liability in Contract Chains]* (Vantaa, WSOYpro, 2007) 1–3.

[23] Lauslahti, Mattila and Seppälä (n 8) 20.

[24] ibid 10.

[25] M Hemmo, *Sopimusoikeuden oppikirja (A Textbook in Contract Law)* (Helsinki, Talentum media Oy, 2006) 96–97. See also Lauslahti, Mattila and Seppälä (n 8) 3–5.

[26] See concerning Finnish law eg M Hemmo, *Sopimusoikeus I* (Helsinki, Talentum media Oy, 2003) 133–36; Hemmo, *Sopimusoikeuden oppikirja* (2006) 88; and Saarnilehto, Annola, Hemmo, Karhu, Kartio, Tammi-Salminen, Tolonen and Tuomisto, *Varallisuusoikeus* (2012) 384–85. In the famous

Likewise, in terms of traditional contract law, using an automat like a vending machine can be considered to contain a feature representing a declaration of intent. The buying process can be characterised as the conclusion of a contract. In this example, intent can be understood to be expressed by the exchange of assets or services, ie by acting upon it in the purchase of items from a vending machine.[27] An automat, with sets of for-sale items and relevant information on prices, methods of payment and products, may perhaps be considered an offer made to a sufficiently limited audience, consisting of those who are willing to buy products from the automat.

Even more generally, in a smart contract, the declaration of intent can be seen to be given through a transaction to the contract system itself: it has been suggested that in smart contracts, the manifestation of the parties' intent can in some cases be identified from the exchange of performances, or participating in a smart contract by performing a transaction in accordance with its terms.[28] According to this view, smart contracts could be considered concluded on the basis of parties' declaration of intent, explained through the offer–acceptance mechanism or by models of tacit agreements or implied contracts. A public smart contract added to the blockchain to which the party has transferred assets for management in the purpose of concluding a contract could be considered as an offer and another party's consistent behaviour as an acceptance of the offer.[29] This requires that the creation of the smart contract and its placement into the blockchain can be seen as a sufficiently individualised offer made to a specified group of addressees and corresponding to the requirements of, for example, the Finnish Contracts Act.[30]

The requirement of separate evidence of the parties' intention may not fit very well to the dynamics and even the very idea of smart contracts, the basic attraction of which lies in their automation and differences from conventional contracts.[31] Some in-depth doctrinal reasoning on this view has been presented in modern American research on the role of consent in contract formation.

The traditional approach to contract law considers a contract as a combination expressions of will and the conscious, objectively manifested intention of parties to be bound to terms.[32] Under an American will-oriented view of form contracts, consenting to form contracts is not about making a promise that a party would need to have actually understood. Instead, it is 'about manifesting consent to be legally bound'.[33] In modern American contract doctrine, the bargain theory of

decision of the Finnish Supreme Court 2010 the driver and the parking company were considered to have concluded a contract by the fact of driving into the parking lot with signage boards indicating a parking charge for non-compliant parking and stating that 'By accepting parking, you accept the terms'.

[27] A similar transaction-based interpretation has also been outlined with regard to smart contracts: Koulu (n 7) 65; Lauslahti, Mattila and Seppälä (n 8) 15.

[28] Koulu (n 7) 54.

[29] Lauslahti, Mattila and Seppälä (n 8) 16.

[30] ibid 21.

[31] ibid.

[32] LH Scholz, 'Algorithmic Contracts' (2017) 20 *Stanford Technology Law Review* 128, 151.

[33] RE Barnett, 'Consenting to Form Contracts' (2002) 71 *Fordham Law Review* 627, 629–30.

contract has been adopted instead of the benefit-detriment model: a bargaining process between the two parties produces something that can be classified as a contract.[34]

In his study on algorithmic contracts and the contract law significance of consent, Scholz draws attention to so-called black box algorithmic contracts in which the foundations of party consent must be outlines in a different way than in form contracts. Parties to, based on consent, form contracts can be, so to speak 'rationally ignorant' about what their consent covers as it is something that exists or at least can be rationally understood in the conclusion of the contract. But in black box algorithmic contracts, there is no fixed set of things of to which a party can be said to be ignorant because what the algorithm is going to do is something emergent and unknown and unpredictable to both parties.[35] In a black box algorithmic contract, an offeror may use an algorithm to choose the contracting partner, price, etc. In black box algorithmic contracts the offeror is not bargaining; it is the algorithm bargaining. This means that this party is in fact not the direct offeror, but the automated agent that is offering on behalf of the offeror, with contractual contents that the offeror has perhaps not fully considered.[36]

According to Scholz, there are serious concerns about whether the bargain theory of contract can be applied to black box algorithmic contracts. This inevitably poses special challenges for the inclusion of black box algorithmic contracts into the category of contracts.

D. Contract Law Position of Parties: Comparison between Smart Contracts and Financial Market Transactions

Each party to a smart contract must: (1) be identifiable; and (2) sign or otherwise indicate acceptance to the agreement and its terms.[37] This all depends on the concept of identity of the party. In applications based on blockchain technology, the parties are primarily unidentifiable. Therefore it had been suggested that the declarations of intent are aimed at parties willing to conclude contracts in the specific matter at offer, as is the case in the vending machine example.[38] But the contract law significance of the identifiable parties can even be elaborated further for the blockchain-based smart contract environment.

The fact that in applications based on blockchain technology the parties are primarily unidentifiable may cause major difficulties for fitting smart contracts into the traditional contract formation patterns. The cryptocurrency wallet address is a one-way unique identifier that guarantees reaching a person's pocketbook, or

[34] Scholz, 'Algorithmic Contracts' (2017) 156.
[35] ibid 152.
[36] ibid 154.
[37] Bourque and Fung Ling Tsui, *Lawyer's Introduction* (2014) 6–7.
[38] Lauslahti, Mattila and Seppälä (n 8) 21.

inbox, but does not reveal the person's identity.[39] Some smart contracts, instead of fulfilling the legal requirements of a contract, can rather be characterised as programs built in the blockchain in which different parties do not appear distinctly.[40]

The problems arising where the users are known only by their pseudonyms and where jurisdiction is in dispute are more relevant to and prevalent in a public chain environment. However, these problems are not insuperable and nearly always arise in large public blockchain environments (such as Bitcoin). If the parties know each other and could have resolved these matters in an analogue transaction, there is no impediment to them resolving or prosecuting a dispute in the usual way.[41]

In digital contracting, the use of the private key infrastructure is a commonly used method of identification. A public key certificate and the corresponding private key that cannot be derived from the public key can be used independently to encrypt information so that only its corresponding key can decrypt (unlock) the information into a meaningful form. Using a combination of such techniques, the smart contract can: (1) be signed; (2) make the parties verifiable; (3) be encrypted; and (4) guarantee the integrity of the code.[42] The public key, which remains publicly visible, is required to receive tokens, and the private key is required to spend them. No tokens can be moved from the public key unless the correct private key is used.[43]

The ability of parties to be identifiable is, of course, of crucial importance with regards to legal liabilities based on the contract. According to Scholz, algorithms should be considered constructive agents for the purpose of contract formation in order to enable finding liability for wrongful acts such as fraud or market manipulation arising from the contracts and to promote algorithmic accountability.[44]

As a point of comparison, the trading mechanisms of securities markets include also anonymous trading. In the automated trading in securities markets, offers and acceptances are fed in the system that then matches the corresponding inputs into contracts, which are in the next stage settled in an automated netting system, distributing the net assets to the participants in trading. In the trading system, no traditional contract relations between identifiable parties can be detected, but there is no doubt about the existence of real sale of securities transactions.[45]

In the case of securities markets trading, the lack of identifiable contractual relations, however, has been seen as an indication for the need for specific

[39] Bourque and Fung Ling Tsui (n 3) 13.

[40] Lauslahti, Mattila and Seppälä (n 8) 21.

[41] P Ryan, 'Smart Contract Relations in e-Commerce: Legal Implications of Exchanges Conducted on the Blockchain' (2017) 7 *Technology Innovation Management* 4, 4–21.

[42] Bourque and Fung Ling Tsui (n 3) 6–7.

[43] Mik (n 2) 22–23.

[44] Scholz (n 32) 169.

[45] See the more detailed presentation (based on Finnish securities markets) in M Rudanko, *Arvopaperimarkkinat ja siviilioikeus (Securities Markets and Civil Law)* (Helsinki, Kauppakaari Oyj, 1998) 40–54, 118–60.

regulation of some aspects that in contract law are left within the sphere of the private autonomy of parties.[46] These aspects include above all manifold and extensive disclosure obligations of issuers and trading parties and rules to eliminate market abuse (like insider dealing and market manipulation). Notably, there are also extensive and detailed sets of legal rules on the very trading on marketplaces. The ultimate goal of the legal provisions is to ensure the smooth and reliable functioning of the markets as well as to achieve and maintain a sufficient level of investor protection.[47]

The anonymity to one another of parties to contracts is not a special issue in financial markets, due to the regulatory arrangement of liability relations between parties.[48] When considering the possibility of similar regulatory measures in 'smart contract markets', remarkable differences from financial markets can, of course, be seen already at first sight. The financial markets form a distinguishable entity because of many factors, including the precise definition of regulated marketplaces, admissible actors, tradable products, etc. The target of regulation can thus be identified exactly enough. Smart contracts lack all these criteria so that it is artificial even to try to detect any clear 'markets' in smart contracts. Contrary to financial markets, the only actors are usually parties to contracts, who are in this sole role unidentified and most difficult to trace as targets of regulation.

Regulatory approaches may, however, be the only means of combatting the apparent disharmony between smart contracts and contract law-based protection of parties – and the already existing grievances and sheer abuses relating especially to blockchain-based smart contracts (see, eg, section V on the infamous DAO case). For regulatory purposes, perhaps some kind of platform for concluding smart contracts on a regulated basis should be defined, precisely enough for regulation, and in contracts concluded on such a platform contract law based or other legal remedies would be available. In the definition of targets as well as finding proper contents of regulation, guidance could perhaps be sought from models applied in financial market regulation. In the cases that remain outside the regulated platforms, the protection of parties could perhaps be at large left to the sphere of the 'code is law' principle, mainly beyond the reach of legal remedies, but possibly with the exception for most flagrant abuses.[49]

Also, in financial markets it has been necessary for the smooth functioning of the markets and investor protection to modify traditional legal views on relationships between parties. For instance, the settlement finality in insolvency proceedings, as

[46] ibid 210–17.

[47] R Veil (ed), *European Capital Markets Law*, 2nd edn (Oxford, Hart Publishing, 2017) 23–30 (§ 2 Concept and Aims of Regulation).

[48] Concerning the structure and objects of European capital markets regulation, a good general picture can be formulated by the list of contents in Veil, *European Capital Markets Law* (2017) xiv–xxxii: public and private supervisory systems, disclosure duties (eg prospectus), regulated trading venues, trading in the markets, settlement of trades, financial instruments, market participants, access to the markets and status of professional intermediaries and investment firms, conflicts of interest, civil and criminal law liabilities and market abuse.

[49] About the slogan 'code is law' see, eg L Lessig, *Code Version 2.0* (New York, Basic Books, 1999) ch 5.

well as the binding nature of financial collateral arrangements toward third parties in insolvency situations have required amendments of contract law, property law and insolvency law rules.[50]

Some structural analogies can be detected between party relations in financial markets and blockchain-based smart contracts, for instance, in the disclosure duties positions. In the forms of smart contracts in which parties are unknown to one another, like in financial markets, these duties cannot be organised on the contract law basis (eg, as disclosure and inquiry obligations of the seller and the buyer) because there are no clear contractual relations and, consequently, neither are there any distinct targets for disclosure duties. Instead, the disclosure obligations have to be directed rather to the markets at large, like the prospectus duty or the ongoing disclosure obligation of issuers of securities. In possible smart contract regulation, the contracting platform could correspond to the 'market' as the main addressee of mandatory information, which would then become to some degree public in this environment.

Another regulatory pattern worth considering also for smart contracts could concern the organisation of and rules for the trading – in this context – making the rules for concluding contracts transparent and establishing solid practices for the behaviour of parties in later stages, including the execution of contracts. Statutory qualifications of platforms ('trading venues') also belong to this regulatory approach.

Also, statutorily set standards for traded products, an integral part of financial market regulation, could be considered – meaning here allowed forms and contents of contracts as well as products suitable as objects of smart contracts. For this purpose, the development of coding possibilities of various contract provisions (see chapter four) and the increasing role of AI should, of course, be taken into account. Likewise, the question arises concerning the limitations of smart contracts solely for the use of experts or professionals who could represent their clients as intermediaries in contractual relationships like investment services providers in financial markets.

Last but not least, there is the possibility of legal protection against 'market' abuses, corresponding insider dealing and market manipulation, designed for smart contract platforms. Relating to this, a (public or private) supervisory system would most probably appear to be necessary. For instance, a crucial question concerns the prevention of the distortion of market mechanisms by means of coding (hacking and cracking). Like in financial markets legislation, the civil and criminal law liabilities should also be defined in legislation.

Aspects relating to algorithmic trading (AT) and high-frequency trading (HFT) that have been considered to contain elements of regulatory interest in financial markets are also worth noticing for smart contracts regulation.[51]

[50] Directive 98/26/EC on Settlement Finality in Payment and Securities Settlement System; Directive 2002/47/EC on Financial Collateral Arrangements.

[51] See Veil (n 47) 477–519.

E. Smart Contracts as Agents

The legal status of systems for concluding smart contracts are of crucial interest for any legal protection of parties, especially in the form of legal liabilities, because potential identifiable carriers of liability are not easily found. There is no liability link from decisions made by an algorithm to the conscious intent of a human actor. Some smart contracts, especially those entered into on unpermissioned platforms practically do not allow for ascertaining the identity of contracting parties, or to establish their legal capacity. In the electronic creation of smart contracts, it is also difficult to find out whether the contracting parties are human agents or robots, which cannot at present be recognised as separate legal personalities and enter into valid contracts establishing rights and duties.[52]

The crucial question is often formulated as a distinction of smart contracts as mere tools or independent agents, acting on behalf of their principal and being capable of having liabilities.[53] Regarding algorithms mere tools could not provide contract law-based solutions to these problems. The general position in law is still that only natural or legal persons have the capacity to act as an agent.[54]

Both contract law theory and pragmatic policy concerns perhaps require an approach to algorithmic contracts that considers algorithms as constructive agents for the purposes of contract formation.[55] Scholz admits that algorithms, given the responsibility to weigh different factors, can act as human agents and, in legal terms, agency law could be applicable. However, he considers that it must be tempered by the 'constructive' qualification because algorithms are not persons and so cannot be regarded as human agents.[56] So-called clear box algorithmic contracts are principally fit for classification as constructive agents if their decisions can be predicted and controlled. As suggested in section II.C above, contracts concluded by clear box algorithms can also contain sufficient intent to commit to a foreseen contractual content, but black box algorithms can create emergent and unforeseen behaviour, not very well-fitting to contract or agency law patterns.[57] For black box algorithms, the status as an independent and liability bearing legal entity may thus be pivotal.

III. Contract Law Specific Aspects

A. Reasoning in Contract Law

To consider the possibilities of automated legal reasoning in the traditional application environment of Finnish law, some basic elements of contract law have first

[52] European Union (n 19).
[53] See, eg Scholz (n 32) and Bourque and Fung Ling Tsui (n 3) 18–19.
[54] Bourque and Fung Ling Tsui (n 3) 18.
[55] Scholz (n 32) 132.
[56] ibid 132, 165.
[57] ibid 136.

to be presented. After that, the capacity of existing smart contract codes and developing AI systems are visited. Parties to a contract governed by Finnish law owe each other what are called duties/obligations of loyalty (good faith). This means that a party to a contract must to a sufficient degree take into account also the interests of the other party. Duties of loyalty in contractual relations take the form of, eg, duty to inform, duty to give notice and duty of care as well as general duties to contribute which are not based on written contractual terms.[58] Also, the principle of reasonableness (fairness) is commonly acknowledged in Finnish contract law. In written law, the basis of the reasonableness requirement can be found, for example, in the general provision governing the adjustment of contract terms in the Finnish Contracts Act (section 36). These contract law principles (loyalty and reasonableness) can be applied as a basis for the protection of the confidence in what is agreed upon between the parties.

The above survey shows that some types of pivotal contract law notions are abstract concepts such as 'good faith' or 'reasonableness'. Intellectual, social or even emotional dimensions of this kind of expression of the human language can appear impossible to translate into code, which has to be built on concrete instruction for actions in an objectively measurable world.[59] It is, however, at present very difficult to try to evaluate the potential or smart contract algorithms or AI to automate full-fledged contract law reasoning, and the possibilities of, for example,distributed networks and asymmetric cryptography still remain to be seen.[60]

For legal reasoning at large, we must start from the epistemology of law. Diverse categories of legal knowledge have to be acknowledged. Materials characterised as legal sources include, depending on the legal system, cases, rules, theories, procedures, hierarchies of authority, norms and meta-rules. Rules consist of 'statutes and codes, constitutional principles, norms of interpretation, rules of criminal and civil procedure, heuristic rules of thumb, "black letter" generalizations abstracted from many actual precedents, "rules of a case" summarizing the main conclusion, or holding, of a case'.[61] The system knowledge of law recognises different hierarchies inherent in legal systems (eg, the Constitution prevails over statutes, etc).

The reasoning within the common law based Anglo-American law *stare decisis* – the doctrine of precedent differs much from, for example, the Continental European (civil law) pattern of legal thinking. To compare the current case with previous ones for similarities and differences is much about seeking analogies and extracting main legal ideas – ratios of decisions. However, the heuristics of determining similarity remains unexpressed in this doctrine. In civil code jurisdictions,

[58] Concerning the principle of loyalty in Finnish contract law, see, eg J Häyhä, 'Lojaliteettiperiaate ja sopimusoppi' ('The Principle of Loyalty and Contract Law Doctrine') (1996) 77 *Defensor Legis* 313.

[59] Mik (n 2) 21.

[60] Mik (n 2) 2.

[61] EL Rissland, KD Ashley and RP Loui, 'AI and Law: A Fruitful Synergy' (2003) 150 *Artificial Intelligence* 1, 2–3.

legal reasoning focuses more on rules and codes.[62] The modes of legal reasoning also depend on judicial assignments like advocacy, adjudication, advising, planning and drafting, and administration, but all of these tasks are about the same kind of normative analysis based on facts and legal provisions.[63]

The application of law contains elements of societal or axiological premises that can hardly be expressed or even consciously recognised.[64] Legal reasoning is a matter of various philosophical, sociological, psychological and economic aspects of judging as is shown, for example, in legal traditions like Law and Economics and Critical Legal Studies.[65] Applying law is not a logical operation in the style of *modus ponens*, because legal concepts are usually ambiguous and need interpretation, and the clear 'isomorphy' relations between legal concepts and real cases are rare.[66] Different interpretations of legal rules are possible, and there are perhaps no only 'right' alternatives. The prevailing interpretation is nothing but what was most persuasive from the point of view of the legal 'audience'.[67] This means that defeasible reasoning and dialectical argument are important in law.[68]

Computational models and especially AI can already now to some degree simulate (or imitate) legal thinking, by the use of its enormous capacity to analyse large amounts of data. This can offer efficient tools to investigate the arguments used by an immense number of legal actors. AI can develop, for example, models of argument and case similarity, extracted from previous materials, developed for use in a current case. It can also provide a way to explore how and how well they work.[69]

Already in an early stage of AI and law research, reasoning with rules (with a special reference to conflict between rules), reasoning with cases, and open texture in legal predicates were addressed. Since then, developing models of argumentation have been a focus of research, producing, for example, a dialogue-based model of legal pleading, and a discourse-based model of legal argumentation. Another topic – most important for common law systems – has been the research on the justifications of legal decisions (*rationes decidendi*) or the impact of the structure of a legal decision on deciding cases.[70]

Legal reasoning is about theory construction, evaluation and application. In AI and law tradition, the law–logics relationship has also been intensely investigated. This approach raises up the question about the purposes motivating legal theories,

[62] ibid 3.

[63] ibid 4.

[64] On the logical and axiological element in legal reasoning, see, eg K Makkonen, *Zur Problematik der Juridischen Entscheidung. Eine strukturanalytische Studie* (Turku, Turun Yliopisto, 1965) and A Aarnio, *The Rational as Reasonable:* A Treatise on Legal Justification (Dodrecht, D Reidel Publishing, 1987).

[65] ibid.

[66] Makkonen, *Zur Problematik der Juridischen Entscheidung* (1965) 143–51.

[67] Aarnio, *The Rational as Reasonable* (1987) 2323. See also Makkonen (n 64) 171–73.

[68] Rissland, Ashley and Loui (n 61) 5.

[69] ibid.

[70] ibid 12–13.

that can be discovered in cases and develop priorities between rules.[71] A core focus has also been in 'operationalising' norms and past rationales for analysing new fact situations, by focusing on the reasons why factors matter as relevant similarities or differences among cases and by using intelligent information retrieval and extraction in the legal domain, in order to reduce and make clear the linkages between cases.[72] Also, ideas about informal logic – especially defeasible reasoning – can contribute to a technology for authoring, analysing and visualising disputational arguments.[73]

It is suggested above that a significant portion of legal reasoning and adjudicative decision-making may be based on a combination of cognitive, volitive and even emotional processes in the human mind, for example, when dealing with the principle of loyalty, protection of contractual confidence, reasonableness and the objective to protect weaker parties in contracts (see section III.C below). These areas of law require legal thinking that is not based only on a quantitative analysis of previous materials or a (deontic) logical analysis of norms and normative systems, but to a remarkable degree on a holistic approach of all intellectual resources of the human mind.

Computational systems and especially AI may have a revolutionary impact on the quantitative analysis of materials and on using logic, including deontic and modal logic to analyse norms, but perhaps also on applying law in areas that require a more intense presence of human mind. This could take place by means of simulating or imitating cognitive and other processes of the human mind, on the basis of infinite material giving guidance on how the human mind acts in similar cases.

This section relates mainly to adjudicative processes in courts and other instances of application of law. But if extensive part of intellectual processes of humans can be coded it can have an impact also of the contents of smart contracts, especially for including ambiguous notions (like reasonableness and good faith) in contract terms, capable of being properly interpreted and executed by a code.

B. Contractual Remedies

It has been stated that smart contracts are, in comparison with traditional contracts, rigid and straightforward, and sometimes impractical or even legally inadmissible, especially in consumer contracts. In equating enforceability with guaranteed performance, they significantly limit the availability of legal remedies like damages, price reduction and rescission of contract. The same rigidness also affects contract law evaluation at large, for instance, concerning the question whether a performance is due, not to speak about the fairness of the contract.

[71] ibid 14.
[72] ibid 14.
[73] ibid 15.

A smart contract that is tamper-proof and self-executing does not allow for taking into account changes in circumstances that perhaps render the execution of the contract less practical or even absurd or illegal. Traditional contracts, on the contrary, are usually flexible and dynamic and allow the parties to retain the ability to decide whether to fulfill their obligations and whether to exercise their rights – or, for example, for business reasons, not to do so.[74]

According to a proposition, the flexibility element could be added to smart contracts by using parallel agreements in the traditional format. This could also allow the alteration and termination of the contract, provided that the parties are unanimous on these issues. The process for amending a smart contract should conform to contract law rules. When an amendment or termination of the contract proposal is found agreeable by all parties, it should be ratified into the contract.[75] Also, the malfunctions of the smart contract due to a coding error may be difficult to prevent. For this, it may be necessary to allocate the risk of their occurrence by prior agreement, according to whether the error originates from factors on one party's or a third party's liability.[76]

C. Protection of the Weaker Party and Adjustment of Contracts

A crucial aspect of smart contracts, when assessed from the perspective of contract law, relates to a reasonable balance between parties to the contract. This emphasis is typical to a model of legal thinking, called social civil justice, influential at least in Finland and other Nordic countries. It aims at protecting the weaker party by helping them to an equal footing with a stronger party in the contractual relationship, for example, merchant–consumer. Also, the mutual trust and loyalty between the parties and the principle of equity of contracts is emphasised (see section III.A above). An unreasonable contract or individual term may, therefore, be amended by the court for reasons of equity (adjustment of contract pursuant to § 36 of the Finnish Contracts Act).[77]

The problem with smart contracts is how the contents of the contract can be presented as a code maintaining the consistency with the mentioned principles that are often able to be expressed only in vague and general wordings (the language aspect; see section IV below). Another problem relates to the difficulties in monitoring the fulfilment of the principles in the automatic enforcement of the contract.

Assumptions about the sophistication of the parties have led to the development of a two-fold contract law, general and consumer contract law. In the former,

[74] Mik (n 2) 12.
[75] Bourque and Fung Ling Tsui (n 3) 9.
[76] Mik (n 2) 11.
[77] See, eg Hemmo (n 25) 19–24 and Lauslahti, Mattila and Seppälä (n 8) 11.

as seen in section II.C), the traditional requirements of mutual assent and consideration are sometimes relaxed.

The principles of contract law will most likely be applied to smart contracts as well. The possibility of evaluating whether a smart contract is consistent with these principles may be a most complicated task. One evident controversy lies between contract law, protecting consumers against sophisticated business actors, and the fact that smart contracts systemically allow powerful parties to benefit at the cost of consumer – and at the same time cause negative externalities on society.[78] As the contract code resides within the merchant's control, the customer usually has neither a chance nor the professional skills (or desire) to review or audit it at any time. It may even be mandatory to keep the code beyond the reach of customers (eg, for data protection reasons), or held by a trusted third party.[79]

On the other hand, automated agents could help to restore consumers' bargaining power by helping them to search an online contract and conclude it on their behalf without relying on e-commerce intermediaries' standard terms or revealing the consumers' identity.[80]

IV. Contract Language and Code

The terms of the smart contracts are written in standard programming languages. The translation of natural language into code means a transition from one linguistic regime to another with quite different communicational tools, structures and even purposes. This leads to a multi-stage interpretation process: first, the contents of the legal prose have to be extracted from contract language; and second, these contents have to be transformed into computer-readable instructions. The interpretation of the legal prose requires legal and commercial knowledge. The core question element is *how* to determine the meaning that must be deemed to have been intended by both parties (the subjective interpretation).[81] Only secondarily, the objective meaning of words and expressions may become relevant.[82]

Standard programming languages are mainly high-level languages, not assembly instructions built on low-level machine instructions or binary code. Thus smart contracts code can possibly include more abstract instructions and even simulate natural languages. The machine language is unambiguous and not technology-specific.[83]

For the coding of a traditional contract, its terms have to be rewritten and its structures reorganised because the contract should be arranged and presented as

[78] Scholz (n 32) 162–63.

[79] Bourque and Fung Ling Tsui (n 3) 3.

[80] J Fairfield, 'Smart Contracts, Bitcoin Bots, and Consumer Protection' (2014) 71 *Washington & Lee Law Review Online Edition*, 36, 47–48. See also Koulu (n 7) 55.

[81] Mik (n 2) 17.

[82] On subjective and objective interpretation see also Hemmo (n 25) ch 24.

[83] Bourque and Fung Ling Tsui (n 3) 7.

a process depicting interdependency: 'if X, then Y, otherwise Z'. This can diminish the need for interpretation.[84] On the other hand, problems with interpretation do not disappear completely, because natural language is inherently imprecise as the meaning of words always depends on the context, and legal language used in contracts may be even more challenging to translate into code than 'normal' natural language.[85]

The increase of precision in the translation of natural language into code has its drawbacks for smart contracts: the rigidity of the contract increases, rendering contract a less suitable tool, for example, for dealing with changed circumstances. Moreover, in this scenario contracts tend to be longer than traditional contracts, which can also increase the possibility of coding errors and other malfunctions.[86]

Also, unambiguity has its disadvantages. Some degree of ambiguity can be even intended by both parties, because it gives space for flexibility, perhaps expected by parties or even necessary for the smooth functioning of the contract in its environment. This potential may appear essential, for example, for assessing contractual performances or for adapting the contract in changed circumstances.[87] Moreover, as was discussed in section III.A, some types of pivotal contract law notions like 'good faith', 'reasonableness' or 'due care and diligence' (with no gauges available for their objective measurement), in all their intellectual, social or even emotional dimensions may be impossible to be translated into code, which has to be built on concrete instruction for actions in an objectively measurable world.[88]

On the other hand, the translation of contract language into code may also decrease the required legal precision, often with no tolerance for approximations.[89] Legal provisions can contain carefully developed expressions that may not tolerate any changes even in single words. Concrete, measurable instructions may lack the potential to understand the nuances of legal reasoning, resulting in inaccurate or even illegal outcomes. The perfect and inevitable execution of smart contracts exacerbates risks related to insufficient legal accuracy.

For possibilities of finding workable solutions to operationalise the complicated and controversial relation between natural language and code, perhaps the potential of AI (and machine learning) that has been referred to in section III.A can have relevance. In the quantitative analysis of enormous materials of linguistic practices, the system can learn to interpret, simulate or imitate processes of these practices and even produce a virtual understanding of syntactic and semantic elements of natural languages, including a form of intuition to distinguish between delicate nuances and shades.

[84] Lauslahti, Mattila and Seppälä (n 8) 13.

[85] Mik (n 2) 17.

[86] Koulu (n 7) 68.

[87] Mik (n 2) 19–20. Contract law also provides means to protect a contract party from abuse by the other party of the ambiguity of the contract.

[88] Mik (n 2) 21.

[89] Mik (n 2) 17.

Also, how the possibilities of visualisation of contracts can help to lower the threshold between natural language and code remains to be seen. The existing state of the art in coding allows for mapping not only a binary logic based scheme but also for the optimisation of principles and discretionary decision-making. The automated visualisation of contracts may help in coding contracts into workable, flexible and sufficiently human smart contracts.[90]

V. Smart Contracts – Legal Rules beyond the Legal System?

Szabo describes courts and legal principles as inconvenient legacies to be made redundant by suitable technologies.[91] It has also been suggested, based on the idea that the use of technology could ensure adherence to the law, that 'code is law' and that technology has normative implications.[92] In fact, pure smart contracts propose a normative change of this kind: the actual code is to be the agreement and there could be no disjunction between the execution and the contract. If there were a traditional contract besides the code, there could be discrepancies between them. In such a situation, it could be argued that the (non-transparent) code deviates from the intent of parties, embodied in the traditional parallel agreement.[93]

The best known and perhaps the most flagrant instance of the code in law-type conflict with the legal realm is the DAO case. The DAO was based on the Ethereum blockchain as a crowdfunding and capital management platform to allocate funds to third-party projects, governed by its computer code, with 'curators' (permitted users). An unknown user exploited a loophole in the computer code of the DAO to drain from it a remarkable amount of currency.

From the point of view of contract law, of course, the misdirected transactions should be reversed and the currency refunded. The 'Blockchain view', on the other hand, considered this solution inconsistent with Ethereum's credentials as an immutable record of past transactions and the irreversibility of its code. The case really concretises the core of the question of respecting contracting parties' intentions.

The solution adopted was based on the idea that the smart contracts built into the DAO were never intended to qualify as binding contracts to the extent that

[90] See also H Haapio and A Rossi, 'Proactive Legal Design: Embedding Values in the Design of Legal Artefacts' in: E Schweighofer, F Kummer and A Saarenpää (eds), *Internet of Things. Proceedings of the 22nd International Legal Informatics Symposium IRIS 2019* (Bern, Editions Weblaw, 2019).

[91] N Szabo, 'Smart Contracts: Formalizing and Securing Relationships on Public Networks' (1997) 2 *First Monday* 2.

[92] See L Lessig, *Code Version 2.0* (New York, Basic Books, 1999) and R Brownsword, *Rights, Regulation, and the Technological Revolution* (Oxford, Oxford University Press, 2013). See also Mik (n 2) 4–5 and 24–25.

[93] Bourque and Fung Ling Tsui (n 3) 5.

they were unsupported by conventional contractual documentation between the parties, allowing their genuine intentions to be surmised. It was the law of contract that was to prevail over the computer code.

Perhaps we can, to some degree, generalise from the DAO example and argue that there still remains a legitimate interest to be able to interpret the genuine intentions of the parties to smart contracts and not to draw far-reaching conclusions of their shared consensus. To exclude any scope for remedial action, aimed at reversing the real-world consequences of the operation of computer code would be absurd – and even in conflict with the idea of the rule of law.[94]

Brownsword speaks about a disruptive wave of law and legal reasoning, the focus of which 'is not on the deficient content of prevailing legal rules, or on gaps, but on the availability of new technological instruments that can be applied for regulatory purposes'.[95] Non-rule technologies ('smart regulation') replacing rules can give direct 'signals at regulatees enjoining them to act in particular ways', or simply impose 'a pattern of conduct upon regulatees irrespective of whether they would otherwise choose to act in the way that the technology now dictates'.

It is a cornerstone of rule of law-based systems that norms become valid only on predetermined conditions, for example, an act of the authorised legislator, ethical quality of the norm or effective application of the norm.[96]

Some pivotal questions are presented by Riikka Koulu: transactions in the blockchain are irreversible, and it is unclear what this would mean for the rule of law and the protection of weaker parties. What assumptions are we making within smart contracts, for example, if we assume the parties to be equal, rational actors? Is there room for taking imbalances in their power relations into consideration? How do we provide an infrastructure with effective redress mechanisms?[97]

[94] European Union (n 52).

[95] R Brownsword, 'Law Disrupted, Law Re-Imagined, Law Re-Invented' (2019) *Technology and Regulation* 10, 12–13 and 16.

[96] ibid 25–26.

[97] Koulu (n 7) 67.

4

Data Protection Issues for Smart Contracts

W GREGORY VOSS

I. Introduction

Smart contracts offer promise for facilitating and streamlining transactions in many areas of business and government. However, they also may be subject to the provisions of relevant data protection laws, if personal data is processed. The term 'data protection' is a European one, which generally is considered a broader concept than 'privacy'. Data protection includes requirements regarding data security, the provision of rights to the individuals to whom the data relate (data subjects) and data processing. In this respect it is a broader concept than the American one of 'information privacy', and sometimes 'data privacy' is used as a compromise term for comparative law purposes to serve as a synonym for data protection.[1] However, data protection is based on transparency, in that those processing data are to do so in a manner that is 'open, fair, appropriate and secure' whereas privacy generally seeks opacity for private information.[2]

Data protection has come to be exemplified by EU legislation, which has helped shape legislation in other jurisdictions around the globe.[3] However, models other than the EU individual rights one exist, such as the US laissez-faire/self-regulation model and the Chinese model centred around national interest.[4] Nonetheless, even in the US current and proposed state data privacy laws are being influenced by EU legislation.[5] This chapter, however, will focus on EU legislation faced with the data protection legal issues that arise through the use of what are called 'smart

[1] WG Voss, 'Obstacles to the Harmonization of Data Privacy Law in Context' (2019) *University of Illinois Journal of Law, Technology & Policy* 405, 408–09.

[2] R Brownsword and M Goodwin, *Law and the Technologies of the Twenty-First Century: Text and Materials* (Cambridge, Cambridge University Press 2012) 308.

[3] Voss, 'Obstacles to the Harmonization' (2019) 411.

[4] WG Voss, 'Cross-Border Data Flows, the GDPR, and Data Governance' (2020) 29 *Washington International Law Journal* 485, 489–93.

[5] Voss (n 1) 498–501.

contracts' – computer processing that executes autonomously.[6] Smart contracts use the blockchain or distributed ledger technology system whereby transactions are stored on various computers (referred to as 'nodes') of a blockchain network, using a consensus algorithm.[7] They also are executed independently of the control of any one actor, according to a computer program (or code).[8] However, the decentralised system of smart contracts using blockchain technology contrasts with the classical centralised system of data collection and storage that the legislators had in mind when they crafted EU legislation,[9] which has raised certain issues that this chapter will detail. Indeed, that legislation was designed and written prior to blockchain technology becoming widely known.[10]

Certain observers have spoken of 'the clash between the GDPR and blockchain technology',[11] referring to the common abbreviation used for the current EU data protection legislation, or of their being 'incompatibile, the digital equivalent of oil and water'.[12] De Filippi and Wright remark that, 'Without strong privacy protections, smart contracts likely will prove unsuitable for legal agreements where confidentiality is crucial.'[13] In this discussion, the reader should keep in mind the distinction between public blockchains, which 'allow anyone to participate in the consensus process, the process for determining which transactions and which blocks are added to the chain',[14] and private blockchains, where participants are known and are bound by terms and conditions.[15] Most legal issues (including privacy ones) arise in connection with public blockchains.[16]

After this introduction, section II briefly explains the GDPR. Section III discusses personal data in smart contracts and section IV delves into details about data protection accountability in the context of smart contracts. Section V investigates data subject rights in the context of smart contracts, section VI covers integrity and confidentiality in the context of the blockchain, and section VII highlights two additional data protection principles relevant in the context of

[6] P De Filippi and A Wright, *Blockchain and the Law: The Rule of Code* (Cambridge, Massachusetts, Harvard University Press 2018) 2.

[7] M Finck, 'Blockchains and Data Protection in the European Union' (2018) 4 *European Data Protection Law Review* 17.

[8] M Finck, 'Smart contracts as a form of solely automated processing under the GDPR' (2019) 9 *International Data Privacy Law* 79.

[9] Finck, 'Blockchains' (2018) 17.

[10] P Van Eecke and AG Haie, 'Blockchain and the GDPR: The EU Blockchain Observatory Report' (2018) 4 *European Data Protection Law Review* 531.

[11] D Meyer, 'Blockchain technology is on a collision course with EU privacy law' *iapp* (27 February 2018), available at iapp.org/news/a/blockchain-technology-is-on-a-collision-course-with-eu-privacy-law.

[12] G Bailey, 'Blockchain And EU Privacy Laws: A Three-Step Guide To Compliance' *Forbes* (22 February 2019), available at www.forbes.com/sites/georgebailey1/2019/02/22/blockchain-and-eu-privacy-laws-a-three-step-guide-to-compliance.

[13] De Filippi and A Wright, *Blockchain and the Law: The Rule of Code* (2018) 83.

[14] E Mik, 'Blockchains: A Technology for Decentralized Marketplaces' in LA DiMatteo, M Cannarsa and C Poncibò (eds), *The Cambridge Handbook of Smart Contracts, Blockchain Technology and Digital Platforms* (Cambridge, Cambridge University Press, 2020) 163.

[15] Mik, 'Blockchains' (2020) 164.

[16] ibid 165.

the blockchain – purpose limitation and data minimisation. Finally, section VIII concludes with the idea that although smart contracts and data protection legislation are not completely incompatible, a good undertstanding of the latter is necessary in order for smart contracts not to violate the legislation.

II. The EU Data Protection Legislative Framework

The current EU data protection legislation is the General Data Protection Regulation (GDPR),[17] which was adopted in 2016, but became applicable on 25 May 2018.[18] The GDPR applies to the processing of the personal data[19] of an individual in the EU when the GDPR's material and territorial scope requirements are met.[20] The concept of processing is a very broad one in the GDPR:

> [A]ny operation or set of operations which is performed on personal data or on sets of personal data, whether or not by automated means, such as collection, recording, organisation, structuring, storage, adaptation or alteration, retrieval, consultation, use, disclosure by transmission, dissemination or otherwise making available, alignment or combination, restriction, erasure or destruction.[21]

Several of these actions would be performed when personal data are included in smart contracts, which involve adaptation and structuring into computer code, dissemination to the various nodes on the blockchain, storage there, disclosure by transmission, use, and so on.

The GDPR has extraterritorial scope and extends to the processing of personal data of those in the EU by data controllers[22] even when they do not have an establishment there, if the processing is related to 'the offering of goods or services, irrespective of whether a payment of the data subject is required, to such data subjects in the Union; or the monitoring of their behaviour as far as their behaviour takes place within the Union'.[23] This is likely to be easy to determine, at least insofar as a permissionless network is concerned, 'since anybody can use an open/permissionless platform, operators of such platforms may be deemed to offer services to data subjects in the EU'.[24] Thus, 'European data protection rules are likely to

[17] Council Regulation on the protection of natural persons with regard to the processing of personal data and on the free movement of such data, and repealing Directive 95/46/EC (General Data Protection Regulation) (EU) 2016/679 [2016] OJ L 119/1.

[18] Article 99 of the GDPR.

[19] For a definition of this term, see text to n 36.

[20] Articles 2–3 of the GDPR.

[21] Article 4(2) of the GDPR.

[22] For a definition of this term, see text to n 60.

[23] Article 3(2) of the GDPR.

[24] J Bacon, JD Michels, C Millard and J Singh, 'Blockchain Demystified' (2017) Queen Mary University of London, School of Law, Legal Studies Research Paper No. 268/2017, 39, available at ssrn.com/abstract=3091218.

apply to many blockchain-based transactions that have little or no connection to Europe'.[25] While the GDPR has a dual objective, protecting 'fundamental rights and freedoms of natural persons and in particular their right to the protection of personal data'[26] and ensuring that the 'free movement of personal data within the Union … be neither restricted nor prohibited for reasons connected with the protection of natural persons with regard to the processing of personal data',[27] it also establishes a limitation on the transfer of personal data to a county outside of the EU to those countries for which 'the Commission has decided that the third country … ensures an adequate level of protection'.[28]

Furthermore, the GDPR provides significant rights to data subjects,[29] and introduces data protection compliance mechanisms such as data protection impact assessments and data protection officers,[30] in addition to data processing registers for most controllers, other than certain SMEs.[31] The GDPR contains various data breach notification requirements,[32] and gives reinforced powers to supervisory authorities,[33] including the power to 'impose a temporary or definitive limitation including a ban on processing',[34] and to levy administrative fines going up to a maximum of the higher of 20 million euros or four per cent of total worldwide annual turnover of the proceding financial year, in the case of an undertaking.[35]

The next section discusses the GDPR concept of personal data in the context of smart contracts.

III. Personal Data in Smart Contracts

This section begins by setting out the definition of 'personal data' (section III.A), then details data not subject to personal data protection (section III.B), developing this through a discussion of anonymous information, anonymised information, and pseudonymisation (section III.C), prior to applying this to the blockchain context (section III.D).

[25] W Maxwell and J Salmon, *A guide to block chain and data protection* (London, Hogan Lovells, 2017) 11.

[26] Article 1(2) of the GDPR.

[27] Article 1(3) of the GDPR.

[28] Article 45(1) of the GDPR.

[29] See text to n 80.

[30] WG Voss, 'Internal Compliance Mechanisms for Firms in the EU General Data Protection Regulation' (2018) 50 *Revue juridique Thémis de l'Université de Montréal* 801–14.

[31] Article 30 of the GDPR.

[32] Articles 33–34 of the GDPR.

[33] Article 58 of the of the GDPR.

[34] Article 58(2)(f) of the GDPR.

[35] Article 83(5) of the GDPR.

A. Definition of 'Personal Data'

The GDPR employs a broad concept of personal data. As the processing of personal data triggers the application of the GDPR this is important. Personal data means:

> Any information relating to an identified or identifiable natural person ('data subect'); an identifiable natural person is one who can be identified, directly or indirectly, in particular by reference to an identifier such as a name, an identification number, location data, an online identifier or to one or more factors specific to the physical, physiological, genetic, mental, economic, cultural or social identity of that natural person.[36]

As a practical matter, this definition extends greatly, because of the fact that the data subject need not specifically be identified by the data; being identifiable suffices. The definition specifically refers to identification numbers and online identifiers, but other examples of what might be considered personal data include not only names and addresses, names used in connection with a telephone number, biometric data, video images of individuals, but also health information, working time information, and in many cases, IP addresses.[37]

B. Data not Subject to Personal Data Protection

However, as indicated in its recitals, and as may be gathered from the definition of 'personal data', which refers solely to information relating to a natural person, the data of companies and other legal persons do not benefit from protection under the GDPR: 'This Regulation does not cover the processing of personal data which concerns legal persons and in particular undertakings established as legal persons, including the name and the form of the legal person and the contact details of the legal person.'[38] In addition, the personal data of those who are deceased are not covered by the GDPR, although EU Member States are given the leeway to legislate in this regard.[39] Furthermore, properly anonymised data are not considered personal data and thus fall out of the scope of the GDPR, as well:

> The principles of data protection should therefore not apply to anonymous information, namely information which does not relate to an identified or identifiable natural person or to personal data rendered anonymous in such a manner that the data subject is not or no longer identifiable. This Regulation does not therefore concern the processing of such anonymous information, including for statistical or research purposes.[40]

[36] Article 4(1) of the GDPR.

[37] WG Voss and KA Houser, 'Personal Data and the GDPR: Providing a Competitive Advantage for U.S. Companies' (2019) 56 *American Business Law Journal* 287, 316–20.

[38] Recital 14 of the GDPR.

[39] Recital 27 of the GDPR.

[40] Recital 26 of the GDPR.

Anonymisation is a procedure that, when properly carried out, allows various new technologies to be used in compliance with the GDPR. Thus, the next subsection details it further.

C. Anonymous Information, Anonymised Information and Pseudonymisation

The GDPR refers to anonymous information as being 'information which does not relate to an identified or identifiable natural person' and anonymised information as 'personal data rendered anonymous in such a manner that the data subject is not or no longer identifiable'.[41] However, further guidance, indicating a risk-based approach, has been adopted:

> To ascertain whether means are reasonably likely to be used to identify the natural person, account should be taken of all objective factors, such as the costs of and the amount of time required for identification, taking into consideration the available technology at the time of the processing and technological developments.[42]

Time and cost, then, are taken into consideration when evaluating whether or not anonymisation is successful and will be considered as such under the GDPR. If so, the data are no longer considered personal data. Advisory guidance indicates that anonymisation must be 'irreversible'.[43] Furthermore, pseudonymised data do not fit within the definition of anonymised information, as the relevant natural person could be identified by using additional information.[44] As a result, they are still treated as personal data subject to the requirements of the GDPR, although pseudonymisation may be used as an element of data security.[45]

D. Application in the Blockchain Context

In the blockchain context, transactional data stored in blocks and public keys may potentially be classified as personal data.[46] Encryption does not remove transactional data from the category of personal data, as it is still possible to access the data using the relevant encryption keys.[47] Furthermore, experts can probably still link the data to an individual, through adequate effort.[48] Likewise, transactional data

[41] Recital 26 of the GDPR.
[42] Recital 26 of the GDPR.
[43] Article 29 Data Protection Working Party, 'Opinion 05/2014 on Anonymisation Techiques' (2014) 5, available at www.pdpjournals.com/docs/88197.pdf.
[44] Recital 26 of the GDPR.
[45] Recital 28 of the GDPR.
[46] Finck (n 7) 22.
[47] ibid.
[48] Maxwell and Salmon, *A guide to block chain and data protection* (2017) 7.

that has gone through a hashing process is still considered personal data, as the hashing is considered a pseudonymisation technique.[49] Hashes are 'mathematical derivations of data that, if properly implemented, cannot be reverse-engineered to expose the data that's being represented – but you *can* use them to verify the underlying data'.[50]

One solution to these issues is to store all personal data off the blockchain, although developers need to be careful not to thwart this by use of metadata that may reveal personal data.[51] For example, 'with respect to metadata, if the platform's users are natural persons, the sender's and recipient's addresses will almost always qualify as personal data'.[52] Another solution would be to restrict use to the business-to-business (B2B) context, as 'if a platform's users are all legal persons (such as businesses) the platform could be designed such that the metadata does not contain information related to natural persons'.[53]

Public keys are likely to be considered pseudononymous data, as connecting them with additional information will permit identification, and these keys cannot be moved 'off-chain',[54] and as such they continue to be considered personal data. The presence of personal data, and their processing, trigger the application of the GDPR, if that legislative instrument's material and territorial scope requirements are met.

Next, this chapter goes into detail about data protection accountability in the context of smart contract.

IV. Accountability in Smart Contracts

This section begins by setting out the concept of accountability (section IV.A), then sets out the definitions of controller and joint controller (section IV.B), prior to discussing guidance from the CNIL and public permissionless blockchains (section IV.C). It continues by detailing the contrasting position of controllers in permissioned blockchains (section IV.D), and concludes with recommendations from the CNIL (section IV.E).

A. The Concept of Accountability

Accountability in the GDPR relates to the concept that someone must be responsible for data protection law compliance. Generally, it is the controller that has

[49] Finck (n 7) 23.
[50] Meyer, 'Blockchain technology' (2018).
[51] ibid.
[52] Bacon, Michels, Millard and Singh, 'Blockchain Demystified' (2017) 40.
[53] ibid 41.
[54] ibid 24–25.

the main responsibility under the GDPR, and they are considered 'key actors in the operationalisation of data protection law as they are the primary bearers of the obligations set by such law toward data subjects'.[55] The GDPR provides that, 'the controller shall implement appropriate technical and organisational measures to ensure and to be able to demonstrate that processing is performed accordance with this Regulation. Those measures shall be reviewed and updated where necessary'.[56] This accountability does not limit itself to the literal content of the GDPR, but may involve an 'ethical assessment'[57] and have as a goal improving corporate data governance.[58] A first determination that should be made is that of the party who is the controller, that is, the party to whom a data subject would turn 'to find out from the controller if his or her data is being processed, and if so, for what purpose, who the data is being shared with, and so on', using their right to access,[59] or the party that a supervisory authority would hold responsible in the event of data protection law violations.

B. Definition of 'Controller' and 'Joint Controller'

The GDPR defines a controller as:

> The natural or legal person, public authority, agency or other body which, alone or jointly with others, *determines the purposes and means of the processing of personal data*; where the purposes and means of such processing are determined by Union or Member State law, the controller or the specific criteria for its nomination may be provided for by Union or Member State law.[60]

However, the GDPR has also added specific reference to joint controllers, meaning that more than one person may have the responsibility for GDPR compliance in the processing of certain personal data. The term 'joint controller' is defined not in the definitions article of the GDPR, but in a specific article devoted to this category of actor – GDPR Article 26. Joint controllers exist, 'where two or more controllers jointly determine the purposes and means of processing', in which case the joint cotrollers are to determine together their respective responsibilities for data protection compliance 'in a transparent manner',[61] which typically means by written contract. Although 'there is no explicit obligation for the arrangement to

[55] LA Bygrave and L Tosoni, 'Article 4(7). Controller' in C Kuner, LA Bygrave and C Docksey (eds), *The EU General Data Protection Regulation (GDPR): A Commentary* (Oxford, Oxford University Press, 2020) 146.
[56] Article 24(1) of the GDPR.
[57] Voss, 'Internal Compliance Mechanisms' (2018) 819.
[58] D Le Métayer, 'Whom to Trust? Using Technology to Enforce Privacy' in D Wright and P De Hert (eds), *Enforcing Privacy: Regulatory, Legal and Technological Approaches* (Cham, Springer, 2016) 427.
[59] T Lyons, L Courcelas and K Timsit, 'Blockchain and the GDPR' (2018) 25, available at www.eublockchainforum.eu/sites/default/files/reports/20181016_report_gdpr.pdf.
[60] Article 4(7) of the GDPR (emphasis added).
[61] Article 26(1) of the GDPR.

be recorded in writing', in connection with transparency requirements vis-à-vis the data subject, it is implied that at the least a summary of the arrangements between the joint controllers should be in writing.[62] The GDPR provides that where joint controllers, or joint processors, or a controller and a processor involved in the same processing, and responsible for damage caused by it, 'each controller or processor shall be held liable for the entire damage in order to ensure effective compensation of the data subject'.[63] Effectively, by a system of joint and several liability this shifts the burden of sorting out the relative responsibilities of the joint controllers to them, through their arrangements, including any provisions as to compensation by one joint controller to the other when it pays out the entire damage compensation.[64]

C. Guidance from the CNIL and Public Permissionless Blockchains

The French supervisory authority, the *Commission nationale informatique et libertés* (CNIL) addresses the identification of data controllers in the blockchain in guidance issued in 2018, while acknowledging that the GDPR was designed for a world where data are managed centrally, unlike the decentralised blockchain model.[65] The CNIL advised that participants in a blockchain may be considered controllers if they have the right to write on the blockchain and send the data on to the miners for validation, as they define the objectives of the data processing and its means, including the data format and use of the blockchain itself.[66] The importance of this fact is that, if each node on the smart contract blockchain is treated as a controller, then they all need to comply with the GDPR.[67] Finck acknowledges that it is likely, in the case of a public permissionless blockchain, that each node is an independent controller (and not a joint controller) as they are 'not subect to external instructions, autonomously decide whether to join the chain, and pursue their own objectives' and do not jointly determine processing purposes and means with other nodes, and they shape the system by their individual behaviour.[68] This causes problems, as it is difficult to determine nodes' number,

[62] C Millard and D Kamarinou, 'Article 26. Joint controllers' in C Kuner, LA Bygrave and C Docksey (eds), *The EU General Data Protection Regulation (GDPR): A Commentary* (Oxford, Oxford University Press, 2020) 587.

[63] Article 82(4) of the GDPR.

[64] Millard and Kamarinou, 'Article 26. Joint controllers' (2020) 583.

[65] CNIL, 'Blockchain: Solutions for a responsible use of the blockchain in the context of personal data' (2018) 1, available at www.cnil.fr/sites/default/files/atoms/files/blockchain_en.pdf.

[66] ibid 1.

[67] LA DiMatteo, M Cannarsa and C Poncibò, 'Smart Contracts and Contract Law' in LA DiMatteo, M Cannarsa and C Poncibò (eds), *The Cambridge Handbook of Smart Contracts, Blockchain Technology and Digital Platforms* (Cambridge, Cambridge University Press, 2020) 15.

[68] Finck (n 7) 26.

identity and location, and nodes only see the encrypted or hashed version of the data and cannot change them, thereby rendering nodes incapable of responding to data protection tasks.[69]

D. Controllers in Permissioned Blockchains

Certain authors assert that in private and consortium blockchain platforms, otherwise known as 'permissioned blockchains' operated by one organisation or a consortium, it may be feasible to identify a central controller; although in a public blockchain, every node may qualify as a controller.[70] Lokke Moerel contends that a form of self-regulation may provide the answer, at least in the case of permissioned blockchains, stating that already 'private and consortium platforms implement membership rules, determining which parties have read or read/write authorization' and also determining who is the responsible entity.[71] Additionally, much as we have seen the rise of platforms as key intermediaries in the Internet infrastructure, Moerel sees the possibility of the rise of new intermediaries in permissioned private and consortium platforms, thus solving the mystery of who is the controller.[72] Furthermore, according to the CNIL, miners are not considered controllers,[73] and an individual using smart contracts strictly for a personal or household activity would also not be considered a controller,[74] as this would fall within an exception to the material scope of the GDPR.[75]

E. Recommendations from the CNIL

The CNIL recommends that the parties carrying out the processing activities with a common purpose identify the controller, perhaps by creating a legal person to play this role, or by appointing one party to make decisions for the group and designating it as the controller.[76] It also comments that the algorithm developer may be a mere supplier or, if it participates in the processing, may be considered a processor or a controller, depending on whether or not it determines the purposes of the processing.[77] A smart contract developer processing personal data on a controller's behalf would be considered a processor, and miners may also be

[69] ibid 26.

[70] L Moerel, 'Blockchain and Data Protection' in LA DiMatteo, M Cannarsa and C Poncibò (eds), *The Cambridge Handbook of Smart Contracts, Blockchain Technology and Digital Platforms* (Cambridge, Cambridge University Press, 2020) 215–16.

[71] ibid 222.

[72] ibid 221.

[73] CNIL, 'Blockchain' (2018) 2.

[74] ibid.

[75] Article 2(2)(c) of the GDPR.

[76] The CNIL refers to French forms of legal persons here – associations and economic interest groups. CNIL (n 65) 2.

[77] ibid 2.

considered processors, thus the CNIL recommends that the miners enter into a contract with the participant, which specifies their respective obligations, pursuant to the provisions of Article 28 of the GDPR.[78] This chapter now turns to the main data subject rights that cause difficulties in connection with smart contracts using the blockchain's distributed ledger technology.

V. Data Subject Rights in the Context of Smart Contracts

This section begins with an introduction on data subect rights (section V.A), prior to discussing two important rights in the context of the compatibility of smart contracts with EU data protection law – the right to rectification and the right to erasure ('right to be forgotten') (section V.B), and an additional right – that not to be subject to a decision based solely on automated processing (section V.C).

A. Introduction on Data Subject Rights

One difficulty that arises in data protection compliance when smart contracts are used is the exercise of data subject rights. This is because of the immutability of smart contracts – by default the code of the smart contracts cannot be changed,[79] while some of the data subject rights involve erasing or changing the data. Data subjects rights, which were expanded in the EU with the adoption of the GDPR, now include a right of access, rights to rectification, to erasure ('right to be forgotten'), to restriction of processing, to data portability, to object to processing, and the right not to be subject to automatic decision-making or profiling (with exceptions).[80] Former European Parliament Member Jan Philipp Albrecht, the rapporteur of the GDPR, commented that:

> Certain technologies will not be compatible with the GDPR if they don't provide for [the exercising of data subject's rights] based on their architectural design … This does not mean that blockchain technology in general has to adapt to the GDPR, it just means that it probably cannot be used for the processing of personal data.[81]

The CNIL considers that the related data subject information rights are not a problem, and the exercise of the right of access and the right to data portability are compatible with the blockchain.[82] However the right to rectification and the right to erasure ('right to be forgotten') deserve more attention, and the right not to be

[78] ibid 3.
[79] DiMatteo, Cannarsa and Poncibò, 'Smart Contracts and Contract Law' (2020) 4.
[80] Voss, 'Obstacles' (2019) 421.
[81] Meyer (n 11).
[82] CNIL (n 65) 8.

subject to a decision based solely on automated processing merits 'careful consideration in advance.'[83]

B. Right to Rectification and Right to Erasure ('Right to be Forgotten')

Specifically, the use of smart contracts in connection with personal data poses problems for GDPR compliance in connection with the 'right to rectification' and the 'right to erasure' ('right to be forgotten') due to the smart contracts' immutability.[84] This section begins with a discussion of the right to rectification (section V.B.i), and continues with a somewhat more developed discussion on the related right to erasure ('right to be forgotten') (section V.B.ii).

i. Right to Rectification

The right to rectification is set out in Article 16 of the GDPR:

> The data subject shall have the right to obtain from the controller without undue delay the rectification of inaccurate personal concerning him or her. Taking into account the purposes of the processing, the data subject shall have the right to have incomplete person data completed, including by means of providing a supplementary statement.[85]

The right to rectification relates to the data quality data protection principle, specifically providing that personal data shall be 'accurate and, where necessary, kept up to date; every reasonable step must be taken to ensure that personal data that are inaccurate, having regard to the purposes for which they are processed, are erased or rectified without delay'.[86] It is a longstanding principle, which virtually mirrors the language of prior EU law,[87] and reflects one of the 'fair information principles' distilled in a 1973 report commissioned by the US Department of Health, Education and Welfare.[88] However it does not sit well with the blockchain, as it is 'technically impossible' to grant a right to rectification 'when cleartext or hashed data is recorded on a blockchain', thus the CNIL strongly recommends 'not to register personal data in cleartext on a blockchain, and to use one of the cryptographic solutions' it discusses.[89] Furthermore the updated data would need to be entered in a new block.[90]

[83] CNIL (n 65) 8–9.
[84] Moerel, 'Blockchain and Data Protection' (2020) 227.
[85] Article 16 of the GDPR.
[86] Article 5(1)(d) of the GDPR.
[87] Article 6(1)(d) of the Council Directive on the protection of individuals with regard to the processing of personal data and on the free movement of such data 95/46/EC [1995] OJ L281/31 Art 6(1)(d).
[88] G González Fuster, *The Emergence of Personal Data Protection as a Fundamental Right of the EU* (Cham, Springer, 2014) 34.
[89] CNIL (n 65) 9.
[90] ibid 9.

ii. Right to Erasure (the 'Right to be Forgotten')

The main provision of the right to erasure ('right to be forgotten'), a related right described as 'more of a detailed elaboration of the already existing right of erasure' than a novelty,[91] is contained in Article 17(1) of the GDPR:

> The data subject shall have the right to obtain from the controller the erasure of personal data concerning him or her without undue delay and the controller shall have the obligation to erase personal data without undue delay where one of the following grounds applies:
>
> (a) the personal data are no longer necessary in relation to the purposes for which they were collected or otherwise processed;
> (b) the data subject withdraws consent on which the processing is based according to point (a) of Article 6(1), or point (a) of Article 9(2), and where there is no other legal ground for the processing;
> (c) the data subject objects to the processing pursuant to Article 21(1) and there are no overriding legitimate grounds for the processing, or the data subject objects to the processing pursuant to Article 21(2);
> (d) the personal data have been unlawfully processed;
> (e) the personal data have to be erased for compliance with a legal obligation in Union or Member State law to which the controller is subject;
> (f) the personal data have been collected in relation to the offer of information society services referred to in Article 8(1).[92]

Where a request for exercise of the right to erasure is made an analysis of the basis for the request must be made, to see if it fits within one of the grounds listed above. If processing of the data is required for contract performance, where the data subject is a party to the contract, then the processing is lawful[93] and likely none of the cases for erasure listed in Article 17(1) would apply. This is consistent with a statement by the Commission during the legislative process prior to adoption of the GDPR, 'personal data may be kept for as long as it is needed to carry out a contract or to meet a legal obligation (for example when citizens have a loan contract with their bank). In short, the right to be forgotten is not absolute'.[94] However, an analysis has to be done to ensure that the processing truly is necessary for contract performance, 'an objective assessment that must be conducted prior to the commencement of the processing'.[95] Futhermore, additional exceptions to this right of erasure apply, such as where the data are necessary for the exercise or

[91] H Kranenborg, 'Article 17. Right to erasure ("right to be forgotten")' in C Kuner, LA Bygrave and C Docksey (eds), *The EU General Data Protection Regulation (GDPR): A Commentary* (Oxford, Oxford University Press, 2020) 477.

[92] Article 17(1) of the GDPR.

[93] Article 6(b) of the GDPR.

[94] European Commission, 'Data Protection Day 2014: Full Speed on EU Data Protection Reform' MEMO 14–60 (27 January 2014), available at ec.europa.eu/commission/presscorner/detail/en/MEMO_14_60.

[95] W Kotschy, 'Article 6. Lawfulness of processing' in C Kuner, LA Bygrave and C Docksey (eds), *The EU General Data Protection Regulation (GDPR): A Commentary* (Oxford, Oxford University Press, 2020) 331.

defence of legal claims.[96] Nonetheless, where the right does apply and when it is exercised by the data subject, the controller must erase the data and, where it has made the data public, inform controllers processing the data 'that the data subject has requested the erasure by such controllers of any links to, or copy or replication of, those personal data'.[97]

While the 'right to be forgotten' is not absolute and a balancing test between data protection and other fundamental rights may need to be applied, a private transaction has less chance of prevailing over data protection than, say, a public interest register such as the Italian public company register in the *Manni* case (decided under EU law prior to the GDPR), or for landownership or trademark ownership ledgers.[98] Thus, where personal data is stored on the blockchain network of any particular smart contract, and an exception does not apply, the right to erasure is problematical as it is almost impossible to delete the data once they are on the blockchain.[99]

The right to erasure creates difficulties in the context of smart contracts using blockchain technology, as blockchain networks are built to create trust by making it impossible to delete or modify transaction records without breaking the chain. 'The whole point of such a blockchain is to ensure that transactions, including the parties to them, are never forgotten in order to enable decentralised trust'.[100] Furthermore, restricting the use of smart contracts to private, permissioned blockchain networks does not remove the problem 'unless that network is designed in a way that each and every piece of data is readable by only the parties that absolutely need to, and can be rectified or erased at the request of the data subject'.[101] While 'it is technically impossible to grant the request for erasure made by a data subject when data is registered on a blockchain', the CNIL has opened the door a bit to exploring technical solutions:

> However, when the data recorded on the blockchain is a commitment, a hash generated by a keyed-hash function or a ciphertext obtained through 'state of the art' algorithms and keys, the data controller can make the data practically inaccessible, and therefore move closer to the effects of data erasure.[102]

Nonetheless, the CNIL reminds the reader that 'these solutions do not, strictly speaking, result in an erasure of the data, insofar as the data would still exist in the blockchain'.[103] Maxwell and Salmon comment that the concept of 'erasure' is still

[96] Article 17(3) of the GDPR.
[97] Article 17(2) of the GDPR.
[98] Moerel (n 70) 228.
[99] R de Caria, 'Definitions of Smart Contracts: Between Law and Code' in LA DiMatteo, M Cannarsa and C Poncibò (eds), *The Cambridge Handbook of Smart Contracts, Blockchain Technology and Digital Platforms* (Cambrdige, Cambridge University Press, 2020) 35.
[100] Lyons, Courselas and Timsit, 'Blockchain and the GDPR' (2018) 25.
[101] ibid 25.
[102] CNIL (n 65) 8.
[103] ibid 9.

open; some supervisory authorities admit that irreversible encryption satisfies the requirement.[104] Furthermore, smart contract mechanisms governing access rights 'can be used to revoke all access rights, thereby making the content invisible to others, albeit not erased'.[105] Certain observers look forward to supervisory authorities issuing guidance evidencing a pragmatic approach in the future.[106]

C. Right not to be Subject to a Decision Based Solely on Automated Processing

Michèle Finck argues that a smart contract 'will only in some circumstances be connected to a legal contract' but always will constitute automated data processing.[107] Thus, by a few keystrokes she cautions that the requisite contract legitimate basis for processing personal data may not exist in many smart contracts and she also holds up the spectre of an additional data subject right – that 'not to be subject to a decision based solely on automated processing, including profiling, which produces legal effects concerning him or her or similarly significantly affects him or her'.[108]

In that case, where the contract legitimate basis does not exist, a potential exception to the prohibition on automated individual decision-making – where 'necessary for entering into, or perfomance of, a contract between the data subject and a data controller'[109] – would also not be available. There would also be significant difficulties using this exception when public and permissionless blockchains 'that can be read and used by anyone are used to execute the smart contract', as this does not jibe with the requirement of a contract between the data subject and the data controller.[110] Furthermore, an exception based on the explicit consent of the data subject[111] would be difficult to use in the context of the immutable blockchain, as the data subject would have a right to withdraw consent at any time, and 'it may be difficult for a data subject to put an end to the data processing in revoking consent' where personal data should then be deleted by the controller.[112] Moreover, withdrawing consent provides a ground for the exercise of the right to erasure.

There are other difficulties related to the prohibition on decisions based solely on automated processing such as complying with the right to human intervention,

[104] Maxwell and Salmon (n 25) 15.
[105] ibid 15.
[106] Van Eecke and AG Haie, 'Blockchain and the GDPR' (2018) 534.
[107] Finck (n 7) 79.
[108] Article 22(1) of the GDPR.
[109] Article 22(2)(a) of the GDPR.
[110] Finck (n 7) 85.
[111] Article 22(2)(c) of the GDPR.
[112] Finck (n 7) 87.

which Finck sees as an unavoidable requirement.[113] In addition, under certain conditions, the use of automated processing may give rise to the requirement that a data protection impact assessment be carried out,[114] as the the blockchain infrastructure used by smart contracts 'involves a high risk from a data protection perspective'.[115]

This chapter now turns to the GDPR's handling of security risks, under a data protection concept that is now referred to as 'integrity and confidentiality'.

VI. Integrity and Confidentiality in Smart Contracts

This section begins by introducing the concept of integrity and confidentiality under the GDPR (section VI.A), prior to developing this subject in the context of the blockchain and smart contracts (section VI.B).

A. Introduction on Integrity and Confidentiality under the GDPR

Security is an important element of EU data protection law, which the GDPR categorises under the 'integrity and confidentiality data protection principle', providing that personal data shall be 'processed in a manner that ensures appropriate security of the personal data, including protection against unauthorised or unlawful processing and against accidental loss, destruction or damage, using appropriate technical or organisational measures'.[116]

The GDPR also takes a risk-based approach in providing that:

> Taking into account the state of the art, the costs of implementation and the nature, scope, context and purposes of processing as well as the risk of varying likelihood and severity for the rights and freedoms of natural persons, the controller and the processor shall implement appropriate technical and organisational measures to ensure a level of security appropriate to the risk.[117]

Various tools may be used to improve security of personal data, such as pseudonymisation and encryption.[118] Furthermore, controllers have responsibility for ensuring the selection of processors that offer 'sufficient guarantees to implement appropriate technical and organisational measures in such a manner

[113] ibid 87.
[114] ibid 90.
[115] ibid 91.
[116] Article 5(1)(f) of the GDPR.
[117] Article 32(1) of the GDPR.
[118] Article 32(1)(a) of the GDPR.

that processing will meet the requirements' of the GDPR and 'ensure the protection of the rights of the data subject', including security requirements.[119]

B. Integrity and Confidentiality in the Context of the Blockchain and Smart Contracts

Integrity and confidentiality (security) is a data protection principle that involves issues in connection with smart contracts using blockchain technology. Not only are there risks of bugs in the computer code, but there are also real dangers of hacking, as evidenced by a case involving the hacking of the Etherum blockchain.[120] In that case, a distributed crowdfunding system, the DAO, was created with corporate governance and operations conducted through the use of smart contracts.[121] Shortly after launching, a hacker profited from a bug in the code to 'siphon off' over $60 million in cybercurrency contributed by users. There was 'no legal or technical way' to recover the funds as things stood, so the leaders of the project had to convince a majority of the nodes to implement a 'hard fork' splitting the blockchain into two paths, which allowed recovery of the funds, but killed off the project.[122] This concept of a 'fork' is explained by ENISA, the European Union Agency for Cybersecurity:

> One of the key aspects of a distributed ledger is that the data held within it, is considered valid because all parties agree to a single 'true' version. In the event that existing participants in a Blockchain decide to include data in a non-compliant manner with established protocols, an event named a fork occurs.
>
> Forks result in a split of the ledger and the consequent creation of two groups, each validating their own version of the ledger. In order for participants to be able to continue to interact with each other, they are required to follow the same fork of the ledger.[123]

However, while the use of a fork is relatively simple on a private blockchain, is is 'a seismic and exceedingly rare event' on a public one.[124] According to Werbach and Cornell, 'Because the only enforcement mechanism was the Ethereum network's computers executing ther terms of the The DAO software code, there was no way to distinguish between a legitimate string of transactions and one with malicious intent'.[125]

[119] Article 28(1) of the GDPR.

[120] V Gatteschi, F Lamberti and C Demartini, 'Technology of Smart Contracts' in LA DiMatteo, M Cannarsa and C Poncibò (eds), *The Cambridge Handbook of Smart Contracts, Blockchain Technology and Digital Platforms* (Cambridge, Cambridge University Press, 2020) 54.

[121] K Werbach and N Cornell, 'Contracts Ex Machina' (2017) 67 *Duke Law Journal* 350.

[122] ibid 351.

[123] ENISA, 'Distributed Ledger Technology & Cybersecurity – Improving information security in the financial sector' (2017) 10, available at www.enisa.europa.eu/publications/blockchain-security/at_download/fullReport.

[124] Meyer (n 11).

[125] ibid 352.

Following a literature review, two scholars identified six security issues connected to smart contracts: 'transaction-dependency, timestamp dependency, mishandled exception, criminal activities, re-entrancy, and untrustworthy data feeds'.[126] These technical issues are too detailed to develop in this chapter, but suffice it to say, they need to be considered in design and development of smart contracts, which highlights the need for careful coding and dovetails with the GDPR requirement of 'data protection by design and by default', including 'data minimisation'.[127] According to ENISA,

> Smart contracts are essentially programs that run on the distributed ledger. They are prone to any faults associated with code. As with any software, the more complex a smart contract is, the more prone to software errors it will be.
>
> Generally, the function, and the security of smart contracts code depends on the author's capabilities.[128]

One technical means proposed to increase security in connection with use of the blockchain is to establish different private keys for signing and encrypting messages across the blockchain distributed ledger. This aspect of good 'key management' would ensure that even if a hacker were to obtain the private key for encrypting messages, and be able to read the data in the smart contract, they would not be able to modify them or otherwise interact with the smart contract.[129] Keys should be stored on secure media.[130] Reference has already been made to the use of cryptography, but the keys must be strong ones and a future threat is quantum computing, which should be taken into account for future-proofing the security measures.[131] ENISA recommends the following good practices as ways to mitigate privacy challenges related to limiting visibility of information to authorised entities and prevent unauthorised access to transactions:

(1) 'Encrypt the transactions, so only the involved counterparties can access the whole information';
(2) 'Use sharding to allow specific transactions to be validated by specific entities';
(3) 'Use pruning to remove data from the ledger at certain period of time, as requested by the regulation';
(4) 'In case an entity must be linked to a key, an authority may keep information of which key belongs to which entity'; and
(5) 'Encrypt ledger with more than one key'.[132]

[126] C Poncibò and LA DiMatteo, 'Smart Contracts: Contractual and Noncontractual Remedies' in LA DiMatteo, M Cannarsa and C Poncibò (eds), *The Cambridge Handbook of Smart Contracts, Blockchain Technology and Digital Platforms* (Cambrdige, Cambridge University Press, 2020) 131.
[127] Article 25 of the GDPR. See section VII.B of this chapter.
[128] ENISA, 'Distributed Ledger Technology & Cybersecurity (2017) 18.
[129] ibid 14.
[130] CNIL (n 65) 10.
[131] ENISA (n 123) 14–15.
[132] ibid 21.

Now, this chapter turns to the purpose limitation and data minimisation concepts in the GDPR.

VII. Purpose Limitation and Data Minimisation

Two additional elements of the data protection principles merit brief attention here. These are the requirement of purpose limitation (section VII.A) and data minimisation (section VII.B).

A. Purpose Limitation

The purpose limitation data protection principle today may be seen to include both purpose specification for the data processing and use limitation. The GDPR provides that personal data shall be:

> [C]ollected for specified, explicit and legitimate purposes and not further processed in a manner that is incompatible with those purposes; further processing for archiving purposes in the public interest, scientific or historical research purposes or statistical purposes shall, in accordance with Article 89(1), not be considered to be incompatible with the initial purposes ('purpose limitation').[133]

The first part of this principle – purpose specification – requires that there be clear communication to the data subject about the use of blockchain technology to process his or her personal data, including a 'specific and explicit' explanation that the data will be processed after the original transaction through the distributed ledger technology.[134] Finck comments that 'legitimate' purposes requirement means not only that there should be a legitimate grounds for data processing under Article 6 of the GDPR (Lawfulness of processing), but that the processing complies with broader applicable legal principles (eg non-discrimination).[135] Furthermore, in this light de Terwangne adds that the purposes 'may not entail a disproportionate interference with the rights, freedoms and interests at stake, in the name of the interests of the data controller'.[136]

The second part of the purpose limitation principle – use limitation (or compatible use) – calls for a case-by-case analysis, and Finck questions 'whether

[133] Article 5(1)(b) of the GDPR.

[134] M Finck, 'Blockchain and the General Data Protection Regulation: Can distributed ledgers be squared with European data protection law?' (European Parliamentary Research Service, 2019) 66, available at www.europarl.europa.eu/RegData/etudes/STUD/2019/634445/EPRS_STU(2019)634445_EN.pdf.

[135] ibid 66.

[136] C de Terwangne, 'Article 5. Principles relating to processing of personal data', in C Kuner, LA Bygrave and C Docksey (eds), *The EU General Data Protection Regulation (GDPR): A Commentary* (Oxford, Oxford University Press, 2020) 315 (citation omitted).

there is a clear linkage of purpose of a single blockchain-based transaction and the continued storage and in the ledger',[137] which refers to the first of the criteria that will now be presented. Indeed, Article 6(4) of the GDPR sets out a list of criteria to be taken into account for a determination of the compatibility of the further processing, where it is not based on the data subject's consent:

(a) any link between the purposes for which the personal data have been collected and the purpose of the intended further processing;
(b) the context in which the personal data have been collected, in particular regarding the relationship between data subjects and the controller;
(c) the nature of the personal data, in particular whether special categories of personal data are processed, pursuant to Article 9, or whether personal data related to criminal convictions and offences are processed, pursuant to Article 10;
(d) the possible consequences of the intended further processing for data subjects;
(e) the existence of appropriate safeguards, which may include encryption or pseudonymisation.[138]

B. Data Minimisation

Data minimisation is often referred to as part of the overriding data quality data protection principle. However, the GDPR separates it out. Personal data are to be 'adequate, relevant and limited to what is necessary in relation to the purposes for which they are processed ("data minimisation")'.[139] Recital 39 not only repeats the text of Article 5(1)(c) of the GDPR, but adds that, 'Personal data should be processed only if the purpose of the processing could not reasonably be fulfilled by other means'.[140] Importantly, de Terwangne comments that 'one may not process an excessively large amount of personal data … But one may not process a single datum either if this would entail a disproportionate interference in the data subject's rights and interests'.[141] Thus, the limitation set out is not only quantitative, but also qualitative. Maxwell and Salmon remark that two features of the blockchain conflict with the data minimisation principle, as well as the storage limitation principle: data traveling through the blockchain are visible to every node and they cannot be deleted from the blockchain.[142] This principle is ripe for advisory guidance, according to Finck, which should include an analysis of the extent to which storing data off-chain may be a way to satisfy the data minimisation principle.[143]

[137] Finck, 'Blockchain and the General Data Protection Regulation' (2019) 67.
[138] Article 6(4) of the GDPR.
[139] Article 5(1)(c) of the GDPR.
[140] Recital 39 of the GDPR.
[141] de Terwangne, 'Article 5' (2020) 317.
[142] Maxwell and Salmon (n 25) 14.
[143] Finck (n 134) 68.

VIII. Cross-Border Data Transfers

The CNIL remarks that 'transfers outside of the European Union (EU) can be particularly problematic, especially in the case of public blockchains'.[144] In that context, participants and miners may span the globe, meaning that personal data could be located most anywhere, and potentially (more likely, probably) in jurisidictons outside the EU that do not benefit from an adequacy decision. Bacon, Michels, Millard and Singh echo this view, especially in the context of permissionless platforms:

> However, widely distributed, permissionless platforms are by design unconstrained by international border: typically anybody, anywhere, can download the entire transaction archive and start processing new transactions as a node or miner. As a result, use of these platforms is likely to entail data transfers to third countries. Since any party in any third country can download the archive, adequacy decisions and appropriate safeguards (including binding corporate rules) are unlikely to provide sufficient coverage.[145]

The CNIL reminds us that transactions on the blockchain involve 'a request to validate the transaction (and therefore potentially personal data) being sent to all miners of the chain' and updates through the addition of new blocks for all participants.[146] The CNIL recommends the use of permissioned blockchains in this regard:

> While appropriate safeguards for a transfer outside the EU may be used in a permissioned blockchain, such as standard contractual clauses, binding corporate rules, codes of conduct or even certification mechanisms, the CNIL observes that these safeguards are harder to implement in a public blockchain, given that the data controller has no real control over the location of miners.[147]

Finck likewise views the difficulties with cross-border transfers on a permissionless (public) blockchain. While on a private permissioned blockchain, it may be possible to obtain data subject consent to a cross-border transfer after providing information about the risks, based on controlled access and applicable terms and conditions, 'it is not obvious how such consent could be acquired in respect of a permissionless chain'.[148]

IX. Conclusion

Contrary to what some commentators may say, smart contracts and data protection legislation are not completely incompatible. However, a good undertstanding of the latter is necessary in order for smart contracts not to violate the legislation.

[144] CNIL (n 65) 5.
[145] Bacon, Michels, Millard and Singh (n 24) 47.
[146] CNIL (n 65) 5.
[147] ibid 5.
[148] Finck (n 134) 28.

This chapter has intended to provide information on some of the challenges of the GDPR through a general presentation of the legislation, followed by a discussion of personal data in the context of smart contracts, and then an analysis of some of the most relevant data protection principles and data subject rights.

Public blockchains provided several issues insofar as EU data protection law is concerned, especially in a B2C context. One solution may be to use only permissioned blockchains for B2C contracts, establishing the identity of the controller through contract. Indeed, the EU Blockchain Observatory is of the opinion that, 'a private permissioned blockchain network operated by a consortium of companies or by a government agency will be better position to apply the letter of the GDPR than a public blockchain network without permission'.[149] Avoidance of the use of personal data on the blockchain is another strategy, when possible, for example in the context of B2B smart contracts between legal persons. The chances of avoiding the use of personal data increase when business to consumer (B2C) transactions are excluded from the use of smart contracts. Next, proper anonymisation results in data no longer being considered 'personal' and thereby is a way to avoid the application of the GDPR, at least downstream, which is to say after the anonymisation.

Accountability is a concern, especially given the increased level of administrative sanctions possible under the GDPR and strengthened supervisory authority powers. In this light, finding the relevant party with responsibility is difficult. Generally, this will be the controller, who bears the brunt of most data protection obligations, although data processors also have potential liability. Defining the roles of the different actors in smart contracts using the blockchain requires careful analysis and the type of blockchain involved – whether this be a public permissionless one or a private permissioned blockchain – will be crucial in this regard.

This chapter has highlighted the main data subject rights that create difficulties in connection with smart contracts using the blockchain. These are essentially the right to rectification and the right to erasure ('right to be forgotten'), given the immutability of the blockchain. In addition, the right not to be subject to a decision based solely on automated processing was worth investigating. Elements of data protection principles – security ('integrity and confidentiality'), purpose limitation, data minimisation – are worthy of study, and have been the subject of sections of this chapter, as have issues related to the GDPR's cross-border personal data transfer requirements.

An industry association representative set out his formula for 'a GDPR-compliant Blockchain solution': 'Keep it private', 'Don't get personal' and 'Set the rules up front'.[150] In other words, stick with a private network, do not handle any personal information, and establish a clear 'common contractual governance framework'.[151] While making use of smart contracts using Blockchain technology GDPR-compliant is not an easy task, those rules provide a good starting point.

[149] Lyons, Courselas and Timsit (n 59) 16.
[150] Bailey, 'Blockchain And EU Privacy Laws' (2019).
[151] ibid.

5

Proactive Legal Design for Health Data Sharing Based on Smart Contracts

ARIANNA ROSSI AND HELENA HAAPIO*

I. Introduction: Scripts, Stacks and the Human Side of Smart Contracts

> The technology of smart contracts neglects the fact that people use contracts as social resources to manage their relations. The inflexibility that they introduce, by design, might short-circuit a number of social uses to which law is routinely put.[1]

Smart contracts are increasingly used in contexts where human choice, oversight and flexibility matter. Still, the human side of smart contracts has gained far less scholarly attention than their technical and legal aspects. Karen EC Levy in her article 'Book-Smart, Not Street-Smart' reminds us of the fact that contracts are deeply social tools, as well as legal ones, and of the risks, if smart contracts are not designed to take into account the social complexities of contracting; while they may facilitate technically perfect implementation and lower transaction costs, they fail to understand or integrate the social world and human behaviour.[2]

The social and human aspects are especially present in the use case that this chapter examines: technological architectures that enable the sharing of health data, with a focus on emerging technologies that would allow a multitude of parties to access and process massive biomedical datasets in a secure and decentralised

* The authors would like to thank the anonymous reviewers for their helpful comments and Jim Hazard for his valuable feedback. The authors would also like to aknowledge Leila Hamhoum for her precious editorial assistance.

[1] KEC Levy, 'Book-Smart, Not Street-Smart: Blockchain-Based Smart Contracts and the Social Workings of Law' (2017) 3 *Engaging Science, Technology, and Society* 1, 1.

[2] ibid 10. 'Automated contracts', according to Levy (ibid) 11, 'tend to focus on contracts' capacity for legal communication, perhaps to the expense of their social capacity'.

manner while providing transparency about such processes and about the permissions granted to specific data uses. This chapter addresses the benefits and challenges related to the construction of user-centric solutions intended to allow individuals to whom the data refers[3] to relinquish rights over their information through the instrument of informed consent. Other parties include researchers and physicians who connect and communicate with those individuals to obtain, collect and use such data; providers of the infrastructure meant to enable the sharing and querying of vast amounts of data; and a variety of organisations, such as research centres, medical institutes and various healthcare facilities that access and analyse that data to enhance the predictive power of their models.[4] To participate in the data sharing economy, these organisations need to comply with applicable laws, for example, by ensuring privacy and transparency of data processing, and adhere to the data permissions established by the participants. In this context, blockchain technologies offer the backbone for the integration with other applications like smart contracts, employed to automate processes, such as participant compensation and real-time data use permissions.

Smart contracts are not necessarily (legal) contracts, especially in our context. Echoing the title of the article by Shaanan Cohney and David A Hoffman, 'Transactional Scripts in Contract Stacks',[5] we might frame them as 'scripts' or 'transactional scripts'. These scripts, which may include consents or permissions, may or may not constitute or be part of (legal) contracts, and they may or may not be human-readable. They seldom stand alone: there is often a 'stack' or a 'chain' (or several stacks or chains) – scripts are the building blocks of contract and consent stacks and chains, which may be quite complex.[6] Given the intricacies of the health data sharing scenario, the expectations and the objectives of the numerous participating stakeholders must be carefully aligned. This complexity calls for proactive legal thinking merged with design thinking, and a legal design intervention based on transparency-enhancing tools.

There is a growing need for easy-to-use solutions, on the one hand, and for complying with operational and legal requirements, on the other. Balancing

[3] In this chapter, the terms 'individuals', 'patients' and '(research) participants' will be used interchangeably. In the context of data privacy, they can also be referred to as 'data subjects'.

[4] TK Mackey, TT Kuo, B Gummadi, KA Clauson, G Church, D Grishin, K Obbad, R Barkovich and M Palombini, '"Fit-for-Purpose?" – Challenges and Opportunities for Applications of Blockchain Technology in the Future of Healthcare' (2019) 17 *BMC Medicine* 68.

[5] S Cohney and DA Hoffman, 'Transactional Scripts in Contract Stacks' (2020) University of Pennsylvania, Institute for Law & Economy Research Paper No. 20-08, available at ssrn.com/abstract=3523515. See also JG Allen, 'Wrapped and Stacked: 'Smart Contracts' and the Interaction of Natural and Formal Languages' (2018) 14 *European Review of Contract Law* 307.

[6] See, eg, the consent receipts (made of machine-readable code and human-readable code) by the Kantara initiative in R Beaumont, C Cooper, S D'Agostino, R Graves, I Henderson, M Hodder, H Honko, A Hughes, T Jones, R Lapes, O Maerz, E Maler, J Pasquale, S Tuoriniemi and J Wunderlich, 'Consent Receipt Specification' (M Lizar and D Turner eds, v1.1.0, Kantara Initiative, 20 February 2018), available at kantarainitiative.org/file-downloads/consent-receipt-specification-v1-1-0.

the needs and interests of the different stakeholders is not always easy. The researchers, planners, developers, builders and users of complex technologies need support and guidance. Contracts, consents and permissions are not easy to work with, even when they stand alone. The inclusion of code, stacks and chains in our context adds a new layer of complexity to the operational and legal issues. But if we think of smart contracts, consents and permissions as *scripts*, *artifacts*[7] or *things*[8] – human-made products like any others – it becomes easier to approach questions related to their functionality, usability, and *quality by design*.[9] Viewing them as *communicative artifacts* and *information products*[10] highlights the notion that they are human-made instruments that intend to convey information for a purpose. In this way, we can remove much of the mystique around them.[11] It then becomes natural that communicating their contents and ramifications can be informed by contract/legal design scholarship and privacy communication design scholarship.

Proactive legal designers can bring a new perspective by identifying and making different expectations and requirements visible early on, helping to embed them from the beginning into the design specifications, building in navigation tools, affordances and signifiers, and asking questions such as: How can we make contract and consent stacks or privacy communication work better? How can we ensure that the smart contract code or script reflects the intention of the stakeholders and does what it is intended to do – and how might design tools and methods assist in managing and using the data inputs and outputs? How can we secure successful and compliant implementation?

Section II begins by introducing the research scenario and the many benefits and challenges involved in health data-sharing transactions based on smart contracts. Section III begins the path towards finding a balance between the different stakeholders' often conflicting needs and goals, integrating data sharing with dynamic consent models and smart contracts, and embedding transparency into health data sharing architectures. After introducing proactive law and legal design, section IV illustrates, with examples, how these can be merged and brought to practice with the help of design patterns. Section V concludes.

[7] MC Suchman, 'Contracts as Social Artifacts' (2003) 37 *Law & Society Review* 91.

[8] AA Leff, 'Contract as Thing' (1970) 19 *The American University Law Review* 131.

[9] Quality by design is a concept introduced in JM Juran, *Juran on Quality by Design: The New Steps for Planning Quality into Goods and Services* (New York, Free Press, 1992). Juran provides a set of steps that can be used to establish quality goals, identify customers, determine customer needs, provide measurement, and develop process features and controls to improve – all very much in line with the design thinking approach adopted in this chapter.

[10] For information products more generally, see E Orna, *Making Knowledge Visible: Communicating Knowledge through Information Products* (London, Gower Publishing, 2005).

[11] Suchman, 'Contracts as Social Artifacts' (2003) 93. 'By seeing contracts as simply one among many types of artifact that we produce and deploy in our daily lives,' Suchman notes, 'we strip them of their legalistic mystique'.

II. Research Scenario

A. Benefits of Health Data Sharing and Reuse

'The value of data lies in its use and re-use' maintains the 2020 European Commission's Data Strategy.[12] This political statement emphasises the necessity of a data-agile ecosystem for the successful development of a competitive economy meant to create a variety of products and services by the private and public sector alike. In the healthcare sector, access to large databases has tremendous value, as it enhances the predictive power of data analysis and provides insights from population health analytics.[13] Yet many medical centres and research facilities are not able to maintain a set of patient records and other data large enough to develop and train their own predictive models, for instance in the case of rare conditions. This is why there is a growing tendency to recur to shared datasets: not only are opportunities for research advancement distributed to a larger network of parties, with the deriving scientific, social and economic implications, but also the efforts to collect, describe and qualify huge amounts of information are not wasted.

Although the possible applications are several, in the medical sector the example of genome data reuse is particularly telling. Nowadays, people increasingly have their DNA sequenced[14] for many reasons of medical and non-medical nature.[15] The data produced is valuable for a number of (commercial and non-commercial) organisations that aspire to leverage an unprecedented amount and variety of information to establish correlations between genetic traits and conditions, supporting thereby preventive medicine. Moreover, genetic data is one of the keys to personalised healthcare, which promotes more efficient, accurate and targeted treatments and prevention strategies for humankind, while it opens new revenue streams for pharmaceutical companies.

[12] European Commission, 'A European Strategy for Data – Communication from the Commission to the European Parliament, the Council, the European Economic and Social Committee and the Committee of the Regions' COM(2020) 66 final, 6.

[13] Mackey, Kuo, Gummadi, Clauson, Church, Grishin, Obbad, Barkovich and Palombini, '"Fit-for-Purpose?"' (2019).

[14] National Human Genome Research Institute (NHGRI), 'DNA Sequencing Fact Sheet', available at www.genome.gov/about-genomics/fact-sheets/DNA-Sequencing-Fact-Sheet: 'Sequencing DNA means determining the order of the four chemical building blocks – called "bases" – that make up the DNA molecule. The sequence tells scientists the kind of genetic information that is carried in a particular DNA segment', for instance changes in a gene that may cause disease.

[15] Motivations include learning about predisposition to heritable disorders, modelling response to medicinal products, uncovering risk of conceiving children with severe genetic conditions and gaining knowledge about ancestry, familial relationships or personal traits. See SA Garner and J Kim, 'The Privacy Risks of Direct-to-Consumer Genetic Testing: A Case Study of 23andMe and Ancestry' (2018) 96 *Washington University Law Review* 1219, 1236.

However, for such opportunities to flourish, the dominant data governance model constituted by data silos needs to be vanquished. Data silos generate value exclusively for those holding the data, not for those who have provided the data, nor for other market players that could create value with that data. Legislative (eg, the General Data Protection Regulation in the EU) as well as other initiatives (eg, MyData[16]) aim to unlock fair digital competition, by developing novel data ownership and sharing approaches. To encourage the free flow of data and pinpoint alternative data governance models based on data sharing, there is a growing need for consumer-centric tools, such as consent and identity management platforms. Such models aspire to rebalance the existing power asymmetry, by placing the users at the centre of processes, restoring their ability to self-determine the permissible use of their information and transforming merely formal digital rights into easily actionable rights.[17] These include, for example, the right to give and withdraw consent for the information flow and to keep track of the parties accessing one's own data, the purposes for which it is accessed and the outcomes of such activities.

B. Issues Concerning Health Data Sharing and Reuse

Great knowledge, however, comes with a cost. The flow and reuse of personal data, especially sensitive health-related information, ought to be protected through legal and ethical means. For services offered in the EU,[18] not only should organisations be able to put such safeguards in place by adopting adequate technical and organisational measures and integrating them in their workflow *by design and by default*,[19] but they are also required to be able to demonstrate compliance, for

[16] The purpose of MyData Global is to empower individuals by improving their right to self-determination regarding their personal data. See MyData.org, 'About' at mydata.org/about.

[17] MyData.org, 'Declaration' (v1.0), available at mydata.org/declaration. According to the Declaration, 'in many countries, individuals have enjoyed legal data protection for decades, yet their rights have remained mostly formal: little known, hard to enforce, and often obscured by corporate practices. We want true transparency and truly informed consent to become the new normal for when people and organisations interact. We intend access and redress, portability, and the right to be forgotten, to become "one-click rights": rights that are as simple and efficient to use as today's and tomorrow's best online services'.

[18] In the EU, the legal protection of medical as well as other personal data is established by Regulation (EU) 2016/679 of the European Parliament and of the Council of 27 April 2016 on the protection of natural persons with regard to the processing of personal data and on the free movement of such data, and repealing Directive 95/46/EC (General Data Protection Regulation) [2016] OJ L119/1 (GDPR), which also poses a number of obligations on organisations collecting and processing data, such as the obligation to implement technical and organizational measures to guard the data from harm.

[19] GDPR, Art 25. See also European Data Protection Board, 'Guidelines 4/2019 on Article 25 Data Protection by Design and by Default' (13 November 2019), available at edpb.europa.eu/sites/edpb/files/consultation/edpb_guidelines_201904_dataprotection_by_design_and_by_default.pdf.

example by maintaining an electronic record of processing activities. Such safeguards should effectively and demonstrably implement data protection principles, including the central tenet of transparency. Transparency aspires to level out information asymmetries and enable the parties providing knowledge about themselves to understand and exert their rights.[20]

Given the value of patient records and the significance of the sector for society, healthcare constitutes one of the favourite attack vectors worldwide. Data breaches can lead to the reidentification of deidentified datasets, exposing patients to the repercussions of data misuse, such as fraudulent activities and discrimination. Healthcare providers may be subject to service disruption, suffer significant financial damage, and face the possibility of litigation.[21] Moreover, a 2019 data breach report[22] observed that the majority of health data losses, theft or accidents due to unauthorised access can be ascribed to internal actors (eg, hospital employees) who either perform unintentional actions exposing vulnerabilities or abuse their authorisations. So the medical sector needs not only to protect itself from external mischievous parties, but also to be vigilant about internal threats, such as human errors in the implementation and enforcement of security policies.[23]

Since information privacy is a non-negotiable precondition for health data analysis, innovative approaches that balance security and confidentiality of personal information with the endavour of keeping high-performance processing capacities are arising. The combination of the respect for user-established rules about permissible data processing and the promotion of transparency about the processing practices is meant to establish a relationship of trust among the stakeholders. Indeed, degradation of trust severely impacts data sharing attitudes and has cascade effects in all data-informed industries.[24] Organisations offering genetic services, for instance, face today intense scrutiny due to questionable practices[25] and yearn to regain people's trust. Enlarging their user base is indispensable to create a prosperous data sharing ecosystem, though. Thus, such organisations have a urgent interest in implementing adequate privacy and security measures as well as user-centric data governance models. Moreover, even business-to-business data sharing lags behind, one reason being 'the lack of trust between economic

[20] European Data Protection Board, 'Guidelines 4/2019' (2019) 14.

[21] A McLeod and D Dolezel, 'Cyber-Analytics: Modeling Factors Associated with Healthcare Data Breaches' (2018) 108 *Decision Support Systems* 57.

[22] Verizon, '2019 Data Breach Investigations Report' (2019) 44–45, available at enterprise.verizon.com/resources/reports/2019-data-breach-investigations-report.pdf.

[23] R Ayyagari, 'An Exploratory Analysis of Data Breaches from 2005–2011: Trends and Insights' (2012) 8 *Journal of Information Privacy and Security* 33.

[24] See, eg, the Facebook–Cambridge Analytica data misuse scandal, H Tuttle, 'Facebook Scandal Raises Data Privacy Concerns' (2018) 65 *Risk Management* 6.

[25] For instance, recent cases of access to consumer genomics services and their databases by law enforcement agencies with the objective of investigating unsolved crimes and the acquisition of genetic data by biopharmaceutical companies to develop new drugs without users' consent or awareness have raised consumers' and authorities' concerns. Garner and Kim, 'The Privacy Risks of Direct-to-Consumer Genetic Testing' (2018) 1221–22.

operators that the data will be used in line with contractual agreements'.[26] Lack of clarity and transparency of the contractual conditions concerning digital services stifles economic development of micro, small and medium enterprises.[27]

III. Seeking a Balance – Identifying, Aligning and Managing Expectations

A. Complexity Caused by the Stakeholders' Conflicting Needs and Goals

In health data sharing scenarios,[28] an elaborate mix of needs and objectives of the various parties is at stake. In user-centric services, individuals impose rules about the permissible use of their data to the organisations collecting or processing the data, often through the instrument of consent. As for the organisations maintaining datasets or providing the sharing infrastructure, they need to establish data governance rules and oversight mechanisms,[29] for instance by clarifying the terms of use of their services and the privacy practices towards the individuals, while also delineating the safeguards under which other parties (eg, research centres) access and process their information. To regulate such access, organisations make data sharing agreements encompassing patients' permissions as well as rules regarding legitimate use of data (eg, in terms of security policies). The research institutes, in turn, need to ensure that their employees respect regulatory requirements as well as their internal privacy and security policies that more or less closely mirror the data sharing agreements. Given the sensitivity of the type of data at hand and the cascade effects of a breach of trust, it is of utmost importance that the expectations pinpointing data sharing among these different actors are clearly set and respectfully honored.

This scenario suggests an intricate process of multi-channel information provision and dynamic consent requests. This ecosystem is even more complicated: it may need to support a blend of analogic and digital means to collect, process and manage the data, as well as to provide information that is necessary for the establishment of the consent and contract relations and their impact. For instance, patients might simultaneously interface with their human healthcare provider as well as with mobile applications and sensors, without necessarily needing to grasp

[26] COM(2020) 66 (n 12) 7.

[27] European Commission, Study on the Economic Detriment to Small and Medium-Sized Enterprises Arising from Unfair and Unbalanced Cloud Computing Contracts – Final Report (European Commission Directorate-General for Justice and Consumers, November 2018) 46–49.

[28] For a review, see C Suver, A Thorogood, M Doerr, J Wilbanks and B Knoppers, 'Bringing Code to Data: Don't Forget Governance' (2020) *Journal of Medical Internet Research* 2.

[29] ibid 2.

the complexity of the underlying sharing architecture. It becomes pivotal, then, to design the appropriate affordances to enable desirable interactions and to foster shared values while inhibiting detrimental actions.

B. Integrating Data Sharing on the Blockchain with Dynamic Consent Models and Smart Contracts

Blockchain technologies are increasingly proposed as solutions to challenges concerning privacy, transparency and accountability for health data sharing.[30] The promoters of such solutions underline the advantages of sharing healthcare datasets without the necessity of trusting a third-party cloud.[31] The adoption of blockchain-based solutions is also intended to successfully manage different stakeholders' needs emerging from labyrinthine data sharing architectures while ensuring confidentiality and verifiability of the information. It is claimed that this digital architecture is able to 'ensure the resilience, provenance, traceability, and management of health data'[32] which originates from a variety of sources, including different data providers, but also manifold devices and sensors (eg, various data produced in the Internet of Medical Things[33]).

The distribution of the data on various databases and machines (ie, nodes) renders the history of transactions immutable and tamper-resistant, thus offering an audit trail.[34] Moreover, the information stored on the blockchain can be secured through advanced encryption schemes.[35] A private ledger (ie, a private network including a limited number of trusted participants) can transparently keep a record of all data access requests and permissions, establishing accountability and allowing patients to scrutinise access to their data. Smart contracts can be conceived to automate the verification of the medical professional accreditation and licensure of participants,[36] thereby ensuring that only parties with verified identities are authorized to engage in data processing activities.

[30] Mackey, Kuo, Gummadi, Clauson, Church, Grishin, Obbad, Barkovich and Palombini (n 4) 12; M Mettler, 'Blockchain Technology in Healthcare: The Revolution Starts Here,' in *2016 IEEE 18th International Conference on E-Health Networking, Applications and Services (Healthcom)* (IEEE 2016) 1–3, available at doi.org/10.1109/HealthCom.2016.7749510; X Yue, H Wang, D Jin, M Li and W Jiang, 'Healthcare Data Gateways: Found Healthcare Intelligence on Blockchain with Novel Privacy Risk Control' (2016) 40 *Journal of Medical Systems* 217, available at doi.org/10.1007/s10916-016-0574-6.

[31] B Shen, J Guo and Y Yang, 'MedChain: Efficient Healthcare Data Sharing via Blockchain' (2019) 9 *Applied Sciences* 3, available at doi.org/10.3390/app9061207.

[32] Mackey, Kuo, Gummadi, Clauson, Church, Grishin, Obbad, Barkovich and Palombini (n 4) 1.

[33] GJ Joyia, RM Liaqat, A Farooq and S Rehman, 'Internet of Medical Things (IOMT): Applications, Benefits and Future Challenges in Healthcare Domain' (2017) 12 *Journal of Communications* 240.

[34] WJ Gordon and C Catalini, 'Blockchain Technology for Healthcare: Facilitating the Transition to Patient-Driven Interoperability' (2018) 16 *Computational and Structural Biotechnology Journal* 227, available at doi.org/10.1016/j.csbj.2018.06.003.

[35] Mackey, Kuo, Gummadi, Clauson, Church, Grishin, Obbad, Barkovich and Palombini (n 4) 1; Yue, Wang, Jin, Li and Jiang, 'Healthcare Data Gateways' (2016) 218.

[36] Mackey, Kuo, Gummadi, Clauson, Church, Grishin, Obbad, Barkovich and Palombini (n 4) 6–7.

Furthermore, patients can use smart contracts to assign digital access rules to their data and embed policies designed to implement those rules,[37] like limiting the access period.[38] Thus, consent traceability is facilitated, since registering authorisations on a permissioned blockchain allows identity verification of the entities viewing or retrieving the data. Their access to specific records can be automatically granted, refused or revoked by the rules established by patients themselves, which would enable easier sharing.[39] Automated notifications can be sent to the parties providing the data, to warn them of recent data accesses or inform them about new data sharing opportunities.[40] These functionalities are crucial for the implementation of dynamic consent models, which enable patients to negotiate in a continuous and nuanced manner the authorized use of their data by certain organisations and for certain activities through time. For instance, people might want to provide new consent to new research activities that were not foreseen at the time of registration or revoke their consent permissions due to changing circumstances.[41]

For these promising models to gain traction, it is necessary to move away from a conceptualisation of consent as a single-point transaction. Digital consent (ie, e-consent) applications[42] play a major role in a feasible micro-management of users' choices and are growing in number and purpose in the biomedical research domain. Their integration with smart contracts embeds the promise of promoting a decentralised data marketplace, where health data sharing can be accelerated by compensating the participants who provide precious information about themselves,[43] yet are traditionally excluded from any benefit (eg, financial

[37] For example, a policy may enforce that separate transactions representing consent are sent from both patients and care providers, before granting viewing permissions to a third party. A Azaria, A Ekblaw, T Vieira and A Lippman, 'MedRec: Using Blockchain for Medical Data Access and Permission Management' in I Awan and M Younas (eds), *2016 2nd International Conference on Open and Big Data (OBD 2016)* (Institute of Electrical and Electronics Engineers IEEE, 2016) 27, available at ieeexplore.ieee.org/document/7573685.

[38] Gordon and Catalini, 'Blockchain Technology for Healthcare' (2018) 227.

[39] ibid 227.

[40] Automated notifications based on smart contracts are employed to warn healthcare providers within the IoT-enabled automated patient monitoring. AD Dwivedi, G Srivastava, S Dhar and R Singh, 'A Decentralized Privacy-Preserving Healthcare Blockchain for IoT' (2019) 19 *Sensors* 7, available at dx.doi.org/10.3390/s19020326.

[41] I Budin-Ljøsne, HJ Teare, J Kaye, S Beck, HB Bentzen, L Caenazzo, C Collett, F D'Abramo, H Felzmann, T Finlay and MK Javaid, 'Dynamic Consent: A Potential Solution to Some of the Challenges of Modern Biomedical Research' (2017) 18 *BMC Medical Ethics* 3.

[42] See, for instance, DB Thiel, J Platt, T Platt, SB King, N Fisher, R Shelton and SL Kardia, 'Testing an Online, Dynamic Consent Portal for Large Population Biobank Research' (2015) 18 *Public Health Genomics* 26; HJA Teare, M Morrison, EA Whitley and J Kaye, 'Towards "Engagement 2.0": Insights from a Study of Dynamic Consent with Biobank Participants' (2015) *Digital Health* (online), available at doi.org/10.1177/2055207615605644. For a review of eConsent in mobile research applications, refer to S Moore, AM Tassé, A Thorogood, I Winship and M Doerr, 'Consent Processes for Mobile App Mediated Research: Systematic Review' (2017) 5 *JMIR mHealth and uHealth* e126, available at doi.org/10.2196/mhealth.7014.

[43] D Grishin, K Obbad, P Estep, K Quinn, SW Zaranek, AW Zaranek, W Vandewege, T Clegg, N César, M Cifric and G Church, 'Accelerating Genomic Data Generation and Facilitating Genomic Data Access Using Decentralization, Privacy-Preserving Technologies and Equitable Compensation' (2018) 1 *Blockchain in Healthcare Today* 1.

benefits, but also return about one's contribution to a study). Transactions established in smart contracts can automate certain processes upon the meeting of predefined conditions. In the given scenario, a research institute can demand access to the decentralised database to query certain data; the data subject is enabled to grant the access, provided that adequate compensation is received; details about the different parties and the transaction are recorded on the blockchain; finally, the research institute is admitted to examine the requested data.[44] Such transactions can be established and multiplied with several organisations accessing the data for their own purposes since the contractual conditions are executed automatically. At the same time, the individual retains control over her data. All transactions are registered on the blockchain and are thereby accessible and transparent.

C. Embedding Transparency into Health Data Sharing Architectures

The complex ecosystem where manifold transactions can be automatically enabled by smart contracts contributes, at least in principle, to establish greater transparency about healthcare data use towards the many parties involved. However, the mere fact of building such a verifiable and traceable architecture does not automatically translate into understandable communications, easily applicable instructions and smooth transactions for human beings. Quite the contrary: automation per se does not guarantee the concretisation of values, such as usability, transparency, compliance or trust. For instance, unclear, cumbersome or abstract security policies might cause employee non-compliant behaviour with the measures and, therefore, data breaches.[45]

Truly informed consent is hindered by the complex mix of legal, medical and technical information through which participants need to orientate themselves when they make decisions about data sharing permissions without the guidance of a practitioner. The manner in which such interactions are laid down can ensure transparency and promote trust, and thereby encourage and increase data sharing willingness – or, to the contrary, demolish them. It all depends on the conscious embedding of values into the design of technologies and interactions, beyond pure functional requirements. Our previous work[46] proposed to apply scholars' reflections about the role and responsibilities of code-writers, engineers and designers in shaping people's digital choices and enabling digital rights[47] to the design of legal

[44] ibid.

[45] For examples of data breaches and related reports, see section II.B.

[46] A Rossi and H Haapio, 'Proactive Legal Design: Embedding Values in the Design of Legal Artefacts' in E Schweighofer, F Kummer and A Saarenpää (eds), *Internet of Things. Proceedings of the 22nd International Legal Informatics Symposium IRIS 2019* (Bern, Editions Weblaw, 2019).

[47] 'As the world is now, code writers are increasingly lawmakers. They determine what the defaults of the Internet will be; whether privacy will be protected; the degree to which anonymity will be allowed;

artefacts. The function of designers and engineers is that of 'choice architects':[48] they organise (digital or physical) environments with the intent of guiding people's actions towards predetermined outcomes.[49]

In data-driven environments, the way options are designed and presented to users has the power of promoting or, on the contrary, discouraging desirable behaviours. For example, consent dialog defaults can be designed to stimulate either privacy-preserving practices or privacy-adverse behaviours (eg, minimal versus maximal data sharing). Legal-medical communication can also be designed to attract attention and foster understanding and engagement of the reader[50] or, on the contrary, be willingly or unwillingly arranged to confuse, dishearten and alienate.[51] In both examples, only the first design promotes the value of transparency into the information and the choices presented to users,[52] establishing a connection with the values of fairness, accountability, trust and autonomy.

The sharing of healthcare data poses complex challenges that are variously related to transparency. Transparency-enhancing technologies (TETs),[53] among which we include legal design patterns, offer operational ways to promote transparency, informed consent and other legal-ethical principles into applicable solutions. Given the complexity of the scenario, it is paramount that the expectations of the various stakeholders are aligned and satisfied. This is where merging proactive legal design with user-centric data management and distributed ledger technologies shows its potential.

the extent to which access will be guaranteed. They are the ones who set its nature.' L Lessig, *Code: And Other Laws of Cyberspace* (New York, Basic Books, 1999) 79.

[48] W Hartzog, *Privacy's Blueprint: The Battle to Control the Design of New Technologies* (Cambridge, Mass, Harvard University Press, 2018) 35.

[49] 'Design decisions establish power and authority in a given setting. They influence societal norms and expectations. When people say they use modern information technologies, what they are really doing is responding to the signals and options that the technology gives them. […] Each design decision reflects an intent as to how information technology is to function or be used.' ibid 8.

[50] A Rossi and G Lenzini, 'Transparency by Design in Data-Informed Research: A Collection of Information Design Patterns' (2020) 37 *Computer Law & Security Review* 1, available at doi.org/10.1016/j.clsr.2020.105402.

[51] On embedding transparency into privacy communication design, see Rossi and Haapio, 'Proactive Legal Design' (2019) 541 and A Rossi, R Ducato, H Haapio and S Passera, 'When Design Met Law: Design Patterns for Information Transparency' (2019) 122–123 *Droit de la Consommation – Consumenterecht DCCR* 79.

[52] The second designs, on the contrary, can be defined as 'dark patterns', ie, design choices that coerce, steer or deceive users into making decisions that are not in their best interest. Definition adapted from A Mathur, G Acar, MJ Friedman, E Lucherini, J Mayer, M Chetty and A Narayanan, 'Dark Patterns at Scale: Findings from a Crawl of 11K Shopping Websites' (2019) 3 *Proceedings of the ACM on Human-Computer Interaction* 81, available at doi.org/10.1145/3359183. See also eg, R Chatellier, G Delcroix, E Hary and C Girard-Chanudet, 'Shaping Choices in the Digital World. From Dark Patterns to Data Protection: The Influence of UX/UI Design on User Empowerment' (Gwendal Le Grand ed, Commission Nationale de l'Informatique et des Libertés CNIL, 2019).

[53] C Zimmermann, 'A Categorization of Transparency-Enhancing Technologies' (v2, last revised 22 July 2015), available at arxiv.org/abs/1507.04914v2.

IV. Proactive Legal Design in Action

A. Merging Proactive Legal Thinking with Design Thinking

For decades, doctors and lawyers have been viewed as professionals serving an *ex post* function: you get sick, you see a doctor. You have a legal problem, you see a lawyer. The need for such services continues, but reactive care is no longer the only alternative. Instead, many health care and legal professionals now work proactively, *ex ante*, participating in the planning or building of new systems or solutions, promoting clients' chances of success and preventing unnecessary problems. In the legal field in Europe, this is known as practicing proactive law;[54] in the US, preventive law.[55] On both sides of the Atlantic, it can also be framed as practicing proactive legal design.[56]

Unlike legal design, which was added to scholars' and practitioners' vocabulary only recently,[57] proactive and preventive lawyering is not new: preventive law originates from the 1950s and proactive law from the 1990s.[58] These approaches, along with collaborative law and similar disciplines, can be viewed as part of a larger movement in law.[59] These approaches differ from conventional legal research and practice, where the focus is mainly on the past – their focus is on the future. Instead of merely looking back to resolve problems that have already occurred, they look forward to enabling desirable outcomes and prevent the causes of problems from arising. They look beyond legal rules, rights and obligations and focus on goals, needs and relationships, seeking to increase awareness, engagement and clarity as to rights and obligations.[60]

[54] See, eg H Haapio, 'Introduction to Proactive Law: A Business Lawyer's View' in P Wahlgren (ed), *A Proactive Approach* (Stockholm, Scandinavian Studies in Law vol 49, Stockholm Institute for Scandinavian Law, 2006); GJ Siedel and H Haapio, 'Using Proactive Law for Competitive Advantage' (2010) 47 *American Business Law Journal* 641; G Siedel and H Haapio, *Proactive Law for Managers: A Hidden Source of Competitive Advantage* (London, Gower 2011); G Berger-Walliser, 'The Past and Future of Proactive Law: An Overview of the Development of the Proactive Law Movement' in G Berger-Walliser and K Østergaard (eds), *Proactive Law in a Business Environment* (Copenhagen, DJØF Publishing, 2012).

[55] See, eg LM Brown, *Preventive Law* (New York, Prentice-Hall, 1950); LM Brown, *Lawyering through Life – The Origin of Preventive Law* (Buffalo, Fred B Rothman & Co, 1986); TD Barton, *Problem Solving and Preventive Law: Lawyering for the Future* (Lake Mary FL, Vandeplas Publishing, 2009).

[56] See, eg Rossi and Haapio (n 46). See also 'Legal Design Alliance' at www.legaldesignalliance.org.

[57] See, eg G Berger-Walliser, TD Barton and H Haapio, 'From Visualization to Legal Design: A Collaborative and Creative Process' (2017) 54 *American Business Law Journal* 347; CR Brunschwig, *Visualisierung von Rechtsnormen – Legal Design* (Zurich, Schulthess Juristische Medien, 2001).

[58] For the origins of the approaches, see the resources mentioned in notes 54–57.

[59] See S Daicoff, 'Law as a Healing Profession: The "Comprehensive Law Movement"' (2005) 6 *Pepperdine Dispute Resolution Law Journal* 1. Daicoff views approaches such as collaborative law; creative problem solving; holistic justice; preventive law; procedural justice; restorative justice; therapeutic jurisprudence; and transformative mediation as 'vectors' of a movement she calls 'comprehensive law'.

[60] ibid. See also S Daicoff, 'The Comprehensive Law Movement: An Emerging Approach to Legal Problems' in P Wahlgren (ed), *A Proactive Approach* (Stockholm, Scandinavian Studies in Law vol 49, Stockholm Institute for Scandinavian Law, 2006).

For a long time, the proponents of proactive law have called for improved legal communication, services and solutions, with the goal of making these more functional, useful and usable. Before the advent of legal design, designers and lawyers lacked access to each others' mindsets, tools and methods. When design met law,[61] reform-minded legal thinkers and designers became natural allies, increasingly drawn into each others' competencies.[62] Mindsets, tools and processes from design started to be adopted across legal fields, from practice to activism to policy-making.[63]

Computer scientists, too, have identified challenges and roadblocks to widespread smart contract adoption and have started to look for new tools and solutions: current smart contracts need programmers, and they cannot be easily generated or understood. Better interfaces and editors are explored to simplify smart contract generation, enabling them to be created by untrained users, without involving programmers and improving their understandability in order to build confidence that the contract does what is intended.[64] In different parts of the world, computer scientists and lawyers alike have started to look for ways to join forces to make smart contracts 'wise'[65] or 'computable':[66] readable and understandable by both humans and computers.

The time has come to merge proactive legal thinking with design thinking and, with the help of technology, to bring them to practice. Putting the user at the centre, we can integrate lawyers' traditional tools, such as templates[67] and clause libraries, with those of designers and technologists, such as design patterns, both at the code level and at the user interface level.

[61] See Rossi and others, 'When Design Met Law' (2019).

[62] For the developments, opportunities and dangers, see A Perry-Kessaris, 'Legal Design for Practice, Activism, Policy, and Research' (2019) 46 *Journal of Law and Society* 185.

[63] ibid. See also A Perry-Kessaris, 'Work in Progress: Doing Socio-Legal Research in Design Mode' (*Approaching Law*, 28 November 2019), available at amandaperrykessaris.org/2019/11/28/work-in-progress-doing-socio-legal-research-in-design-mode.

[64] K Purnell and R Schwitter, 'Towards Declarative Smart Contracts' in *The 4th Symposium on Distributed Ledger Technology* (Griffith University, 10 December 2019) 18, available at symposium-dlt.org/SDLT2019-FinalProceedings.pdf.

[65] J Hazard and H Haapio, 'Wise Contracts: Smart Contracts that Work for People and Machines' in E Schweighofer, F Kummer, W Hötzendorfer and C Sorge (eds), *Trends and Communities of Legal Informatics. Proceedings of the 20th International Legal Informatics Symposium IRIS 2017* (Wien, Österreichische Computer Gesellschaft, 2017).

[66] See, eg J Cummins and C Clack, 'Transforming Commercial Contracts through Computable Contracting' (University College London, 23 March 2020), available at arxiv.org/abs/2003.10400 and, more generally, the UCL Computable Contracts research page (www.ucl.ac.uk/computer-science/research/research-groups/financial-computing-and-analytics/computable-contracts), identifying legal design for contracts as one of the four key areas to be addressed in order to achieve the vision.

[67] For open-access templates, see, for example, the Lambert Toolkit containing university and business collaboration agreements, including, a fast-track model agreement produced by Public Health England to evaluate potential treatment options for Ebola and Zika very rapidly and to share the results with stakeholders for a coordinated global response; see Intellectual Property Office, 'University and business collaboration agreements: Lambert Toolkit' (Gov.uk, 6 October 2016, last updated 3 April 2019), available at www.gov.uk/guidance/university-and-business-collaboration-agreements-lambert-toolkit. For data sharing agreements and informed consent templates, various forms can be found doing a Google search on the Internet.

B. Design Patterns: Bringing Proactive Legal Design to Practice

When communicating and handling complex legal, technical and medical information, it is important to consider what the users are trying to achieve, and then present information in such a way that the users know what they are expected to do and not do. In order to ensure that users can find and act upon the information, a balance needs to be found between functionality and precision, and between precision and ease of use. According to David Sless, communicating organisations often ask the wrong question: 'They ask, "What information should go into the document?," when they should be asking, "What actions should people be able to perform, easily and quickly, with the information given?"'[68]

After finding the answer, what do designers do? They know that if people do not read the information, find what they need or understand what they find, inadvertent non-compliance will occur. Readers' (and non-readers') problems easily become writers' problems: avoidable complexity causes unnecessary risks. To protect people against themselves and prevent cognitive accidents, designers seek to simplify the user experience. There are three main building blocks to simpler communication: 1) empathise with the users' needs and expectations; 2) distill the communication, boil it down to its essence; and 3) clarify.[69]

Designers seeking clear communication do not overwhelm people with too much information. Instead, they guide them through it, making sure people can skim through headings and sections and easily find relevant information. They explain procedures in a step-by-step fashion and with the help of explanatory diagrams. They use companion icons and clear and visible headings that answer or anticipate typical user questions, and so on. These information design techniques need not be reinvented – they can be identified, shared and reused as design patterns.

i. The Goal of Design Patterns

In recent years, on several continents, researchers and practitioners have started to explore new ways of presenting complex legal information, for example, in the context of contracts[70] and privacy communication,[71] seeking to make legal

[68] D Sless, 'Designing Documents for People to Use' (2018) 4 *She Ji: The Journal of Design, Economics, and Innovation* 125, 131.

[69] See A Siegel and I Etzkorn, *Simple: Conquering the Crisis of Complexity* (New York, Twelve, 2013).

[70] See, generally, G Berger-Walliser, RC Bird and H Haapio, 'Promoting Business Success through Contract Visualization' (2011) 17 *The Journal of Law, Business & Ethics* 55; H Haapio, *Next Generation Contracts: A Paradigm Shift* (Helsinki, Lexpert Ltd, 2013); TD Barton, G Berger-Walliser and H Haapio, 'Contracting for Innovation and Innovating Contracts: An Overview and Introduction to the Special Issue' (2016) 2 *Journal of Strategic Contracting and Negotiation* 3; H Haapio and TD Barton, 'Business-Friendly Contracting: How Simplification and Visualization Can Help Bring It to Practice' in K Jacob,

communication simpler, more accessible and actionable.[72] Design patterns and pattern libraries offer a systematic way to identify, collect, and share good practices. In essence, design patterns are reusable solutions to a commonly occurring problem: something that practitioners can develop, collect and share. Pattern libraries, in turn, are collections or catalogues of patterns.

The original idea of design patterns stems from Christopher Alexander and others,[73] who collected reusable architectural solutions. The idea was later applied to the digital world and gained widespread acceptance with Erich Gamma and others.[74] Since then, design patterns have been extensively used in many other fields, including computer science and interface and UX design.[75] Over the last few years, design patterns and pattern libraries have even made their way to contract design,[76] privacy design[77] and legal design.[78]

D Schindler and Strathausen (eds), *Liquid Legal: Transforming Legal into a Business Savvy, Information Enabled and Performance Driven Industry* (New York, Springer International, 2017); S Passera, *Beyond the Wall of Contract Text: Visualizing Contracts to Foster Understanding and Collaboration within and across Organizations* (Aalto, Aalto University, 2017); H Haapio, R De Rooy and T D Barton, 'New Contract Genres' in E Schweighofer, F Kummer, A Saarenpää and B Schafer (eds), *Data Protection / LegalTech. Proceedings of the 21th International Legal Informatics Symposium IRIS 2018* (Bern, Editions Weblaw, 2018).

[71] See, generally, Rossi, Ducato, Haapio and Passera (n 51), with references.

[72] Margaret Hagan, the Director of the Legal Design Lab at Stanford Law School, has collected different models to present complex legal information, see 'Examples of Legal Communication Designs' in Stanford Legal Design Lab, 'Legal Communication Design', available at www.legaltechdesign.com/communication-design, and generally, M Hagan, 'Law by Design', available at www.lawbydesign.co.

[73] C Alexander, *A Pattern Language: Towns, Buildings, Construction* (Oxford, Oxford University Press, 1977).

[74] E Gamma, R Helm, R Johnson and J Vlissides, *Design Patterns: Elements of Reusable Object-Oriented Software* (Upper Saddle River NJ, Addison-Wesley, 1995).

[75] See, eg J Tidwell, *Designing Interfaces*, 2nd edn (Sebastopol CA, O'Reilly Media, 2014); selected patterns from the book are featured at designinginterfaces.com/patterns.

[76] H Haapio and M Hagan, 'Design Patterns for Contracts' in E Schweighofer, F Kummer, W Hötzendorfer and G Borges (eds), *Networks. Proceedings of the 19th International Legal Informatics Symposium IRIS 2016* (Vienna, Österreichische Computer Gesellschaft, 2016); R Waller, J Waller, H Haapio, G Crag and S Morrisseau, 'Cooperation Through Clarity: Designing Simplified Contracts' (2016) 2 *Journal of Strategic Contracting and Negotiation* 48, 64–65; H Haapio and S Passera, 'Contracts as Interfaces: Exploring Visual Representation Patterns In Contract Design' in DM Katz, R Dolin and MJ Bommarito and R Dolin (eds), *Legal Informatics* (Cambridge, Cambridge University Press, forthcoming). See also International Association for Contract & Commercial Management (IACCM), S Passera and H Haapio, 'IACCM Contract Design Pattern Library, available at contract-design.iaccm.com; and Stanford Legal Design Lab, 'Contract Design Pattern Library' www.legaltechdesign.com/communication-design/legal-design-pattern-libraries/contracts.

[77] H Haapio, M Hagan, M Palmirani and A Rossi, 'Legal Design Patterns for Privacy' in E Schweighofer, F Kummer, A Saarenpää and B Schafer (eds), *Data Protection/LegalTech. Proceedings of the 21th International Legal Informatics Symposium IRIS 2018* (Bern, Editions Weblaw, 2018); Rossi and Lenzini, 'Transparency by Design in Data-Informed Research' (2020). See also Stanford Legal Design Lab, 'Privacy Design Pattern Library', available at www.legaltechdesign.com/communication-design/legal-design-pattern-libraries/privacy-design-pattern-library. For privacy interface design and data permission design in the context of this chapter, see, eg, Sage Bionetworks, 'Privacy Policy' (Privacy Toolkit), available at designmanual.sagebionetworks.org/privacy-policy.html.

[78] For an overview of legal design patterns, see, eg Rossi, Ducato, Haapio and Passera (n 51). See also Stanford Legal Design Lab, 'Legal Design Pattern Libraries', available at www.legaltechdesign.com/communication-design/legal-design-pattern-libraries.

Consider a situation where the goal is to impact, guide and support decisions and actions, for example at the participant onboarding state. For research to succeed, researchers need to meet participants' concerns and design experiences that pinpoint transparency, autonomy and trust.[79] Here a genre shift from legal documents to user guides can help. User guides are organised around practical tasks, to support action.[80] With the help of technology, static user guides can be turned to apps, playbooks and interactive self-help solutions.[81]

In recent years, new resources have become available that help researchers make decisions about how and when to collect and use data about people and effectively communicate their related messages. Sage Bionetwork provides biomedical researchers with a privacy toolkit of design tools and patterns with accompanying use cases to assist them in using the appropriate patterns in their mHealth and other applications.[82] Another valuable resource is offered by IF, providing a curated catalogue of design patterns ('data patterns').[83] Similarly, design patterns ('multimedia components') for eConsent applications have been gathered[84] to promote informed decision-making about participation in clinical research studies, with the secondary goal of gaining a better insight into the participant experience to improve it.[85] By using design patterns at the appropriate time, participants are helped to understand the types of data that are being collected and how they have the ability to change their data sharing permission, with the goal of building a trusted partnership between researchers and participants.[86]

[79] For further scenarios and helpful design patterns in the context of mobile health research, see V Barone, W MacDuffie, Y Guan and S Simon, 'The Privacy Toolkit for Mobile Health Research Studies – Providing Biomedical Researchers with A Catalog of Privacy Design Patterns for Their Digital Studies' (Privacy Forecast, 2019), available at privacy.shorensteincenter.org/mobilehealth. See also S Moore and M Doerr, 'The Elements of Informed Consent. A Toolkit' (M Doerr ed, v3.0, Sage Bionetworks 2019), available at sagebionetworks.org/wp-content/uploads/2020/01/SageBio_EIC-Toolkit_V3_21Jan20_final.pdf.

[80] User guide format is one of the design patterns included in the IACCM Contract Design Pattern Library. See IACCM, S Passera and H Haapio, 'User Guide Format' (IACCM Contract Design Pattern Library), available at contract-design.iaccm.com/user-guide-format. Good user guides often apply other design patterns included in the Pattern Library; for example, clear layout, skimmable headings, numbered steps, companion icons, icon systems and other visualisations. See IACCM, S Passera and H Haapio, 'Pattern Families' (IACCM Contract Design Pattern Library), available at contract-design.iaccm.com/families-overview.

[81] See, eg H Haapio, 'Legal Design in Action: From Text-Only Guidebooks to Digital, Visual Playbooks' in E Schweighofer, F Kummer and A Saarenpää (eds), *Internet of Things. Proceedings of the 22nd International Legal Infomatics Symposium IRIS 2019* (Bern, Editions Weblaw, 2019).

[82] Sage Bionetworks, 'Privacy Toolkit for Mobile Health Research Studies', available at sagebionetworks.org/tools_resources/privacy-toolkit-for-mobile-health-research-studies; Sage Bionetworks, 'Informed Consent' (Privacy Toolkit), available at designmanual.sagebionetworks.org/informed-consent.html.

[83] IF, 'Data Patterns Catalogue', available at catalogue.projectsbyif.com.

[84] TransCelerate Biopharma Inc, 'EConsent: Implemetation Guidance Version 1.0' (2017), available at www.transceleratebiopharmainc.com/wp-content/uploads/2017/11/eConsent-Implementation-Guidance.pdf.

[85] ibid 7.

[86] See, eg Barone, MacDuffie, Guan and Simon, 'The Privacy Toolkit for Mobile Health Research Studies' (2019).

ii. Examples of Design Patterns

One of the main goals of design patterns is to share solutions enabling users to notice, explore, retain and interact with information. The selection of patterns needs to be based on what is suited to express a certain communicative goal for a particular user group in a particular context. For those in charge of producing information, the focus changes from clear and concise writing or drafting to *designing communication experiences* with and for multiple user groups. This also involves responding to and balancing different needs and requirements.

The following sections summarise three *experience design patterns* that can be employed for health data sharing to foster transparency, accountability, autonomy and trust.

a. Navigable eConsent Process[87]

Scenario: Consider a participant who has adhered to the biomedical data sharing model under exploration. Before being able to make her record available for a new research activity, she is required to provide informed consent via the dedicated mobile application. She needs to prove that she has understood the reason why and by whom her data will be analysed, the inherent benefits and risks and her rights as both a research participant and a data owner.

Problem: The consent process can be long, complex and information-heavy, while choices can, as a result, be unclear and overwhelming. Moreover, the traditional researcher's additional explanations and comprehension assessment must be remotely self-administered.[88]

Solution: Informed consent is conceptualised as a whole informative process, turning a legalistic form into an engaging and easy-to-navigate experience that drives the participant to a decision that can be described as informed. This translates into breaking down the consent process into different stages, giving an overview of the various steps of the consent process before it starts, and combining simple text with images, videos or other visual means[89] to support comprehension in each phase. The navigation of the participant is thereby supported through the various informative stages until she lands on the actual options for data use authorisation. An assessment of the participant's understanding can also be devised as a precondition that, when met, automatically activates the possibility to grant consent.

[87] Sage Bionetworks, 'Informed Consent' (n 82).

[88] Moore, Tassé, Thorogood, Winship and Doerr, 'Consent Processes for Mobile App Mediated Research' (2017).

[89] eg, comics, see WM Botes, 'Visual Communication as a Legal-Ethical Tool for Informed Consent in Genome Research Involving the San Community of South Africa' (doctoral thesis, University of South Africa, 15 November 2017). See a portion in Rossi and Lenzini (n 50) 12–13.

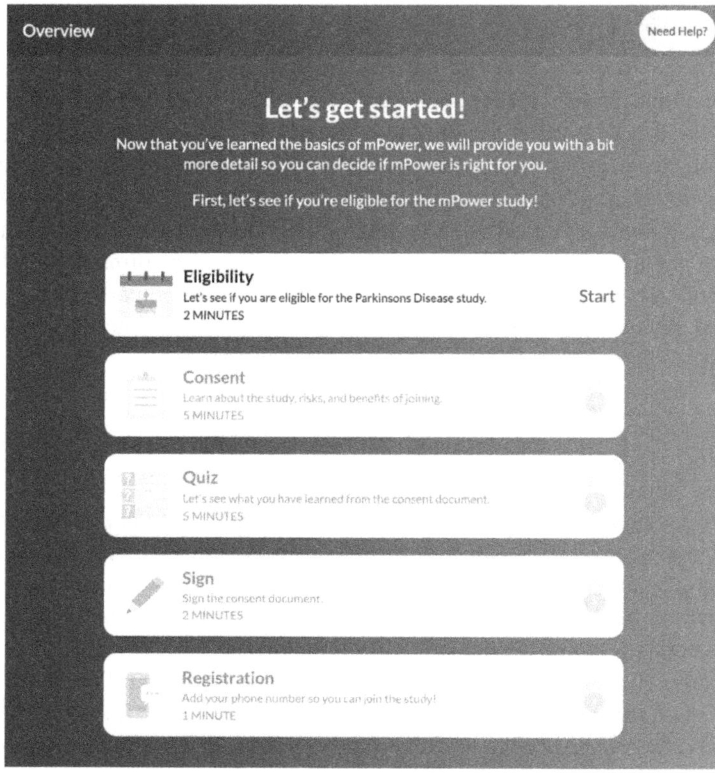

Figure 5.1 eConsent steps for participation in a research study on Parkinson's disease[90]

b. Just-in-time, Dynamic Data Use Permissions[91]

Scenario: Consider a research institute that intends to access its patients' sensitive data collected by IoT devices and sensors and combine it with other data, eg, the patients' medical history already retrieved. Researchers need to send a timely request to the patients where they ask permission to activate sensors and start information collection.

Problem: In traditional consent models, information about possible data uses is provided at a single point in time (eg, at registration), rendering it ineffective for the understanding of the consent options[92] in future uses. Permission options that are not clearly relevant for the task at hand (eg, activating a sensor at the time

[90] Sage Bionetworks, 'Overview' (mPower 2.0), available at parkinsonmpower.org/study/overview. Used with permission.

[91] Sage Bionetworks, 'Just-in-Time Permission' (Privacy Toolkit), available at designmanual.sagebionetworks.org/just-in-time-permission.html.

[92] F Schaub, R Balebako, AL Durity and LF Cranor, 'A Design Space for Effective Privacy Notices' in *SOUPS 2015 Proceedings of the Eleventh Symposium On Usable Privacy and Security* (USENIX 2015) 6, available at www.usenix.org/sites/default/files/soups15_full_proceedings.pdf.

of registration) might be found invasive and cause distrust. They might alienate people from participation or nudge them to refuse permission.[93] Moreover, certain analysis capacities or processing purposes are not foreseeable at the moment of registration. Yet, as scientific progress advances and the network of participating institutions enlarges, the number and variety of possible reuses are enriched.

Solution: A dynamic, just-in-time permission model uses modern communication strategies and technological means to provide the participants with relevant information at the moment when they need to authorise or refuse the collection of data.[94] A dynamic approach enables participants to receive notifications, engage them in the provision of granular authorizations for specific research activities and update their preferences about data access by certain organisations.[95]

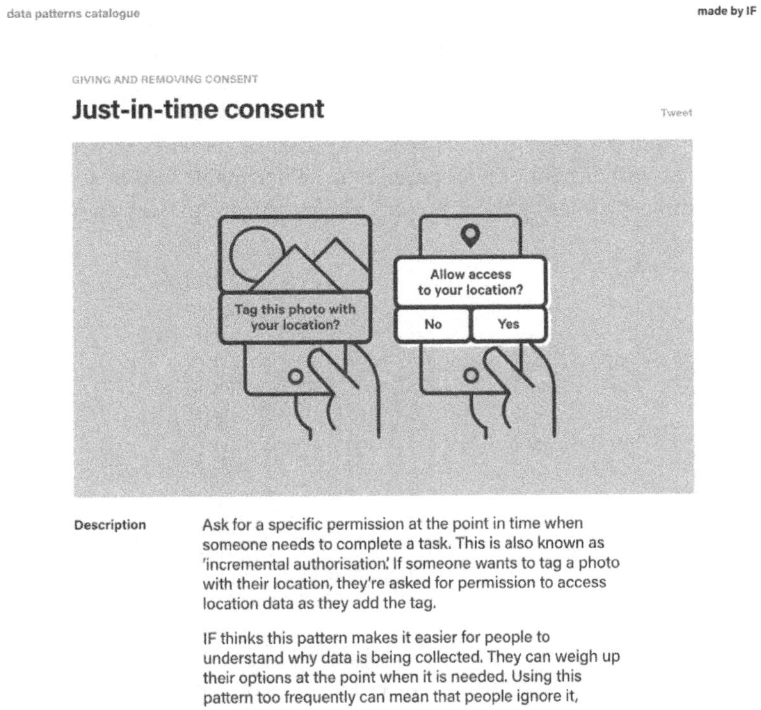

Figure 5.2 Excerpt from IF catalogue of design patterns: just-in-time consent[96]

[93] Sage Bionetworks, 'Just-in-Time Permission' (n 91).

[94] Just-in-time permissions oppose widespread models of broad consent, where participants initially agree to a framework for future research of specific kinds, but are not informed of those unforeseeable or undefined aspects that only emerge as the research unfolds. Due to the incompleteness of information at the moment of decision-making, detractors of this model argue that participants can not be considered informed, therefore broad consent is illegal and unethical. For a discussion, see K Solum Steinsbekk, B Kåre Myskja and B Solberg, 'Broad Consent versus Dynamic Consent in Biobank Research: Is Passive Participation an Ethical Problem?' (2013) 21 *European Journal of Human Genetics* 897.

[95] Budin-Ljøsne and others, 'Dynamic Consent' (2017) 3.

[96] IF, 'Just-in-Time Consent' (Data Patterns Catalogue), available at catalogue.projectsbyif.com/patterns/just-in-time-consent. Licensed under CC BY 4.0: creativecommons.org/licenses/by/4.0.

c. Data Usage Logs[97] and Consent Receipts[98]

Scenario: Imagine an individual who has carefully set dozens of data use permissions. The parties accessing the data must be able to demonstrate compliance with the established permissible use (ie, to demonstrate accountability).

Problem: The expectation that participants memorise or autonomously record their preferences is irrealistic. Moreover, they are unable to check the actual data practices of the other parties and contrast them with the permissions they granted and the declared practices. Without such feedback, participants do not know whether and how the sharing system is functioning, which might cause distrust.

Solution: Data usage logs keep a record of all parties' access to datasets, thereby serving the goal of transparency for all stakeholders involved. It enables participants to receive a tangible return about the helpfulness of their cooperation. This approach can be combined with consent receipts issued as proof of consent for each data use authorised by the participant. The records can be contrasted to find out whether such permissions have been respected or rather breached by certain parties. It is an instrument of transparency for participants and of accountability for organisations processing those records while respecting users' rights.

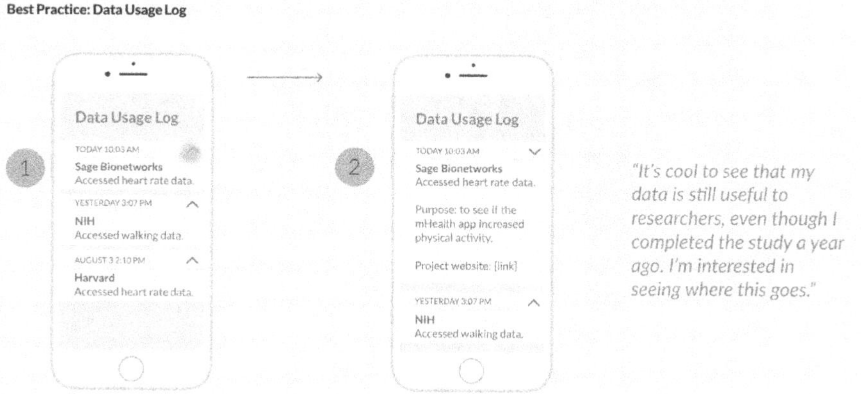

Figure 5.3 Excerpt from SageBionetworks Privacy Toolkit: data usage log interface for biomedical research purposes[99]

[97] Sage Bionetworks, 'Data Usage Log' (Privacy Toolkit), available at designmanual.sagebionetworks.org/data-usage-log.html. See also IF, 'Activity Log' (Data Patterns Catalogue), available at catalogue.projectsbyif.com/patterns/activity-log.

[98] Kantara consent receipt specification, Beaumont, Cooper, D'Agostino, Graves, Henderson, Hodder, Honko, Hughes, Jones, Lapes, Maerz, Maler, Pasquale, Tuoriniemi and Wunderlich, 'Consent Receipt Specification' (2018).

[99] Sage Bionetworks, 'Data Usage Log' (n 97). Used with permission.

V. Conclusion

This chapter has explored the human side of smart contracts, framing them as communicative artefacts that intend to convey information for a purpose. In this context, smart contracts are not just technical or legal tools, but also deeply social tools that impact and are impacted by human behaviour. Our emphasis has been on the application of proactive legal design for the promotion of transparency, autonomy, accountability and trust in the context of health data sharing. This pursuit requires finding a balance between the different stakeholders' often conflicting needs and goals, and embedding transparency into health data sharing services.

We have explored the opportunities that design patterns offer to respond to recurring challenges, so as to translate expectations and values into design-oriented requirements. The user interface layer, when properly designed and built, allows users to translate their intentions into a form that meets their needs, helps them reach their objectives and is legally sound. Our examples illustrate how design patterns offer concrete solutions to increase awareness, engagement and clarity about rights and obligations, with the aim of achieving desirable outcomes and preventing the causes of problems from arising. Although we consider the possible applications to be manifold, we have focused on the design of dynamic informed consent and user-established permissions for information access and use to foster a trustworthy data sharing economy. Future work will explore how proactive legal design can help make, use and humanise smart contracts and promote transparency, trust and compliance in data sharing agreements, security policies and other contexts.

6

A Multilayer Safeguard Mechanism to Optimise the Potential of Smart Contracts in B2C Transactions

STEFAN WRBKA

I. Introduction

In 1993 the European Economic Community, a predecessor of the European Union (EU), responded to the increased use of standard form contracts (SFCs) with the adoption of the Unfair Contract Terms Directive (UCTD).[1] The UCTD did not intend to stop the use of SFCs. Rather, it aimed to strike a balance between the business side interest in utilising standardised contractual templates to save time and transaction costs and the consumer side interest in enjoying contractual clarity and mandatory protective standards. One of the achievements of the Directive was that by striking this balance it succeeded in strengthening the use of SFCs in conformity with legal principles.

Advancements in digital technology (in combination with legal expertise) are often considered to increase contractual certainty, to speed up the contractual negotiation, conclusion and execution phases and to lower transaction costs. With the rise of smart contracts – understood as computer program codes or protocols that automate the verification, execution and enforcement of specific terms and conditions of 'real' contracts[2] – the idea to save both time and money reached

[1] Council Directive on unfair terms in consumer contracts 93/13/EEC [1993] OJ L95/29.

[2] In a comparable vein, eg OECD, 'Blockchain Technology and Corporate Governance – Technology, Markets, Regulation and Corporate Governance' (2018) 9, available at www.oecd.org/officialdocuments/publicdisplaydocumentpdf/?cote=DAF/CA/CG/RD(2018)1/REV1&docLanguage=En: 'A smart contract is basically a software program to execute certain tasks if certain conditions are met. The program code comprises the initiation, verification, execution and enforcement of the terms and conditions of a contract between two or multiple parties. The code itself and all of its executions in chronological order are recorded in the blockchain using the same consensus and security mechanisms as other transactions'. See also M Corrales, M Fenwick and H Haapio (eds), *Legal Tech, Smart Contracts & Blockchain* (Singapore, Springer, 2019); M Fenwick and S Wrbka, 'Rechtsfragen der digitalen Transformation' in HG Fill and A Meier (eds), *Blockchain – Grundlagen, Anwendungsszenarien und Nutzungspotenziale* (Wiesbaden, Springer Vieweg, 2020); M Fries and BP Paal (eds), *Smart*

the next level.[3] These purported advantages do not come risk-free, however. The key concerns include possible data risks, the low level of the average smart contract user's digital knowledge and the limited impact of (some) contractual parties when it comes to designing and executing smart contracts. The latter two points, in particular, are of prime concern in business-to-consumer (B2C) transactions. Under normal circumstances, consumers have neither the competence nor the required knowledge or capacity to influence smart contract mechanisms. They might even have no actual insight whatsoever into the underlying digital process.

Regardless of whose side one takes, it is clear that within a couple of decades the business world has shifted from a predominantly paper-based to an increasingly paper-free economy. The role people used to play in contractual lifecycles started to change significantly.

This chapter considers these arguments and aims to explore ways smart contracts could and should be regulated to tap their full potential without neglecting both contractual parties' interests and underlying legal principles. As such, the central claims are twofold: firstly, smart contracts – digital, computer-code-based translations of transactional relationships – show similarities with SFCs; secondly, regulators need to find ways to install a (multilayer) safeguard mechanism to ensure that smart contracts are used in an unobjectionable way. To achieve this goal, the contribution builds upon prominent parametres – legal transparency, legal certainty and consumer protection – and draws parallels to respective mechanisms that aim to safeguard them.

The chapter starts with remarks on the evolution of digitalisation and the smart contract phenomenon. It continues with a summary of the alleged benefits of smart contracts before turning to their possible risks and challenges. An excursion to SFCs and their impact on B2C contracts, in particular, shifts the focus to more conventional contract designs. This builds the basis for the key argument of the present analysis, ie, for the suggestion that regulators could and should learn a lesson from the development of SFC regulation and additional B2C tools to support the law-compliant use of smart contracts.

II. The Emergence of Smart Contracts

For centuries, trade and the conclusion of contracts had largely taken place face-to-face. With new technologies emerging, commercial transactions began to

Contracts: Schlaue Verträge? (Tübingen, Mohr Siebeck, 2019); C Molina-Jimenez, E Solaiman, I Sfyrakis and ICL Ng, 'On and Off Blockchain Enforcement of Smart Contracts' (2018), available at arxiv.org/pdf/1805.00626.pdf; A Savelyev, 'Contract law 2.0: "Smart" contracts as the beginning of the end of classic contract law' (2017) 26 *Information & Communications Technology* 116 for comparable definitions.

[3] See, eg, C Hein, W Wellbrock and C Hein, *Rechtliche Herausforderungen von Blockchain-Anwendungen: Straf-, Datenschutz- und Zivilrecht* (Wiesbaden, Springer Gabler, 2019).

explore alternative channels. Telephones and telegrams are early examples of such technologisation. The second half of the twentieth century saw the emergence of more refined and advanced means of communication. The rise of the Internet, in particular, can be considered as a key development in this respect. New computer- and software-based instruments allowed for creating and harnessing alternative marketplaces that functioned 'invisibly' in the sense that they did not operate via real or physical business premises, but rather on intangible platforms detached from conventional business facilities. This more recent form of transacting – commonly referred to as e-commerce[4] – (allegedly) creates extra benefits for the transacting parties. A broader range of selection and a wider possible audience are arguably two of the most significant features in this respect. Within a couple of decades, entrepreneurs had developed cheaper, faster and more easily accessible ways to conclude commercial contracts.

It was not before the final decade of the twentieth century, however, that e-commerce succeeded in reaching broader and more diverse segments of society, ie, segments other than professional stakeholders. Slowly but steadily, the number of (non-professional) consumers that were willing and able to take part in online transactions began to rise.[5] Regulatory stakeholders responded to and further facilitated this trend with early key legislation and policy decisions that aimed to simplify the use of the Internet and to protect the interests of those using it. At the EU level, for example, the European Commission's 1997 Initiative in Electronic Commerce was among the first instruments that advocated for a comprehensive support of the e-commerce market while acknowledging the importance of safeguarding the rights of the 'weaker' or less-experienced stakeholders involved. The ultimate aim of the policy-stakeholders was clear – e-commerce was seen as one of the most promising tools, if not the most promising tool, to maximise cross-border trade and to establish prosperity throughout the society. At a more global level, this view was shared and further expanded notably by the Organization for Economic Cooperation and Development (OECD). The OECD stated that e-commerce was 'a central element … for economic growth, jobs and improved social conditions'.[6] Put differently, the OECD hoped that e-commerce would prove advantageous not only for providers of goods and services, but for the society in general.

Parallel to the emergence of the conventional e-commerce market, computer scientists started to develop more 'progressive' and less conventional forms of

[4] For an overview of the development of e-commerce law see, eg M Fenwick and S Wrbka, *International Business Law* (Oxford, Hart, 2017) 159 with further references.

[5] A Davidson, *Social Media and Electronic Commerce Law*, 2nd edn (Oxford, Oxford University Press, 2016) 5.

[6] OECD, 'A Borderless World: Realising the Potential of Global Electronic Commerce' (1998) 3, available at www.oecd.org/officialdocuments/publicdisplaydocumentpdf/?cote=SG/EC(98)9/FINAL&docLanguage=En.

data processing that heralded a 'digital revolution'[7] / 'digital transformation'.[8] Automated algorithms, cloud-based storage facilities and additional digital advancements, such a nanotechnologies, various types of artificial intelligence (AI) and distributed ledger technologies (DLTs) were the result of this. The blockchain technology – arguably the most well-known DLT form – is of particular interest in the present context, because it builds the basis and enables the use of smart contracts – instruments that can be utilised to monitor and execute contractual performance and enforcement. An important key feature of the blockchain technology is that it allows for processing commercial and personal data in a decentralised environment free from the 'interruption' or 'interference' by third parties.[9] These new platforms can be easily accessed from anywhere and at any time (based on the condition that the relevant stakeholders have the required technical instruments) and – so the argument of blockchain advocates – are a safer way of storing information. The key blockchain elements – the 'blocks' – store individual facts, information or transactional records, which, if and once connected to a 'thread' – a blockchain – can tell a conclusive 'story'. Access to a blockchain can be granted to the public, but can also be limited to selected individuals. Utilising a blockchain and adding new information to it both require identity and authenticity checks of digital IDs that rely on a complex digital model of automated data verification and validation. Only participants that are granted access rights would have the chance to participate in such a private (or 'permissioned') peer-to-peer network. The non-existence of tangible data makes it comparatively difficult for external regulators and authorities to monitor blockchain-based processes, but at the same time appealing to those stakeholders that are looking for digital ways of interaction.

[7] See, eg, A De Franceschi (ed), *European Contract Law and the Digital Single Market: The Implications of the Digital Revolution* (Cambridge, Intersentia, 2016); R Schulze and D Staudenmayer (eds), *Digital Revolution: Challenges for Contract Law in Practice* (Baden-Baden, Nomos, 2016); D Gerard, EM de Rivery and B Meyring (eds), *Dynamic Markets, Dynamic Competition and Dynamic Enforcement: The impact of the digital revolution and globalisation on competition law enforcement in Europe* (Bruxelles, Bruylant, 2018); DA Zetzsche, RP Buckley, DW Arner, and JN Barberis, 'Regulating a Revolution: From Regulatory Sandboxes to Smart Regulation' (2017) 23 *Fordham Journal of Corporate & Financial Law* 31.

[8] See, eg F Xavier Olleros and M Zhegu (eds), *Research Handbook on Digital Transformations* (Cheltenham, Edward Elgar, 2016); DL Rogers, *Digital Transformation Playbook: Rethink Your Business for the Digital Age* (Columbia Business School Publishing, 2016); RF van Beeman, R Graf von Pfeil and GF Tanja, *Legal Tech and Digital Transformation: Competitive Positioning and Business Models of Law Firms* (Horsell, Globe Law and Business, 2018); OECD, 'OECD Science, Technology and Industry Scoreboard 2017: The digital transformation' (2017), available at www.oecd.org/sti/oecd-science-technology-and-industry-scoreboard-20725345.htm; Fenwick and Wrbka, 'Rechtsfragen der digitalen Transformation' (2020) 2.

[9] Oscar Borgogno, for example, argues that smart contracts have the potential to 'eliminat[e] the [contractual] default risk at almost no cost without any external human intervention' – see O Borgogno, 'Smart Contracts as the (new) Power of the Powerless? The Stakes for Consumers' (2019) 6 *European Review of Private Law* 885, 886. One has to note, though, that the often-found argument that smart contracts would operate without the necessity to involve third parties seems to ignore the fact that other third parties replace those more conventional, 'obsolete' intermediaries. Without the help of digital experts, it is impossible to design suitable digital frameworks that allow for the implementation of ordinary contracts.

III. The Alleged Benefits of Smart Contracts

Smart contracts are – despite their name – not real contracts, but special, digital tools that are based on computer codes or protocols that translate a contract into automated terms and conditions.[10] They are utilised in particular to support the contractual performance and enforcement of real contracts. As argued on a different occasion, smart contracts have the potential to revolutionise trade and the lifecycles of contractual relationships for two main reasons. Smart contracts are designed to monitor contractual relationships with the help of objectively verifiable triggering conditions and could – if necessary – ensure contractual performance via imposing automated enforcement consequences or penalties on a party if that party fails to fulfill predefined smart contract-implemented parametres.[11] Because of their likely impact on the 'enjoyment' of contractual rights and their supervisory function with respect to contractual duties, it is justified to say that smart contracts are the 'next step of the digital transformation'.[12] But what is it that makes them so attractive for (particularly) the business side? In short, it is the mix of alleged cost-efficiency, simplified enforcement procedures and swifter contractual performance supervision.

Advocates of DLT in general and smart contracts, in particular, argue that respective instruments help to save transaction costs. A look at the typical e-commerce / smart contract setting might exemplify this statement. With the online conclusion of a contract the contractual terms and conditions are immediately translated into smart contract language. The result of this – a digitalised monitoring and enforcement instrument – would assess whether the contractual obligations are performed in the right way. If a performance issue was detected, smart contracts would react and the underlying algorithms would trigger a predefined mechanism that responds to the contractual breach by imposing a 'penalty' on the breaching party. Penalties could take various forms, reaching from additional buyer's payments (eg, via debiting fines from registered credit cards) and issuing seller's paybacks (eg, by crediting amounts to the seller's account) to interrupting the use of services or the infringed party's contractual performance. Automatic notification letters or emails that announce further steps in case the breach continues could round this off. Compared with human intervention by additional employees or third parties ('repo men'), this – as hoped by smart contract advocates – eventually helps to save money.

Against this background, smart contract-based mechanism can be understood as a shortened and simplified way of executing contractual parameters.

[10] In a similar vein, eg Borgogno, 'Smart Contracts' (2019) 884, where he calls the term 'smart contracts' 'misleading as, from a strictly legal perspective, they are not proper contracts, but a self-help remedy aimed at automating the performance of contractual obligations'.

[11] Fenwick and Wrbka (n 2) 51.

[12] In a comparable vein, eg ibid 41.

The process is shortened, because it can be exercised without the necessity to undergo lengthy court proceedings. It is simplified, because it can be achieved without the need to rely on the help of a 'repo man'[13] or third party intermediary that decides on possible consequences. The algorithmic translation of possible consequences in the form of 'If A occurs, then execute B' automates contractual enforcement and – once being fully operational – might lead to a significant reduction of enforcement and (hopefully) transaction costs. However, accomplishing true 'automation' needs to meet one challenge, in particular. The order 'If A occurs, then execute B' – precise as the definitions of A and B might be – requires a mechanism that, or an actor who, feeds the system with the required information to allow smart contracts to respond appropriately. Just think of a case in which a compensation payment should be made if certain parameters were fulfilled, eg, if a flight was delayed or cancelled. How does the system generate the necessary information, ie, the data that the compensation requirements are actually fulfilled? The answer is a tool that is commonly known as oracle.[14]

The term 'oracle' refers to third parties that collect off-chain information and then feed that information into the system. Integrating oracles could be a necessity to maximise the quality of smart contract-based mechanisms. One of their major drawbacks – as seen from a smart contract industry perspective – lies in the fact oracles are usually human beings and that bringing them in might actually mitigate one of the biggest advantages of smart contract-based mechanisms – that they work without (human) third-party intervention. Put differently, consulting oracles could undermine the potential benefits of having a 'slenderised' monitoring and enforcement instrument. One possible future solution to this would be a further development of oracles in the sense that one creates AI-based, fully automated oracles. Answering the question of how this can be achieved is not the purpose of this chapter. What can be said, however, is that at the time of writing such endeavour still seems to be a long way off – but so were smart contracts a couple of decades ago. Linking different data sources together and utilising synergised information from one point to another could be an intermediary solution. Take our compensation example again. Delay and cancellation information could directly and automatically be sent to the smart contract interface without the need for a human oracle to enter the data.

One of the most obvious and intriguing possible advantages over smart contract-less contractual performance and enforcement lies in the potential of 'elegantly' saving time. Smart contract-based mechanisms aim to replace (or at

[13] In this vein, eg Fenwick and Wrbka (n 2) 50.

[14] See, eg R Baron and M Chaudey, 'Blockchain and Smart-Contract: A Pioneering Approach of Inter-Firms Relationships? The Case of Franchise Networks' (2019, available at ssrn.com/abstract=3378477; Borgogno (n 9) 891; A Egberts, 'The Oracle Problem – An Analysis of how Blockchain Oracles Undermine the Advantages of Decentralized Ledger Systems' (2017), available at ssrn.com/abstract=3382343; M Fenwick and S Wrbka, 'Rechtliche Fragen' in HG Fill and A Meier (eds), *Blockchain kompakt – Grundlagen, Anwendungsoptionen und kritische Bewertung* (Wiesbaden, Springer Vieweg, 2020).

least to push back) conventional means of dispute resolution (litigation and ADR). Being convinced that 'nothing can be done' to double-check smart contract-triggered consequences, in particular those stakeholders that traditionally show a considerable low level of legal and technological knowledge, might refrain from taking legal action unless they receive proper information. It becomes obvious that this – in a transactional context – might first and foremost affect consumers. (We will return to this 'non-information' issue later.) What should be noted at this point is the possibility for smart contract-based mechanism designers and users to benefit from and build on the generally low motivational level of consumers to launch an action. As shown, for example, by a Eurobarometer study on consumer access to justice, only a minority – 13 per cent – of consumers who fail to reach an amicable solution with their contract partner would actually consider going to court.[15] Smart contract-based mechanisms 'craftily' preempt the 'argument' stage (and counteract efforts of simplifying conventional redress schemes eg, with the help of small claim procedures or ODR tools). Technically speaking, smart contracts do (of course) not exclude consumers from complaining or taking legal action, but – considering the low level of consumer willingness to sue – imposing penalties automatically and immediately on a consumer party would (in practice) intensify already existing consumer redress concerns. The higher the number of consumers that refrain from launching legal proceedings, the higher is the 'chance' that unilaterally chosen consequences prevail over solutions decided by neutral third parties. (We will return to this concern in more detail at a later point.)

To sum up, smart contracts might have enormous potential to revolutionise trade, the contracting processes and lifecycles of contracts across multiple sectors of the economy.[16] One can rightfully assume that smart contracts can become extremely powerful in practice and significantly influence contractual party performance, most notably because they might eventually replace the law as regulatory schemes and become a new version of 'the law'.[17] It is the possible scale

[15] European Opinion Research Group, 'European Union Citizens and Access to Justice' (2004) 195 *Eurobarometer* 9, available at www.medsos.gr/medsos/images/stories/PDF/eurobarometer_11-04_en.pdf. The study showed that the key reasons why consumers are unwilling to go to court are the additional financial risk of losing the case (in particular in those jurisdictions that apply a loser pays principle) as well as concerns regarding the length of legal proceedings and their overall complexity – see European Opinion Research Group (ibid) 32.

[16] For comments on the possible impact of smart contracts on trade and the industry see, eg R Brownsword, 'Regulatory Fitness: Fintech, Funny Money, and Smart Contracts' (2019) 20 *European Business Organization Law Review* 5; P Catchlove, 'Smart Contracts: A New Era of Contract Use' (2017), available at papers.ssrn.com/sol3/papers.cfm?abstract_id=3090226; I Kounelis, G Steri, R Giuliani and D Geneiatakis, 'Fostering consumers' energy market through smart contracts' (2017), available at ieeexplore.ieee.org/document/8015343; M Lang and M Müller, 'Blockchain and Smart Contracts in the Energy Industry – A European Perspective' (2019), available at www.twobirds.com/~/media/pdfs/blockchain-and-smart-contracts-in-the-energy-industry--article.pdf; SD Levi and AB Lipton, 'An Introduction to Smart Contracts and Their Potential and Inherent Limitations' (2018) Harvard Law School Forum on Corporate Governance & Financial Regulation, available at corpgov.law.harvard.edu/2018/05/26/an-introduction-to-smart-contracts-and-their-potential-and-inherent-limitations.

[17] For details on this issue see, eg P De Filippi and A Wright (eds), *Blockchain & the Law: The Rule of Code* (Cambridge/Mass, Harvard University Press, 2018).

of significance that asks for a more holistic and neutral look at smart contracts. The following sections will discuss the challenges smart contracts face and selected tools that might be of help to answer them.

IV. The Downsides and Possible Risks of Smart Contracts

In the digital era it is only natural that innovators are looking for ways to simplify and standardise procedures by switching to and developing online tools. This trend characterises, in particular, the trade and industry sectors. Just think of the disruption of conventional, ie, centralised and hierarchical organisational forms of enterprises that began with the emergence of platform companies (such as Facebook, Instagram, Uber, Netflix, etc).[18] Smart contracts are one mechanism that contributes to the further rise of digitalisation. But true to the motto 'where light, there is shadow', one has to recognise that there are possible issues. One of the biggest concerns found in the pertinent literature is that digitalisation appears to be promoted for the sake of digitalisation itself and often neglects party fairness.[19]

This concern seems to be of great significance, in particular, when it comes to commercial contracts. The main reason for this lies in the fact that digital codes might be technologically superior to their creators (ie, to human beings), but inferior when it comes to flexible decision-making, finding answers for unforeseen scenarios and making compromises. Unlike human beings, machines, software and codes lack the capacity to react to special circumstances in situations that ask for special treatment. Making judgments, in particular, seems a 'mission impossible' if the necessary information is lacking and possible decisions are neither predefined nor integrated into the automated system. Admittedly, human decision-making can be time-consuming, but – in the end – ensures fairer results than inflexible, auto-generated 'answers'. Just think of the typical way smart contracts are designed: The most simple design form – 'If A occurs, then execute B' – guarantees clear results, but might come at the cost of justness or reasonableness. One might, for

[18] See, eg S Galloway, *The Four: The Hidden DNA of Amazon, Apple, Facebook & Google* (New York, Portfolio/Penguin, 2017); A Moazed and NJ Johnson, *Modern Monopolies: What it Takes to Dominate the Twenty First Century Economy* (New York, St Martin's Press, 2016); GG Parker, MW van Alstyne and SP Choudary, *Platform Revolution: How Networked Markets are Transforming the Economy and How to Make them Work for You* (New York, Norton, 2016). See also Fenwick and Wrbka (n 2) 40, where the authors discuss the phenomenon of disrupting conventional company structures as one consequence of the 'digital transformation' ('*digitale Transformation*').

[19] For selected points of criticism in the context of smart contracts, in particular, see KEC Levy, 'Book-Smart, Not Street-Smart: Blockchain-Based Smart Contracts and The Social Workings of Law' (2017) 3 *Engaging Science, Technology, and Society* 1; E Mik, 'Smart Contracts: Terminology, Technical Limitations and Real World Complexity' (2017) 9 *Law, Innovation and Technology* 269; J Sklaroff, 'Smart Contracts and the Cost of Inflexibility' (2017) *166 University of Pennsylvania Law Review* 263.

example, have good reasons to ask, 'Why did A occur?' or 'Why did it not occur?' Today's smart contracts inevitably fail to take these subquestions into consideration and simply execute what ought to be executed under 'sterile' (or ordinary) conditions. The combination of this inflexibility and the aim to replace or push back conventional enforcement mechanisms creates the risk that automated performance and enforcement tools do not necessarily reflect true party intentions, as particularly pointed out in the 'relational contractual theory' literature on smart contracts.[20] This issue becomes even more complex if one considers that contractual parties might willingly create scenarios that, by definition, require further (party) clarification. Parties could, for example, use ambiguous / more flexible language to allow for later decision-making to respond to certain, not yet foreseeable circumstances. In this vein, Eliza Mik criticises that (smart contract) 'developers fail to recognise that in contract law, ambiguity is a feature, not a bug'.[21] Regardless of whether they intentionally fail to do so, the biggest challenge in this respect is the fact that smart contracts are still unable to make innovative decisions if needed.

Taking the effectiveness and efficiency of smart contracts into consideration, they might still look more attractive than conventional contract performance and enforcement tools. Judgmental inflexibility is, however, not the only concern. Another issue relates to the alleged transaction cost savings and lower prices that might result from this, as indicated in the preceding section. The first question that arises in this context is whether smart contracts really reduce transaction costs. To answer this question, one needs to clarify what the term 'transaction costs' actually means. In a simplified way, transaction costs can be grouped into two broader categories – *ex ante* (transaction) costs and *ex post* (transaction) costs. The first category – *ex ante* costs – looks at costs that arise prior to and at the time of the conclusion of a contract. In particular, when referring to conventional, paper-based contracts, they can be further subdivided into initiation and negotiation costs (ie, costs that relate to the marketing and negotiation phases) on the one hand and direct agreement costs (ie, costs that arise in close context with the conclusion of the contract) on the other. The *ex post* group adds another cost pillar and focuses on the time after the conclusion of the contract. *Ex post* costs can be subdivided into handling and performance costs (ie, costs that relate to the parties' contractual performance), possible contract amendment or renegotiation costs (in case the parties want to reconsider contract terms) and possible enforcement costs (ie, costs that relate to third-party enforcement).

Undeniably, smart contracts have the potential to significantly reduce enforcement costs. This understanding rests on the consideration that contractual enforcement becomes automated in the sense that judges and other third-party enforcers (repo men) are replaced or pushed back by digitalised processes.

[20] In this vein, eg Fenwick and Wrbka, 'Rechtliche Fragen' (2020) 124. For more details see, eg Levy (ibid)18.

[21] Mik, 'Smart Contracts' (2017) 289.

However, some caveats should be made. First, a total replacement and thus a general reduction of enforcement costs can, of course, take only place in those scenarios in which the party negatively affected by the automated enforcement mechanism does not take recourse to courts or other conventional dispute-settlement institutions (ADR). Second and under the condition that the enforcement seeking party eventually wins a possible litigation or ADR case, the loser-pays principle, which still dominates continental European jurisdictions, leads to the result that the winning party receives full payment and would not have to carry any enforcement costs. Third, refined enforcement mechanisms (eg, small claim procedures and ODR) additionally mitigate the cost risk for the enforcement-seeking party. Hence, when it comes to enforcement costs, smart contract-based mechanisms might have some advantages, but some features of conventional redress minimise the gap.

What can be concluded with respect to the other transaction cost layers? In a generalised way, one can note that smart contracts do not – or at least not significantly – reduce transaction costs other than enforcement costs. Automating contractual performance and enforcement via the translation of 'true' contracts into digital language does not have any positive effect on *ex ante* costs. On the contrary, smart contracts could (at least in the short and medium-term) actually increase *ex ante* costs by adding a new cost layer. This results from the consideration that third parties – external programmers and internal, employed IT engineers – are needed to design, create and install smart contract codes for and in translation of contract terms into digital language. In a considerable number of scenarios these 'smart contract installation costs' might further rise due to the necessity to install an infrastructure that is capable of handling smart contract tools. The cost issue is additionally maximised by the need to draft contracts more 'carefully' and in more detail, if contractual performance and enforcement should be automated. This consideration rests on the fact that in order to minimise the risk of wrong translations into code, contracts need to define each possible enforcement step and decision in detail. This might require the investment of further financial means, because the average contractual parties would depend on additional legal and technical expertise to understand which contractual information is needed. Compared with conventional contract transaction costs, one can thus conclude that the balance between *ex ante* and *ex post* costs might significantly tilt towards *ex ante* costs.

Like the *ex ante* cost layer, the *ex post* pillar might also be subject to an increase. Smart contract-based mechanisms have the potential to take the pressure off the courts and ADR institutions. Regardless of their quality or level of sophistication, however, smart contracts still require human support and intervention. As explained above, IT experts are needed to prevent and solve technical malfunctions, because the average contract parties do not necessarily have the capacity and technical knowledge to achieve this. Hence, smart contract administrators would be needed to monitor and restore the functioning of smart contract-based mechanisms (if and where needed). Ideally, smart contract administrators combine technical and legal knowledge and could additionally function as a contact point for enquiries by the contract parties. Smart contract administrators do not come cost-free, though, and might increase handling and performance costs as well as contract amendment or renegotiation costs.

Even if one arrived at the conclusion that smart contracts lead to cost savings (for the smart contract utilising contract party / business), one still has to question whether this is of any advantage for *both* parties. A look at relevant discussions shows that there is no convincing evidence that businesses are actually willing to pass on cost savings to the respective contract party. One might just as well suggest that cost reductions are, rather, used to increase profits by way of extending the profit margin while leaving prices as they are. In a similar vein is Geraint Howells and Jean-Sébastien Borghetti's reply to a Court of Justice of the European Union judgment that discussed the consequences of cost reductions. Howells and Borghetti point out that claims according to which both contract parties would benefit from cost savings are mere speculation.[22]

An additional concern directly relates to technological aspects. As already pointed out, one of the key disadvantages of smart contracts is the fact that computer codes and protocols – unlike human beings – cannot generate new or innovative solutions or even make a well-balanced decision that takes aspects into consideration that initially were unforeseeable or which are impossible to clearly predefine. It is this impossibility to translate certain legal terms and legal mechanisms into computer code language that might be a major drawback in particular in more intricate contractual scenarios. Even for legal experts, striking the correct 'fairness' balance is oftentimes a challenge. But adding respective decision-making features to smart contracts seems impossible or – at the very least – extremely difficult. This leads Oscar Borgogno to conclude that (in the middle and long term) the utilisation of smart contracts might ask for a new generation of lawyers – lawyers with 'new skills in the field of computer sciences (such as coding) so as to be able to design and understand sophisticated smart contracts'.[23] At the moment, however, stakeholders that are able to meet the outlined challenges seem to be missing.

It is, however, a different concern that links smart contracts to the implementations of the following section. Smart contracts are of particular popularity among those stakeholders that seek to simplify contractual performance and enforcement by way of automated standardisation. This implies that smart contracts are used first and foremost in commercial transaction scenarios that aim at a high(er) number of customers. High-volume B2C e-commerce cases, ie, contractual settings that rest on similar keypoints or parametres in a high number of cases, are arguably a paramount example of this. This might further be generally the case in trade,

[22] G Howells and JS Borghetti, 'Product Liability' in HW Micklitz, J Stuyck and E Terryn (eds), *Cases, Materials and Text on Consumer Law* (Oxford, Hart, 2010) 452, where the authors discuss the issue of cost savings and possible price reductions in the context of strict product liability.

[23] Borgogno (n 9) 890 fn 18.

industry and service settings that inherently aim at a high number of possible customers. Just think of the travel industry, postal services or energy procurement. It is the large number of parties potentially affected by the imposed use of smart contracts in combination with the unique smart contract characteristics that give cause for concern. The smart contract industry primarily focuses on automated process standardisation and often tries to achieve this by circumventing conventional, legal performance and enforcement procedures. This is facilitated by the fact that automated enforcement tools are difficult to govern for actors other than their creators. In a 2017 blockchain and smart contract statement, the OECD framed this distinctness of smart contracts as follows:

> [I]f a code of law or any regulation can be embedded as a smart contract in a blockchain, then breaking the law is tantamount to breaking the code. In other words, the only way to infringe the law is to 'crack' the computer code. This is potentially a very powerful tool not only to automate contractual transactions but also to automate legal supervision and enforcement.[24]

What does this mean for the present analysis? The short answer is that smart contracts complicate fair decision-making and – unlike neutral third parties (courts and ADR institutions) – are not a guarantee that mandatory laws are respected. It is justified to say that legal compliance faces new, more complex challenges in the digital era. Particularly in a B2C context this might be worrisome, because B2C transactions are governed by a comparatively broad set of mandatory legal provisions that aim to ensure a level playing field and contractual fairness. With the help of providers of smart contract technology, smart contract utilising parties can comparatively easily impose any factual legal consequence on their contract partner simply by issuing / generating automated (unilaterally chosen) decisions. This is undeniably very appealing for stakeholders with an interest in smart contracts, in particular for those that aim to apply such mechanisms in a larger number of parallel cases. The lack of neutrality of smart contract-based mechanisms can easily undermine or complicate party fairness and the protection by mandatory law. One of the key issues with smart contracts can thus be seen in their potential to hamper protection offered by mandatory laws and traditional, neutral dispute resolution schemes that both aim to ensure true party balance in cases where one of the two parties is believed to be in a stronger position than the other. This clearly contradicts one of the targets enshrined in the UCTD[25] that was emphasised more recently by the 2003 Alternative Dispute Resolution Directive. The UCTD aims to prevent businesses from forcing significantly lopsided, unfavourable contract terms on their counterparts. With reference to Article 3(3) of the UCTD, Point 1(q) of the Annex of the Directive emphasises the importance of conventional dispute resolution and declares contractual terms unfair that 'exclude[e] or hinder the consumer's right to take legal action or exercise

[24] OECD, 'Blockchain Technology and Corporate Governance' (2018) 9.
[25] For details of this Directive see section V below.

any other legal remedy, particularly by requiring the consumer to take disputes exclusively to arbitration not covered by legal provisions'. Article 10(1) of the ADR Directive summarises the preference for (traditional) courts as follows:

> Member States shall ensure that an agreement between a consumer and a trader to submit complaints to an ADR entity is not binding on the consumer if it was concluded before the dispute has materialised and if it has the effect of depriving the consumer of his right to bring an action before the courts for the settlement of the dispute.

Without suitable 'safety mechanisms', smart contracts would undermine the importance and rationale of these statements.

All of these arguments show that – in the absence of convincing evidence – the question of what the true advantages of smart contracts actually are remains unanswered (in particular with respect to average consumers). This does not mean that smart contracts should not be applied any further. Digitalisation has become part of our daily lives and obviously has its benefits. Nevertheless, a tailor-made regulatory framework might be needed to reply to the challenges outlined in this section.

V. Possible Ways Forward

As indicated in the previous section, realising the full potential of smart contracts while treasuring protective achievements of consumer law might pose a regulatory challenge. Regulation should not be too strict to allow smart contracts to develop, but at the same time must not fail to ensure that overriding, justifiable legal principles are respected. One specific approach that has been taken more recently relates to regulatory experimentation.[26] Regulatory (blockchain) sandboxes[27] (hereinafter 'sandboxes') date back to 2016, when the UK Financial Conduct Authortiy (FCA) announced their introduction to give blockchain enterprises the opportunity to test the waters in a comparatively safe environment under 'softer' authority supervision. The FCA would allow hand-picked enterprises to apply innovative technical solutions (Fintech in a broader sense) and ask them to provide the authorities with feedback on application processes in return. The unique feature of sandboxes lies in the attenuated regulatory interference of business activities within the sandbox. It is not the aim of this contribution to comment on the potential of sandboxes. But what should be noted is that they obviously incentivise enterprises to further develop digital solutions (including smart contracts), while providing authorities with invaluable insights into this new form of technology.

[26] On regulatory experimentation in the context of the blockchain technology see, eg ML Bennett, 'How to think about law, regulation and technology: Problems with "technology" as a regulatory target' (2013) 5 *Law, Innovation & Technology* 1; J Black, 'Paradoxes and Failures: 'New Governance Techniques and the Financial Crisis' (2012) 75 *Modern Law Review* 1037.

[27] See on this, eg Fenwick and Wrbka (n 14) 130.

Depending on the concrete design, however, sandboxes might not be the perfect or final solution to effectively reply to concerns of possible legal breaches of smart contracts. Sandbox enterprises undeniably are under a significantly high degree of authority supervision. However, not all potential smart contract providers are necessarily covered. Sandboxes cannot prevent reckless non-sandbox stakeholders from launching legally 'questionable' smart contract projects that cannot be monitored by sandbox authorities. Additional, more comprehensive mechanisms might be needed to close gaps that sandboxes cannot.

One of the possible instruments that come to mind shows parallels to a model that – at the EU level – was first introduced in the 1990s to reply to a first wave of contractual standardisation. With the help of standard form contracts (SFCs) enterprises aimed to simplify and standardise contractual frameworks. In this sense, one can note that SFCs and smart contracts – despite their conceptual differences – both seek to simplify and standardise processes in a high number of comparable cases and that a brief look at SFCs and pertinent legislation might offer solutions that could be applied to safeguard party fairness also in smart contract scenarios.

With the advent of pan-EU consumer legislation in the late 1980s and early 1990s the EU took the initiative to address issues that had been considered as particularly harmful to maintaining a level playing field for both parties to B2C contracts. One of the first instruments was the UCTD,[28] which introduced common minimum standards to balance contractual interests.[29] The legislator believed that the most promising way to ensure an acceptable fairness level rested primarily on two complementary thoughts. The first relates to the concept of unfair, non-negotiated contract terms defined as follows:

> A contractual term which has not been individually negotiated shall be regarded as unfair if, contrary to the requirement of good faith, it causes a significant imbalance in the parties' rights and obligations arising under the contract, to the detriment of the consumer (Article 3(1) of the UCTD).

[28] For background information and comments on the UCTD see P Nebbia, 'Unfair Contract Terms' in C Twigg-Flesner (ed), *The Cambridge Companion to European Union Private Law* (Cambridge, Cambridge University Press, 2010) 216; T Wilhelmsson and C Willett, 'Unfair Terms and Standard Form Contracts' in G Howells, I Ramsay and T Wilhelmsson (eds), *Handbook of Research on International Consumer Law* (Cheltenham, Edward Elgar, 2010) 158; J Stuyck, 'Unfair Terms' in G Howells and R Schulze (eds), *Modernising and Harmonising Consumer Contract Law* (Munich, Sellier, 2009) 115; L Tichý, 'Unfair Terms in Consumer Contracts' in H Schulte-Nölke and L Tichý (eds), *Perspectives for European Consumer Law: Towards a Directive on Consumer Rights and Beyond* (Munich, Sellier, 2010) 59; HW Micklitz and N Reich, 'The Court and Sleeping Beauty: The Revival of the Unfair Contract Terms Directive (UCTD)' (2014) 51 *Common Market Law Review* 795.

[29] This 'minimum harmonisation approach' is enshrined in Art 8 of the UCTD as follows: 'Member States may adopt or retain the most stringent provisions compatible with the Treaty in the area covered by this Directive, to ensure a maximum degree of protection for the consumer.' Later attempts to replace the instrument with a set of fully harmonised provisions – thus depriving Member States to maintain stricter standards even if and where reasonable and well-established – failed. One of the more recent (unsuccessful) moves was the 2008 Proposal for a directive on consumer rights. Its Arts 34 and 35 sought to replace the UCTD with a fully harmonised set of absolutely and presumably unfair contract terms (black and grey list), but eventually did not make it into the 2011 Consumer Rights Directive.

and

> A term shall always be regarded as not individually negotiated where it has been drafted in advance and the consumer has therefore not been able to influence the substance of the term, particularly in the context of a pre-formulated standard contract (Article 3(2) of the UCTD).

The second consideration refers to the fact that the Directive obliged Member States to ensure that qualified entities can take legal action against unfair contract terms on behalf of the collective interests of consumers. Article 7(1) of the UCTD aims to secure that unfair contract terms can be fought for the sake of collective consumer interests and grants Member States some leeway to design a suitable mechanism. A minimum common standard is ensured via the applicability of the Injunctions Directive.[30] Point 5 of Annex 1 of the 2009 Injunctions Directive lists the UCTD as one of the legislative pieces for which broad injunctions should be used. If successful, a judgment would have effect not only in a particular case, but *pro futuro* with respect to similar cases.[31] In addition to these two key strategies, the Directive sought to improve the overall understandability and legal certainty of contract terms[32] by asking for the use of 'plain, intelligible language' and an 'interpretation most favourable to the consumer'[33] in cases of ambiguity.

Extensive studies have evaluated the UCTD over the years. Two of the most noteworthy studies are the 2008 'EC Consumer Law Compendium' ('Consumer Law Compendium')[34] and the 2017 report on the Study for the Fitness Check of EU consumer and marketing law ('Consumer Law Fitness Check Study').[35] Both covered EU consumer legislation at a broader level and discussed the UCTD as one of the key regulatory pieces. The Consumer Law Compendium pointed out that one of the key achievements of the UCTD is that unfair contract terms are now combatted in all Member States, although there are still some considerable differences when it comes to the type of possibly covered contract terms.[36] Diversity can further be found when it comes to the design of national protection

[30] Directive 2009/22/EC [2009] OJ L110/30. This is in line with the original injunctions regime as introduced by the 1998 Injunctions Directive (Directive 98/27/EC [1998] OJ L166/51) – see Point 7 of the Annex of the 1998 Injunctions Directive.

[31] See, in particular, Art 7 of the UCTD.

[32] See, in particular, sentence 1 of Art 5 of the UCTD.

[33] Sentence 2 of Art 5 of the UCTD.

[34] H Schulte-Nölke, C Twigg-Flesner and M Ebers (eds), *EC Consumer Law Compendium: The Consumer Acquis and Its Transposition in the Member States* (Munich, Sellier, 2008).

[35] Civic Consulting, 'Study for the Fitness Check of EU consumer and marketing law – Final report Part 1 – Main report' (2017), available at ec.europa.eu/newsroom/document.cfm?doc_id=44840.

[36] Some Member States limit the scope to contract terms that are not individually negotiated by the parties, while others go beyond the minimum standard of the Directive and cover individually negotiated clauses as well. For a summary of the national implementation of the UCTD with respect to the material scope of national law, see Schulte-Nölke, Twigg-Flesner and Ebers, *EC Consumer Law Compendium* (2008) 339. In the course of the national implementation of the Directive some Member States went one step further and revised or introduced comparative schemes also for non-B2C cases – see Schulte-Nölke, Twigg-Flesner and Ebers (ibid) 362.

schemes.[37] Overall, the study pointed out that the Directive had clearly raised the bar of protection and emphasised the importance of ensuring a fair (ie, non-abusive) contract environment. Regardless of the concrete approach a Member State would take, it can be summarised that all relevant jurisdictions have successfully installed mechanisms that seek to safeguard collective consumer interests in limiting the use of unfair contract terms. One factor that might explain the success of the UCTD enforcement tools is the fact that competent authorities oftentimes are in a better situation to combat unfair contract terms, be it because of a superior degree of legal knowledge, better financial resources or a higher motivation to fight abusive contract terms – all compared with average consumers. Although collective (injunctive) mechanisms cannot replace individual compensatory redress, they surely have the potential to increase the overall level of legal compliance. This consideration is significant because of the risk that power and knowledge imbalance between enterprises and consumers might facilitate legal abuse.[38] The CJEU has confirmed this consideration. In *Océano Grupo Editorial SA v Roció Murciano Quintero*, for example, the court noted that:

> [The UCTD is] based on the idea that the consumer is in a weak position vis-à-vis the seller or supplier, as regards both his bargaining power and his level of knowledge. This leads to the consumer agreeing to terms drawn up in advance by the seller or supplier without being able to influence the content of the terms.[39]

Nine years after the publication of the Consumer Law Compendium the European Commission released the result of a second study with coverage of the UCTD. The 2017 Consumer Law Fitness Check Study emphasised the importance of the UCTD as follows:

> It can be concluded that the benefits of the UCTD for consumers mainly derive from preventing and stopping abuses of standard terms in contracts, which involve asymmetries of information between contracting parties leading to market failure. The obligations of the UCTD for traders concerning transparency and fairness of standard contract terms and the possibility to declare the nullity of an unfair contract term address this market failure and thereby increase consumer welfare.[40]

The study arrived at this result after having conducted a detailed analysis that had included feedback from more than 23,000 respondents from all Member States

[37] Some Member States have opted for administrative proceedings, others for court actions, some for enforcement by public authorities, others by private bodies – see Schulte-Nölke, Twigg-Flesner and Ebers (n 34) 405. For the variety of legal 'contractual unfairness' concepts introduced at the Member State level that range from absolute nullity to relative nullity of (partial or whole) clauses to the possibility to alter, amend or adjust contract terms – in several cases in combination with possible compensation claims – see Schulte-Nölke (n 34) 388.

[38] In the language of the Directive this concern sounded as follows: 'acquirers of goods and services should be protected against the abuse of power by the seller or supplier, in particular against one-sided standard contracts and the unfair exclusion of essential rights in contracts' – see Recital 9 of the UCTD.

[39] Judgment of 27 June 2000, Joined Cases C-240/98 to C-244/98 – *Océano Grupo Editorial SA v Roció Murciano Quintero*, ECLI:EU:C:2000:346 [25].

[40] Civic Consulting, 'Fitness Check' (2017) 158.

(plus Iceland and Norway), two comprehensive 'mystery shopping' projects in 12 Member States and four behavioural consumer experiments in eight Member States.[41] Based on the results of these processes, the study arrived at the conclusion that the UCTD and its collective enforcement mechanisms are of utmost importance to ensure a level playing field for B2C transactions. Potential information gaps, in particular, were found to be significant obstacles for consumers to enforce their rights. The 2017 Consumer Law Fitness Check Study based the necessity of a 'safety net'[42] inter alia on the following findings:

> Businesses in most countries are considered to be quite well aware of the application of the horizontal EU consumer legislation in the regulated sectors. They are obliged to comply with the (legislation implementing the) UCTD and as a result, they should be well-informed of its requirements. Although the knowledge of businesses is deemed sufficient by most stakeholders, violations of the legislation on unfair contract terms occur frequently.[43]

and

> It is the awareness (or rather lack of awareness) of consumers of the requirements of the UCTD-both in the regulated sectors and also in general-that turns out to be an important concern.[44]

Combining the results of the two studies, one can draw in particular five important conclusions. First, the average enterprise is well aware of applicable laws (although some enterprises might still lack sufficient legal knowledge). Second, some (but, of course, not all) enterprises abuse laws to exploit consumers. Third, the average consumer does not have sufficient knowledge regarding applicable laws, in particular, when it comes to the question of what constitutes fairness and what breaches it. Fourth, enforcement instruments are needed to defend consumer rights, because it is unrealistic to assume that the average consumer is able to pursue his or her legal interests. Fifth, if left unpursued, reckless business behaviour would have a negative impact not only on consumers, but also on competitors.[45]

Possible counterarguments that the UCTD might put a too heavy burden on businesses, because the regime might necessitate a more thorough design and constant monitoring of SFCs come (close) to nothing. The Consumer Law Fitness Check Study explained that the costs for annual SFC reviews amount – on average – to '0.009 percent of annual turnover' in the considered business sectors.

[41] European Commission, 'Consumer Market Study to Support the Fitness Check of EU Consumer and Marketing Law – Executive Summary' (2017) 1–2, available at publications.europa.eu/en/publication-detail/-/publication/9ee338d4-a7e5-11e7-837e-01aa75ed71a1.

[42] Civic Consulting (n 35) 185.

[43] ibid 179.

[44] ibid 180.

[45] ibid 156. See in addition pp 157–58 for consumer benefits that result from the enforcement mechanisms of the UCTD; p 69 for comments on the overall effectiveness of the UCTD, p 74 for data with respect to UCTD cases decided by courts and p 88 for a comment on the collectiveness notion of UCTC enforcement.

Advice offered free of cost by interest business representative groups and public bodies might further contribute to the fact that compliance costs do not carry significant weight.

The benefits of ensuring a level playing field to allow for self-determined market participation cannot be denied. This leaves us with two questions: First, what do SFCs and smart contracts have in common? Second, why is it advisable to learn from the UCTD experience when dealing with smart contracts?

At first sight, SFCs and smart contracts do not share any conceptual features. SFCs are utilised by businesses, because it is arguably the easiest – at least the most efficient and effective – way to design a legal framework that satisfies the needs of the framework user. Smart contracts, on the other hand, do not create an 'original' legal framework, but merely translate contractual provisions into code. Three interrelated considerations, however, explain the considerable similarity of SFCs and smart contracts.

First, both SFCs and smart contracts can significantly impact contractual performance processes. SFCs aim to incorporate specifically crafted legal provisions into a contract, which usually deviate from statutory or 'default' law. Smart contracts focus on monitoring contractual performance and enable the smart contract using party to easily answer possible failures in performance by the other party.

Second, both instruments are precontractually crafted by or on behalf of the same party – in a B2C context – by or on behalf of the business party. The other party – in a B2C context, the consumer – has no or little influence on the design of SFCs and smart contracts.

Third, both rest on standardised models and procedures and potentially affect a large number of consumers in a comparable way. Possible breaches of mandatory consumer laws by SFCs and smart contracts would impair not only the interests of individual consumers, but additionally collective interests and hence pose a 'multilayer interest' risk.[46]

These considerations show that SFCs and smart contracts have actually more in common than what could be expected at first sight. Returning to the second of our two questions ('What can smart contracts learn from the regulation of SFCs?'), it is important to note the complexity of smart contracts. Just as is the case with the abundance of legal norms that aim to protect consumers and the confusion that this might create, smart contracts might not easily be understood by consumers. Taking the abusive potential of both SFCs and smart contracts into consideration, it is only consequential to ask for consumer support in smart contract situations in a similar way as is already successfully the case with SFCs. As is currently the case, smart contracts largely operate far away from neutral supervision (with the

[46] For details on the concept of multilayer interests see the contributions in S Wrbka, S Van Uytsel and M Siems (eds), *Collective Actions – Enhancing Access to Justice and Reconciling Multilayer Interests?* (Cambridge, Cambridge University Press, 2012).

exception of the aforementioned regulatory sandbox initiatives). To improve and guarantee compliance with consumer laws, it is necessary to provide for mechanisms that have the potential to intervene where and when needed. The UCTD experience shows that this might best be achieved by neutral third-party stakeholders that have the competence to effectively address possible consumer pitfalls. Respective authorities and private bodies ideally combine legal knowledge with technical expertise, and by doing this are promising actors in attempts to safeguard and restore contractual performance and enforcement fairness. Third-party intervention schemes should (of course) not be seen as an obstacle for the further development of technical solutions. Rather, they act as facilitators and assist in creating a safe, reliable space for parties to engage in B2C-transactions without legal worries or concerns. One can also say that SFC-regulation-based mechanisms have the potential to function as a safety mechanism in a largely unregulated smart contract environment. In the end, consumer interests are the interests most likely negatively affected by under-regulated environments. With SFC-regulation-based mechanisms, a reasonable balance can be found to reach the highest possible degree of mutual trust.

SFC-regulation-based mechanisms are promising tools to improve legal compliance and to ensure party fairness. One of the shortcomings, however, lies in the fact that such mechanisms typically do not vest authorities with (autonomous) investigative competencies. What might be needed are complementary processes that pave the way for corrective mechanisms. This should ideally happen at a larger scale and allow for constructive authority feedback in case misbehaviour is detected. Respective tools could add a 'softer' mechanism and avoid lengthy court proceedings. Not every case of non-compliance is the result of deliberate legal abuse. Non-sufficient legal knowledge might just as well be the reason why an enterprise does not follow the law. By introducing a mechanism that takes account of both issues – proactive investigation and graded enforcement that begins with informal feedback – the development of law-abiding smart contracts might further benefit.

One thinkable initiative could implement consumer protection ideas that were introduced by 'sweeps', a set of control tools coordinated at the EU level by the European Commission.[47] The mechanism dates back to the early 2000s when EU stakeholders discussed possible non-judiciary means to strengthen consumer law compliance. The result was the adoption of the Regulation on Consumer Protection Cooperation (CPC Regulation)[48] in 2004. One of its unique features was the introduction of a cross-border cooperation mechanism (other

[47] For detailed comments on the potential of sweeps in general see, eg S Wrbka, *European Consumer Access to Justice Revisited* (Cambridge, Cambridge University Press, 2015) 64.

[48] Regulation (EC) No 2006/2004 of the European Parliament and of the Council on cooperation between national authorities responsible for the enforcement of consumer protection laws [2004] OJ L364/1 as amended by Regulation (EU) No 954/2011 of the European Parliament and of the Council amending Regulation (EC) No 2006/2004 on cooperation between national authorities responsible for the enforcement of consumer protection laws [2011] OJ L259/1.

than ordinary courts) commonly known as 'sweeps' or – in the language of the regulation – as '[c]oordination of market surveillance and enforcement activities'.[49] Under the sweeps, designated public authorities do not answer individual issues, but address preselected topics with respect to a broad range of entrepreneurs throughout the EU. On an annual basis, the European Commission picks a 'prominent' theme[50] under which the designated authorities conduct their market monitoring activities. The authorities screen hundreds of pertinent stakeholders and contact them in case of regulatory breach with individual feedback that allows the relevant enterprises to restore legal compliance. Overall, sweeps constantly have shown comparatively positive effects on securing compliance with consumer laws. Regardless of the concrete topic, sweeps have repeatedly evidenced legal irregularities of the majority of screened businesses prior to feedback 'intervention'.[51] The most noteworthy and positive effect of sweeps lies in their significant impact on 'misbehaving' businesses. European Commission data explains that in a large number of cases national sweep authorities have successfully 'convinced' law-breaking businesses to comply with consumer laws.[52] And in those cases, in which businesses are unwilling to end their illegal practices, national authorities could exercise their powers to force businesses to stop unlawful activities (or even to cease the business operations).[53]

Sweeps are a monitoring mechanism that perfectly complements the more 'experimental' sandboxes and SFC-regulation based tools. Particularly in situations that ask for a large-scale screening of smart contract environments, they could develop their full potential. As repeatedly shown over a stretch of more than a decade, coordinated actions by national authorities can significantly increase the level of legal compliance by applying relatively soft force. Regardless of whether returning to law-compliant behaviour happens voluntarily or not, both prudent businesses, as well as consumers, would benefit from the consequences, not least, because sweeps have the potential to strengthen mutual trust.

Sweep-inspired actions would undeniably benefit from interdisciplinary cooperation between technical / digital experts and legal specialists. Knowledge exchange between these two stakeholder groups can achieve two goals in

[49] Article 9 of the CPC Regulation.

[50] The range of topics is broad and includes major areas in which B2C incidents are reported. The sweeps carried out thus far include the following: Airline sweep (2007), mobile phone content sweep (2008), electronic goods sweep (2009), online ticket sales sweep (2010), consumer credit sweep (2011), digital contents sweep (2012), travel services sweep (2013), guarantee of consumer electronics sweep (2014), pre-contractual information requirement sweep (2015), price comparison and travel booking websites sweep (2016), telecommunications and other digital services sweep (2017) and price transparency and drip pricing sweep (2018). For details see, eg Wrbka, *European Consumer Access* (2015) 66. and – with respect to recent sweeps – the information provided by the European Commission on sweeps, available at ec.europa.eu/info/live-work-travel-eu/consumers/enforcement-consumer-protection/sweeps_en, both with further references.

[51] For details and data see Wrbka (n 47) 66.

[52] ibid 66 with further references.

[53] ibid 66 with further references.

particular. First, sweeps can ensure that possible loopholes of regulatory sandboxes are patched. Second, sweeps – with the exception of having to go the 'long run' in exceptional cases – avoid excessive litigative costs. There is more: sweeps can further be deployed to address an additional challenge for smart contract-based contractual performance and enforcement mechanisms that must not be underestimated. Proponents of blockchain-based tools would argue that respective digital environments are absolutely (or at least by a large extent) safe. Arguably the biggest issue with this statement is that the argument has not been convincingly proven yet. To the contrary, hacking attacks have shown the vulnerability of digitalisation. The 2016 'The DAO' incident, where approximately 30 per cent of funds collected by Christoph Jentzsch for his decentralised, investor-directed venture capital fund project were hacked and stolen, is one of the best known examples. It shows that safety concerns are valid and need to be taken seriously.[54] Sweeps can help discovering relevant security issues in a large-scale project that runs across the EU. This would provide smart contract designers with invaluable, representative feedback.

VI. Concluding Remarks

In 2017 the OECD commented on smart contracts legislation and regulation as follows: '[R]egulating a business without adequate comprehension of its true nature is often possible via complex and hence costly regulation, which in turn becomes a barrier to entry for innovative start-ups.'[55] This statement reflects a very business-sided perspective on smart contracts. Legislation and regulation are considered as an obstacle for businesses to create and utilise smart contract-based instruments. Unfortunately, the statement fails to accept the justifiably supreme role of law. Law did not emerge to limit the freedom of parties, but to ensure fairness and to prevent exploitation of the weaker ones. In a business context, corporate and business governance have dominated the regulatory processes over the years to reflect this idea. It is the rule of law – and not the rule of code – that is best adapted to safeguard and balance the interests of *all* parties involved in a transaction. Digital codes have the potential to further realise this idea while simplifying procedures and saving time and money. Undeniably, however, the concern remains that – in the absence of a proper legal framework – the potential of digital codes in general and smart contracts, in particular, could burst their banks and undermine or subvert the achievements of law. Particularly in a B2C context, possible negative impacts of smart contract abuse become very obvious. This shall not mean that

[54] Michael Weidner, head of the Fraunhofer Institute for Secure Information Technology, for example, asks for 'IT seat belts' and argues that the institute has discovered security bugs in approximately 80% of the most popular IOS and Android applications tested in a representative study – for details see R Hutsteiner, 'IT braucht Sicherheitsgurte' (2019), available at science.orf.at/stories/2988307.

[55] OECD (n 2) 20.

smart contracts are an undesirable development. But to create a win–win situation for both parties – businesses and consumers – strategies need to be found and implemented to guarantee that automated contractual performance and enforcement tap its full potential without ignoring the need to obey the law and preserves the rationale behind law.

The suggestions made in this chapter aim to provide some ideas on how this complex challenge can be met. The pertinent literature repeatedly – and justifiably – lists regulatory sandboxes as one way to test specific, innovative regulatory mechanisms in this new digital environment. However, regulatory sandboxes cannot function as standalone mechanisms. Collective 'correction' tools and specific guidance should be introduced to establish the best possible regulatory / legal infrastructure for smart contracts to operate. This chapter discussed two complementary ways to achieve this. Based on similarities between the use of smart contracts and SFCs, the point was made that the regulation of digital processes should learn from SFC legislation that has successfully been put to the test. SFC experience showed that party interests do not necessarily stand in each other's way, but that SFC benefits can be maximised while guaranteeing a satisfactory degree of party fairness. Our short excursion into authority control mechanisms – the example of EU sweeps – visualised an additional tool to support the plausible use of smart contracts. The big incentive of sweep-based tools lies in the fact that they have a significantly positive impact on safeguarding and restoring legal compliance, while providing businesses with guidance and invaluable information on mandatory law.

The market has made a choice and paved the way for further digitalisation of contractual performance and enforcement. To guarantee a high standard of party trust, legislators and regulators must not fall behind. Utilised in a well-balanced way, the combination of regulatory sandboxes, SFC-regulation based tools and sweep-based devices could emerge as the long-awaited safety belt to accomplish this endeavour.

7

Feeding Smart Contract Legal Requirements with Semantic and Event Detection Logic Structures from Modern Service-Oriented Supply Chains

STYLIANOS TSARSITALIDIS, MARCELO CORRALES COMPAGNUCCI, GEORGE KOUSIOURIS AND ALAN DAHI*

'Software is eating the world …'[1]
'… and the law is next.'[2]

I. Introduction

The idea of 'software eating the law' has been around for more than six decades. In his seminal paper on this issue, Layman Allen suggested a new approach to drafting using certain basic notions of symbolic logic as a 'razor-edged tool for drafting and interpreting legal documents'.[3] According to Allen, this would help eliminate the ambiguity in legal texts that is the cause for different possible interpretations of the legislator's actual intent. It would permit a more precise and efficient method of legal reasoning as well as drafting.

* The work presented in this paper has received funding under the AffectUs extension, a TagItSmart Open Call 1 Extension project co-funded by the European Union (EU) Horizon 2020 programme under Grant number 688061.

[1] M Andreessen, 'Why Software is Eating the World' *Wall Street Journal* (20 August 2011), available at www.wsj.com/articles/SB10001424053111903480904576512250915629460.

[2] K Chan, 'Software is Eating Law' *Law Tech Asia* (25 September 2016), available at lawtech.asia/software-is-eating-law.

[3] LE Allen, 'Symbolic Logic: A Razor-Edged Tool for Drafting and Interpreting Legal Documents' (1957) 66 *Yale Law Journal* 833.

The study of logic is concerned with forms of reasoning. It is therefore essential for all pursuits, including law. John Stuart Mill famously called logic 'the art of reasoning' and later the 'art of thinking'.[4] Elaborating (or coding) a smart contract is very similar to the concepts behind symbolic logic as it uses logical expressions through the use of symbols and variables, instead of plain language.

This chapter follows a similar symbolic logic structure; in particular, it explores how semantics and event detection in the AffectUS semantic framework can support smart contract implementation requirements in modern supply chains. The framework incorporates concepts in a machine-readable way that tracks the distribution of goods that may be the subject of intellectual property rights (IPRs). It includes concepts that enable the modelling of ownership, dependencies and supply chain relations, as well as embedding of logical rules that can detect potential violations in goods management or distribution.

These declarations are expressed in the Ontology Web Language (OWL):

> '[A] Semantic Web language designed to represent rich and complex knowledge about things, groups of things, and relations between things. OWL is a computational logic-based language such that knowledge expressed in OWL can be exploited by computer programs, eg, to verify the consistency of that knowledge or to make implicit knowledge explicit.'[5]

AffectUs is a service-oriented system that links to other baseline systems (such as product monitoring platforms (eg, evrythng.com) and correlates information between stakeholders.[6]

The system retrieves the semantic declarations and uses an internal logic to detect various exceptions from a normal situation (such as a product ID in two different places as an indication of counterfeit existence, delay in product delivery, etc), while exploiting smart tag indications with relation to quality aspects of the delivered goods (such as maximum encountered temperature along the product's journey).

Upon detecting such events, the system notifies all affected stakeholders – producers and consumers of the product – through notification endpoints that they have defined. The usage of these rules and semantic concepts can help future efforts generate smart contracts that will provide a more effective and multilayered end-to-end supply chain solution.

This chapter is divided into five sections. Section II briefly discusses the intersection between blockchain technology and smart contracts in modern supply chains. Section III explains the AffectUS platform for enabling ecosystems of connected objects. Section IV delves into detail concerning the legal requirements in the supply chain and their technical implementation. Section V concludes.

[4] C Hookway, *The Pragmatic Maxim: Essays on Peirce and Pragmatism* (Oxford, Oxford University Press, 2012) 87.

[5] W3C Ontology Web Language, available at www.w3.org/OWL.

[6] G Kousiouris (2019) 'A Microservice-based Framework for Integrating IoT Management Platforms, Semantic and AI Services for Supply Chain Management' 5 *ICT Express* 141.

II. Blockchain and Smart Contracts in Modern Supply Chains

Blockchain and smart contracts are already two of the most hyped terms of the twenty-first century. It has been said that the combination of these two innovations can revolutionise the world.[7] Some think that bankers, notaries and even lawyers might soon have to offer new services and reinvent the way they do business or risk becoming redundant and obsolete.[8] Blockchain and smart contracts will also allow users to exert more control over their data, assets and identities.[9]

Blockchain is a type of immutable and distributed digital ledger.[10] 'Immutable' means that it cannot be edited since it is very difficult to change (alter or remove) something once an entry is added to the blockchain.[11] 'Distributed' because there is a network of several independent computers (nodes) connected together and the blockchain is shared among all the participants of the network. 'Digital ledger' because it is a computerised record of all transactions made. It is similar to a large database (almost like a shared Excel table) that contains all the information in rows or cells.[12]

More specifically, the blockchain is a data structure composed of time-stamped and cryptographically linked blocks.[13] This means that each block has a cryptographic hash code (a unique fingerprint) of the previous code, which is used to authenticate the transaction source, circumventing the need for a central intermediary. Put simply, a hash code can basically be used to verify the integrity of the data and files.[14]

[7] A Gazdecki, 'Five Ways Blockchain Could Change the World' *Forbes* (7 September 2018), available at www.forbes.com/sites/forbestechcouncil/2018/09/07/five-ways-blockchain-could-change-the-world.

[8] B Cenkus, 'Will Smart Contracts Finally Rid the World of Lawyers?' *Hackernoon* (2 February 2018), available at hackernoon.com/even-the-best-smart-contracts-wont-put-lawyers-out-of-work-anytime-soon-a224736e0235.

[9] M Horasan, 'Blockchain Technology and Finance' in N Tüfecki (ed), *Innovative Approaches in the Business World* (New York, Hiperlink Yayinlari, 2018) 185; M Corrales Compagnucci, M Fenwick and H Happio, 'Tomorrow's Lawyer Today? Platform-Driven LegalTech, Smart Contracts & the New World of Legal Design' (2019) 22 *Journal of Internet Law* 3.

[10] M Corrales Compagnucci, M Fenwick and N Forgó, 'Disruptive Technologies Shaping the Law of the Future' in M Corrales Compagnucci, M Fenwick and N. Forgó (eds), *New Technology, Big Data and the Law* (Singapore, Springer, 2017) 7.

[11] This feature is very attractive for organisations of various sectors. However, as the DTCC 2016 White Paper on Blockchain technology pointed out, 'immutability' is not particularly attractive to eg, the financial sector as there are many errors and frauds in the real world that may need corrections and clarifications. See A Walsch, 'Open-Source Operational Risk: Should Public Blockchains Serve as Financial Market Infrastructures?' in D Lee Kuo Chuen and RH Deng (eds), *Handbook of Blockchain, Digital Finance, and Inclusion, ChinaTech, Mobile Security, and Distributed Ledger, Vol. 2* (London, Academic Press, 2017) 247.

[12] R Sandor, *Electronic Trading and Blockchain: Yesterday, Today and Tomorrow* (London, World Scientific, 2018) 20.

[13] A Rayes and S Salam, *Internet of Things from Hype to Reality: The Road to Digitization*, 2nd edn (Berlin, Springer, 2019) 272.

[14] G Baralla, 'A Blockchain Based System to Ensure Transparency and Reliability in Food Supply Chain' in G Mencagli, DB Heras, V Cardelli, E Casalicchio, E Jeannot, F Wolf, A Salis, C Schifanella,

Cryptography and hash code are the two linchpin components of the blockchain that make the supply chain a secure environment to improve product traceability. They are how the blockchain permits the secure transfer of instances of value such as money, assets, property and identity credentials on the Internet without the involvement of an intermediary, eg, a bank or government agency.[15]

Blockchain and other distributed ledger technologies (DLT) have found applications in areas that go beyond the Fintech sector.[16] They are being used to improve product traceability and provenance throughout the extended supply chain.[17] The modern supply chain is a complex network of partners and suppliers dispersed across the world; there are multiple entities that in turn act as consumers and then producers of goods in order to complete the chain.[18]

Due to this multifunction and multiparticipant ecosystem, it has become increasingly difficult to manage the supply chain across various axes, such as detection and protection against counterfeiters, automated payment release upon satisfactory delivery, etc. Furthermore, satisfaction may be declared through various parameters including timely delivery, state of the delivered goods, liability for damages of products along the chain, etc.

For these purposes, therefore, smart contracts are seen as a potentially innovative tool to automatically execute the agreements between the various involved parties. At the most basic level, smart contracts are 'machine readable transaction protocols which create a contract with predetermined terms'.[19] This is the definition first introduced by the American cryptographer Nick Szabo in 1994. In a later paper, Szabo came up with better definition: 'a set of promises, specified in digital form, including protocols within which the parties perform on these promises'.[20] He called these new contracts 'smart' because they are far more functional than the classic inanimate paper-based versions of the same agreement.[21]

RR Manumachu, L Ricci, M Beccuti, L Antonelli, JD Garcia Sanchez and SL Scott (eds), *Euro-Par 2018: Parallel Processing Workshops: Euro-Par 2018 International. Turin, Italy. August 27–28, 2018. Revised Selected Papers* (Berlin, Springer, 2019) 385.

[15] M Swan, 'Blockchain for Business: Next Generation Enterprise Artificial Intelligence Systems' in P Raj and G Chandra Deka (eds), *Advances in Computers. Vol. 111. Blockchain Technology: Platforms, Tools and Use Cases* (London, Academic Press, 2018) 128.

[16] M Corrales Compagnucci, T Kono and S Teramoto, 'Legal Aspects of Decentralized and Platform-Driven Economy' in M Corrales Compagnucci, T Kono, S Teramoto, N Forgo and EPM Vermeulen (eds), *Legal Tech and the New Sharing Economy* (Singapore, Springer, 2020) 3.

[17] LOP, 'Un(b)locking Traceability with Blockchain?', available at www.lop.ai/unblocking-traceabillity-with-blockchain.

[18] SS Perera, MGH Bell and MCJ Bliemer, 'Modelling Supply Chains as Complex Networks for Investigating Resilience: An Improved Methodological Framework', available at www.australasiantransportresearchforum.org.au/sites/default/files/ATRF2015_Resubmission_118.pdf.

[19] K Lauslahti, J Matila, T Hukkinen and T Seppala, 'Expanding the Platform: Smart Contracts as Boundary Resources', in A Smedlund, A. Lindblom and L Mitronen (eds), *Collaborative Value Co-creation in the Platform Economy* (Berlin, Springer, 2019) 66.

[20] N Szabo, 'Smart Contracts: Building Blocks for Digital Markets' (1996), available at www.fon.hum.uva.nl/rob/Courses/InformationInSpeech/CDROM/Literature/LOTwinterschool2006/szabo.best.vwh.net/smart_contracts_2.html.

[21] ibid.

Smart contracts are not necessarily related to the traditional concept of a contract as we know them in the legal field. They are in essence computer programs stored in the blockchain or DLT as a code. As such, their logic and state are shared between the nodes of the network; given the appropriate triggering input (eg, delivery of a good in a supply chain entity), the relevant contract may be executed (eg, transfer of funds from the receiver to the producer). They could also be referred as 'algorithmic contracts' because they are programmed with a set of rules under which the involved parties to that smart contract convey to interact with each other.[22] The main goal of smart contracts is to automate transactions.

Smart contracts are programmed using a generic 'If-Then-Rule'.[23] The logic behind shapes the structure of the programming language. For instance, if A = B, then C = A, else C = D.[24] This also follows the same kind of logical argument applied to 'syllogisms' or a deductive way of reasoning to arrive to a conclusion based on two or more propositions that are presumed to be true.[25]

One of the main challenges of smart contracts is how to translate and embed complex legal issues into computer code as well as document the complex concepts in a supply chain ecosystem and their inter-relations. This is an ongoing debate and bottleneck for software developers and lawyers. We propose that the best approach is through a pseudo code. This is essentially a representation of a program sequence or algorithm that is not intended to be run directly on a machine, but that is used to outline the program without using any specific programming language. Pseudo code is a method to develop a computer software *before* it is coded.[26]

In other words, the pseudo code describes how the software developer would implement an algorithm before deciding the syntactical language details. Fundamentally, it is a generic text containing some keywords that provide a specific set of instructions to code the programming language itself. Then, the pseudo code can be easily translated into a specific language and source code[27] which could be embedded into the architectural design of the blockchain.[28]

In this chapter, we present a set of supply chain semantic concepts that can indicate relations as well as dependencies between supply chain participants,

[22] N Vyas, A Beije and B Krishnamachari, *Blockchain and the Supply Chain: Concepts, Strategies and Practical Applications* (London, Kogan Page, 2019) 57.

[23] M Corrales Compagnucci, P Jurčys and G Kousiouris, 'Smart Contracts and Smart Disclosure: Coding a GDPR Compliance Framework' in M Corrales Compagnucci, M Fenwick and H Haapio (eds), *Legal Tech, Smart Contracts and Blockchain* (Singapore, Springer, 2019).

[24] M Corrales Compagnucci, *Big Data, Databases and 'Ownership' Rights in the Cloud* (Singapore, Springer, 2020) 242.

[25] J Corcoran, 'Ancient Logic and its Modern Interpretation' Proceedings of the Buffalo Symposium on Modernist Interpretations of Ancient Logic', 21–22 April 1972 (New York, Springer, 1974).

[26] See M Corrales Compagnucci, M Fenwick and H Haapio, 'Digital Technologies, Legal Design and the Future of the Legal Profession' in M Corrales Compagnucci, M Fenwick and H Haapio (eds), *Legal Tech, Smart Contracts and Blockchain* (Singapore, Springer, 2019).

[27] D Brooks, *Problem Solving with Fortram 90: For Scientists and Engineers* (Berlin, Springer, 1997) 27.

[28] See M Corrales Compagnucci, P Jurčys and G Kousiouris, 'Smart Contracts and Smart Disclosure: Coding a GDPR Compliance Framework' in M Corrales Compagnucci, M Fenwick and H Haapio (eds), *Legal Tech, Smart Contracts and Blockchain* (Singapore, Springer, 2019).

as well as pseudo code that can detect a number of events affecting the supply chain operation using the AffectUs semantic framework explained below. As such, the provided logic can be used either as part of the triggering mechanism of a blockchain system or potentially even as part of the smart contract logic used during the investigation of fulfilment of the contract.

III. The AffectUs Framework

AffectUs is an extension module to the H2020 TagItSmart (TIS) project. It is essentially a service-oriented system that links to other baseline systems such as the evrythng.com monitoring platform for IoT systems, through which individual items can be tracked and monitored during their journey across a supply chain. The framework monitors the course of the product along the whole supply chain network from producer to consumer (including factories, warehouses, distribution centres, retail stores, etc). If something unexpected happens eg, product delay, it notifies the producer and potential consumer of the product (eg, if a business waiting for the product to be used as raw material). This enables a more sustainable, secure and transparent supply chain.[29]

Possible use cases of such a system include: evidence of creatorship; provenance to authenticate key product information; registering and clearing intellectual property (IP); providing evidence of genuineness and/or quality of the product; establishing and enforcing IP licence agreements or exclusive distribution networks; and making payments in real-time to IP owners. Finally, it may also be used for the detection of counterfeit products, retrieval of stolen goods as well as parallel-imported products.[30]

Based on this end-to-end visibility and authenticity through item-level real-time intelligence and analytics, a number of rules can be applied on top, from simplistic to more complex ones, in order to enable various event detection logics such as counterfeit products, product delay, transit effects on product quality, etc. Consider the situation where a product's near field communication (NFC) tag appears simultaneously in two different locations. NFC is a wireless technology which enables the transfer of data to another NFC device, such as a smart phone. NFC tags contain small microchips and antennas where small datasets are encoded. The actual amount of data varies depending on the NFC chip used.[31] If this data were duplicated, this often implies that a counterfeiter may have removed the NFC tag from the genuine item and reapplied it to the counterfeit product. Smart tags are programmed with relevant information and

[29] See evrythng.com.

[30] B Clark, 'Blockchain and IP Law: A Match Made in Crypto Heaven' *WIPO Magazine* (February 2018), available at www.wipo.int/wipo_magazine/en/2018/01/article_0005.html.

[31] NFC Tags Explained, Seritag (22 April 2020), available at <seritag.com/learn/using-nfc/nfc-tags-explained.

then connected to almost any kind of product, allowing users to read them with a smartphone or another NFC-capable device. However, given that the item is tracked and monitored through its journey from the factory to the retail location, it is easy to detect whether the specific item has found its way to a specific location in a legitimate or not manner. The ability to process such journey data (combined with a semantic annotation of the supply chain structure indicating the involved entities) opens up a number of analytics capabilities and reasoning rationale that may span across various domains, starting from supply chain performance (eg, in terms of delays experienced in each step) to IP issues.

The AffectUs platform can, for example, identify abnormal situations with relation to the state of a supply chain, based on AI models created from historical data regarding transition times from stage to stage and events identified and linked to the chain structure. Imagine that a product manufacturer declares that it is using a specific product as raw material in a supply chain. The system retrieves this product's information and – through an internal logic system and predefined endpoints – detects various exemptions from a normal situation. Similarly, it can apply simple 'If-Then-Else' rules (as the ones mentioned above) through which aspects such as multiple occurrences of the same product ID appearing in different locations, can be communicated to the product manufacturer and other stakeholders in the supply chain.

IV. Legal Requirements in the Supply Chain Context and their Technical Addressing

Modern supply chains are characterised by a globalised network of participants, acting either as suppliers or receivers (or both) of goods along the production line. Different systems and stakeholders need to cooperate and synchronise in order to efficiently and optimally deliver raw materials and manufactured goods. Furthermore, a set of requirements emerge that have to do with either legal, technical or organisational aspects. These requirements are presented below, along with high-level technical descriptions as to how they are addressed in the context of AffectUs and TagItSmart. These would need to be taken under consideration in the smart contract rationale that may be implemented as an extension to the framework (or in any other framework) for more automated supply chain contract management.

1. How does one overcome organisational boundaries between companies needing to exchange internal information, in an effort to achieve higher transparency, early warning and notification along the supply chain?

For a holistic management of the supply chain, information needs to be shared between the IT systems of different companies in an automated manner. This is especially important in cases where real-time monitoring is needed, which implies the integration between the different, proprietary and obviously confidential systems. Which information is shared, for how long, under which circumstances and filters, and with what authorisation/authentication means is critical in order to balance the needs for internal confidentiality and data-sharing.

On the technical side, this can be achieved via well-known standards and processes such as OATH (open authentication[32]). Based on this process, the owner of a resource such as a data collection may enable sharing of that resource (or a specific subset of it based on given criteria) to a specific third party via well-defined interfaces and means of acquisition. Acceptance of the third-party request is validated by the data owner based on the access characteristics (eg, the entity that accesses them, the subset of data the access relates to and reason for access, as well as potential time interval of access validity) and enabled based on that validation.

> This process is implemented in the creation of a new account on LinkedIn. LinkedIn asks if you want to grant access to your Gmail account in order to retrieve your contact list and directly propose the LinkedIn accounts that use these email addresses to replicate your existing contact network on LinkedIn. If you reply positively, LinkedIn redirects you to Gmail, where you need to login (thus validating your identity) and define the level of access you want to give to LinkedIn (eg, the contact list and nothing else). Once you agree, a relevant token is created; based on that token, LinkedIn can then access the contact list (and only that) in order to provide the described functionality.

2. How does one incorporate more practical functional aspects, such as monitoring of the supplies, especially when dealing with sensitive material that require, for example, that the temperature of the product is within certain thresholds?

In many cases of supply chain operation, the nature of the goods dictates that specific handling is enforced during their transit, storage and retail environments. A common example may be food and pharmaceutical materials with temperature, humidity and other values. In many cases the requirements differ in strictness, such as not dropping below or above a certain threshold at all for health safety/effectiveness reasons, not remaining below the threshold for a specific interval or just indicating the correct level of the threshold that can aid in better management of the product (eg, reading the temperature of wine bottles in a refrigerator so that the ones that are currently at the proper serving temperature are selected).

[32] IETF RFC 6749: The OAuth 2.0 Authorization Framework (2012), available at tools.ietf.org/html/rfc6749.

Advances in the Internet of Things (IoT) domain have led to the emergence of smarter barcode tags that are parametre-sensitive (eg, temperature, humidity, luminosity, etc). These tags exploit advances in ink technology that permit a dynamic reflection of the parametre level. At any given point, the printed barcode, which can be read with a common barcode scanner, can change depending on the measured parametre. The type of ink uses means the change can be either permanent or transient. Thus, for example, if a batch of ice-cream or medicine is exposed to temperatures higher than x°C, the barcode is permanently changed so that upon scanning you are warned that the product is no longer safe to consume. In more relaxed cases, such as the wine bottle selection, the ink applies a transient effect indicating the current temperature of the bottle.

3. If the monitoring system shows that the goods are unusable, how can the system help in investigating responsibilities and/or liability for the damage?

During the transportation of a product as part of a supply chain, many different entities may be involved across the chain. For example, transportation services, logistics services, storage services, wholesale and retail points, etc. Thus, when a specific batch travels down the chain, a potential mishandling may occur at any given point in the chain, rendering the goods unusable and causing damages for the involved entities. A major question is assessing when the mishandling took place and which entity (in charge of the product at that time) should be held liable for these damages.

Given that the smart ink functionality is applied as mentioned in the previous step, and that products are scanned when they change organisational boundaries (for example when they are delivered from one entity to the next), this liability may be evident from the bar code alteration caused during the time the good was under the supervision of that entity. To be on the safe side, suitable event detection should also exist in the case one entity forgets or deliberately skips the relevant scanning process at the borders of responsibility. A relevant structure of such an event message appears in the following machine understandable JSON example:

```
'eventConditionName':'stage_change',
'statename': 'skipped',
'Details': {
      'timestamp': value,
      'thing_id': value,
      'prev_stage': value,
      'new_stage': value
      }
}
```

What this message implies is that a situation has been detected in which a product instance (aka a 'thing') has been scanned at a supply chain stage, but this stage is not the one that was anticipated (eg, it is in the stage after the one that is anticipated). So if the thing is originally at stage i, travels to i+1 and then to i+2, it should be scanned at all stages, but based on the available data the scans appear to be only from stages i and i+2. This indicates that a specific scan action has been skipped at stage i+1, which creates ambiguity on the liability for a potential mishandling of the product (has that happened in the i–>i+1 or i+1–>i+2 stage?). Thus, it should be foreseen in the smart contract that if such an event is detected and the product is found damaged at i+2 stage, the entity held liable should be the one that forgot to implement the scan at stage i+1. Furthermore, in order to be fully immutable, this information could be inserted in a relevant blockchain, thus rendering it part of the product history, preventing its reuse or reselling to another party without being aware of the incident.

4. How can the system aid in detecting potential IPR violations with relation to the produced goods, such as counterfeit products?

Counterfeit products exist in many domains and modern supply chains are equipped with some means to mitigate them. Common ways include the existence of a barcode tag that, when scanned (by the potential customer), may indicate whether the specific barcode has been produced by the respective company. However, this does not cater for all cases, given that a counterfeit product may also copy a legitimate barcode ID, thus misleading the potential customer. Therefore, a complete process should be able to document for each item its supposed location, the involved intermediate processing steps, the supplier that purchased it, how many times it has been sold, etc. Thus, a supply chain model that includes documentation of such steps may apply a set of rules in order to investigate whether a product transition from one stage to another is legitimate or whether a relevant alert should be issued for potential IPR violation. This implies definition of the supply chain structure (such as location of the intermediate steps, the order and types of stages eg, at_the factory, at_retail, in_transit, at_customer etc), mapping of the incoming scans to a given stage type (eg, based on location, based on digital signature included during the scan, etc) and checking stage sequence for a given product ID in order to discover anomalies in transitions that should not exist (eg, the same product ID appearing at multiple locations, appearance of a product ID after it has been recycled, etc).

5. How does one incorporate aspects that reach up to the end of the chain (ie, the recycling stage of the product, if applicable) and how does this affect the overall process, given that it may involve issues with relation to data protection of the citizen and may enable violations such as data triangulation?

In many cases such as retail loyalty programs, the purchase of a specific product may be logged in the retailer's IT system along with the purchasing user's ID or other details (including personal information). Thus, if a supply chain system intends to link different stages including retail acquisition point or disposal of the good in a recycle bin, then this potentially personal information could be released to this system, whereas the user has only given permission to the loyalty program owner/retailer to process their data. Thus, in this case special attention must be given by the loyalty program owner/retailer when granting information to the supply chain monitoring system to hide any personal data from the exchange, allowing only (for example) sharing of the product ID purchased, the location from which it was purchased, and the location in which it was recycled. This relates also to the OATH-based method described previously, in which the declared shared resource should follow the requirement posed from the given case.

6. How can the system enforce other rules that have to do with limitations in terms of goods distribution?

Common cases for this include the pharmaceutical sector, in which there are a lot of goods that need a prescription, or the entertainment sector, in which there may be separate arrangements per country of distribution, etc. In this case, and based on the specific domain constraints, suitable rules should be prescribed (eg, in smart contracts) in order to enable the validation for each individual product item release. Thus, a set of rules can be identified based on the aforementioned analysis, which can be applied either as smart contracts, as ontological/semantic constraints, direct if-then-else structures in a programming logic, or a combination of the above.

Initially, the system needs to determine a set of potential states and their sequence, for example 'OutOfProduction'→'In Transit'→'At Retail'→'At End User'→'At Recycle Bin'. The locations for each of the stages can be multiply defined for each stage based on the supply chain structure. Then another set of relationships need to exist that indicate the semantic concepts and their links. These can be later on used to enforce rules associated with the detection of specific events or conditions similar to the ones mentioned above. Even though the details of this set-up go beyond the scope of this chapter and extend into the use of semantics and ontologies in IT systems, the rationale is that these relationships are defined as textual triples of Subject–Predicate–Object which can later on be understood and processed by relevant programming logic. Examples of such relationships that can be determined are portrayed below:

Subject	**Predicate**	**Object**	**Comments**
Product	isAffectedBy	EventType	A product is in general affected by an EventType eg, temperature.
Producer	Produces	Product	Who produces a product?

(continued)

(Continued)

Subject	Predicate	Object	Comments
Consumer	consumes	Product	Entity that consumes a product. Populated indirectly through the incorporation of the dependent input product as part of the supply chain structure.
Handler	handles	Product	The entity that is responsible for the handling of a product at a given stage. Can be the owner or (eg) a transport company.
SupplyChain	hasStage	StageEnumeration	Supply Chain (as concept, or draft for a new 'Instance') has Stages.
ChainStage	isOfType	StageEnumeration	Out of production, in transit, at retail, etc. Used in the illegal state detection event.
Chainstage	hasLocation	Location	Location that conforms to the Geo-JSON standard description. Necessary to map incoming scan data to stage type.
ChainStage	hasPrevious	ChainStage	Necessary to indicate the proper sequence of stages (dictated also by the need for out of sequence skipped scans detection).
ChainStage	hasNext	ChainStage	Same as above.
Chainstage	hasInputs	Product	ChainStage can have one or many products as inputs. Necessary for inferring usage and dependencies.
Chainstage	hasOutputs	Product	ChainStage can have one or many products as outputs. Outputs may be different from inputs.

(continued)

(Continued)

Subject	**Predicate**	**Object**	**Comments**
Domain-specific triples (pharmaceutical domain example)			
Product	needs	PrescriptionInstance	Definition of the need to have a prescription for a given (pharmaceutical) product.
PrescriptionInstance	hasOwner	Consumer	Owner of the specific prescription (implies that prior to release by the retailer, a check needs to be performed on whether the specific person has an active prescription for the specific product).
PrescriptionInstance	isActive	True/False	This is to indicate whether the specific prescription is still active (true). Set to false if it has already been served. Other options can be included as well, such as prescription duration (if applicable) etc.

For each of the aforementioned abstract relationship types, a number of individuals is then created during program execution exploiting the real time data in order to concretise a specific relationship, eg, 'consumer with ID 5 consumes product with ID 2'.

The overall system sequence resembles the following form:

1. Get scanned data.
2. Pass scanned information through semantic structure and elevate to the necessary concept level (eg, which stage the item is currently, what entity consumes this item etc.).
3. Apply programming logic to detect events (rules in OWL or if-then-else cases or smart contract constructs).

In the following, examples relevant to the questions posed in the previous paragraphs of such if-then-else rules are given. The examples could serve as triggering inputs or smart contract clauses. Lines starting with '//' are comment lines, indicating the rationale of the rule.

//If no violation is detected in the scan (eg, in terms of temperature thresholds), and the stage //is not the final retail one (that should enable return of product), the next scanned stage can //only be the next in the supply chain, assuming that a contract has already be signed for its //delivery. Therefore a transition to i–1 should be considered as illegal.

Rule 1: if in stage i and stage i is not at consumer and scan is ok

next scanned stage may only be stage i+1

//If the product is at retail, then product return should be foreseen, therefore next scan could //be of either stage i+1 or i–1

Rule 2: if in stage i and stage i is at consumer

next stage may be i+1 (recycling) or i–1 (in case of returned product)

//If the product is scanned at the reception point but it has been compromised (eg, exposed //to higher temperatures than appropriate) the receiver should not accept the delivery and //should notify the product owner for the product state.

Rule 3: if scan indicates threshold violation and actor is not current handler

refuse to accept delivery

notify product owner

//If a notification comes at the product owner based on the previous rule, a process should //be initiated against the handler of the product at the stage after which the violation has been //detected

Rule 4: if scan indicates threshold violation and actor is product owner

start liability claim against handler

//The skip event is created when a product is bypassing, or skipping, one or more stages

Rule 5: if in stage i and previous stage was i–2 or less

alert for skipped scan

//'counterfeit' events can be if the same product/thing ID appears in multiple stages (eg, //already recycled but also available for sale) or at multiple locations of the same stage (eg, //multiple locations of the same retailer)

Rule 6: If product ID appears in more than one stages at the same time

Alert for potential counterfeit

Rule 7: If product ID appears in more than one locations of the same stage at the same time

Alert for potential counterfeit

This rule list is obviously not exhaustive, and based on one's needs and available semantic concepts, it can be extended in further useful cases of supply chain management and serve as input for a smart contract implementation.

V. Conclusion

Blockchain and other DLT have already found its applications in areas that go beyond the Fintech sector. They are already being used to improve product traceability and provenance throughout the extended supply chain. The modern supply chain is a complex network of partners and suppliers dispersed across the world, with multiple different entities across the path, acting in turns as consumers and then producers of goods in order to complete the chain. Due to this multirole and multiparticipant ecosystem, it has become increasingly difficult to manage the supply chain across various axes, such as detection and protection against counterfeiters, automated payment release upon satisfactory delivery, etc. Furthermore, satisfaction may be declared through various parametres including timely delivery, state of the delivered goods, who is responsible for damages incurred upon the products along the chain, etc.

This chapter elaborated a relevant pseudo code that may be used as a requirement as well as initial implementation sketch for the creation of a smart contract based on the AffectUs:TagItSmart semantic framework, that incorporates the aforementioned concepts in a machine-understandable manner, including semantic aspects of the supply chain roles and actions. AffectUs:TagItSmart is a service-oriented system that links to other baseline systems (such as product monitoring platforms eg, evrythng.com) and correlates information between stakeholders.

To this end, a number of such relationships have been described in order to model actors and roles in the chain, that can be populated by specific instances during runtime and based on the available data. The system retrieves the semantic declarations and uses an internal logic to detect various exceptions from a normal situation (such products ID in two different places which is an indication of counterfeit existence, delay in product delivery, etc), while exploiting smart tags indications with relation to quality aspects of the delivered goods (such as maximum encountered temperature along the product's journey). When detecting such events, relevant rules have been defined that can be used to notify affected stakeholders (producers and consumers of the product, handlers, etc). Thus, they can serve as a direct input towards efforts that need to create smart contracts or define the events upon which these contracts will be calculated and validated.

8

The Historical Significance of Blockchain and Smart Contracts

MARK FENWICK AND ERIK PM VERMEULEN

I. Introduction

In some ways, it is unfortunate that smart contracts – self-executed agreements in the form of computer code hosted on a blockchain – are labelled 'contracts'. Observers of smart contracts – particularly lawyers – tend to pick up on this term and focus on how such technologies are often not 'really' contracts. At least, they are not always contracts, in the strict sense of legally enforceable agreements comprising a predefined set of elements – in Anglo-American law, for example, an intention to create legal relations, offer and acceptance, consideration, legality and capacity.

Whilst the observation that a smart contract is not a legal contract is valid in many cases, it is often made as a part of a larger argument to defend the continued relevance of contract law and diminish the significance of these technologies. Here, we won't examine the issue of the continued relevance of contract law as a means of structuring commercial transactions – this claim seems obvious and uncontroversial. However, the suggestion or implication that smart contracts and blockchain, more generally, will not play an important role in transforming business operations is more contentious. Comparing smart contracts to traditional contractual arrangements often appears to be a strategy to diminish the significance of these technologies and to obscure their transformative potential. At least, this seems to be a likely effect, even if it is not intended.

In this chapter, we suggest that a comparison between 'smart' and 'old world' contracts is an incomplete approach that obscures the broader significance and disruptive potential of these technologies. Instead, we argue that the historical significance and future value of smart contracts should not be judged by reference to contract law, but – instead – we should acknowledge the diverse functions that such technologies might play across diverse fields of business and the law. This chapter therefore locates the emergence of smart contracts and blockchain, more generally, in the context of ongoing technology-driven changes in business, in particular a shift towards more decentralised business forms that leverage digital technologies in their organization, operations, and corporate governance.

The closed, hierarchical modern corporation, which was so successful in an earlier phase of industrial capitalism, is less suited to the demands of an innovation-driven digital age and flatter, more open and distributed forms of organising business have emerged. This chapter suggests that the emergence and proliferation of smart contracts can be located in this broader historical shift and that, by doing so, it can help us better understand the impact and significance of these technologies.

The chapter is structured around two substantive sections. Section II examines the disruption of hierarchical organisational forms (particularly the modern corporation) by digital technologies and examines the emergence of blockchain and smart contracts in the context of this narrative. Section III looks more specifically at some current use cases of smart contracts that, for the moment, at least, might be considered marginal, but which, nevertheless, have the potential to disrupt traditional business forms. Specifically, we examine recent attempts to reimagine the company (decentralised autonomous organisations; DAOs) and financial services (decentralised finance; 'DeFi').

II. 'Decentralisation is Coming!'

For the last three centuries, economic and political life has been dominated by centralised, hierarchical organisations.[1] Such organisations are characterised by a central source of authority; a formal hierarchy with clearly defined powers and roles; and, standardised operational systems and procedures dictated by that central authority/hierarchy. This type of organisation has exerted an enormous influence on modern culture and society.[2]

In a business context, centralised, hierarchical organisational forms have been central to the emergence and global expansion of capitalism.[3] Corporations are the most prominent example of such structures, and the advent and proliferation of the corporate form have been a defining feature of modern

[1] A Aneesh, 'Technologically Coded Authority: The Post-Industrial Decline in Bureaucratic Hierarchies' stanford.edu, available at web.stanford.edu/class/sts175/NewFiles/Algocratic%20 Governance.pdf.

[2] The most influential account of this organisational form and its role in the emergence of capitalism is that of Max Weber, See, eg M Weber, *Max Weber on Law in Economy and Society* (Cambridge, MA, Harvard University Press, 1954).

[3] J Bakan, *The Corporation* (New York, Free Press, 2001) 5 ('Over the last 150 years the corporation has risen from relative obscurity to become the world's dominant economic institution'); J Micklethwait and A Wooldridge, *The Company: A Short History of a Revolutionary Idea* (London, Weidenfeld, 2005) 1 ('The most important institution in the world is the company; the basis of the prosperity of the West and the best hoped for the future of the rest of world').

economic development.[4] Recall the rapid growth of such corporate structures during the rise of mass production in the Industrial Revolution.

Moreover, other types of centralised, hierarchical organisation (banks and other financial service providers, for instance) played a crucial role as facilitators (or intermediaries), allowing third parties to engage in various business transactions. Finally, highly centralised nation-states provided the supporting infrastructure – both political and legal – that allowed such businesses to operate effectively.

As such, centralised, hierarchical organisational structures supported by the appropriate formal processes and procedures have been hugely influential in 'getting things done' efficiently and creating and maintaining trust in the modern world.[5]

Moreover, previous technological revolutions led to a concentration of such organisations, as society adapted to the uncertain meaning, effects, and risks of technological advances by pooling (ie, centralising) authority. Regulatory models – company law and corporate governance, for example – have been designed to support and sustain such closed, hierarchical forms of business organisation.[6]

In recent decades, however, an interconnected series of technological innovations – specifically those associated with the ongoing Digital Revolution – have reshaped social life and disrupted centralised organisational form.[7] Consider the following developments: cheaper, smaller and more robust digital hardware (initially PCs but, more recently, smartphones); global communication networks and mass connectivity (the Internet)); and, cloud-based storage of Big Data and automated algorithms.

These overlapping developments provide the foundation and necessary infrastructure for an ongoing process of 'digitalisation' in which technology disrupts every aspect of our lives.[8] The economic, cultural and social impact of these changes is so significant that it makes sense to speak of a 'digital transformation'

[4] See, eg SR Brown, *Merchant Kings: When Companies Ruled the World, 1600–1900* (London, Macmillan, 2010); CA Cooke, *Corporation, Trust and Company: An Essay in Legal History* (Manchester, Manchester University Press, 1950); O Gelderblom, *Cities of Commerce: The Institutional Foundations of International Trade in the Low Countries, 1250–1650* (Princeton, Princeton University Press, 2013).

[5] DR Dalton, WD Todor, MJ Spendolini, GJ Fielding and LW Porter, 'Organization Structure and Performance: A Critical Review' (1980) 5 *Academy of Management Review* 49.

[6] See generally T Hadden, *Company Law and Capitalism* (London, Weidenfeld & Nicolson, 1972); H Wells (ed), *Research Handbook on the History of Corporate and Company Law* (London, Edward Elgar, 2018).

[7] A Horlacher, P Klarner and T Hess, 'Crossing Boundaries: Organization Design Parameters Surrounding CDOs and their Digital Transformation Activities' Americas Conference on Information Systems, available at pdfs.semanticscholar.org/a623/ff3e690caea7fb6d5a014bd59220470f4915.pdf.

[8] See, eg S Denning, 'Why Mindset is Driving the Age of Agile' *Forbes* (20 August 2018), available at www.forbes.com/sites/stevedenning/2018/08/20/why-mindset-is-driving-the-age-of-agile/#1dc209d35631; I-Scoop, 'Digital Transformation: Online Guide to Digital Business Transformation' I-Scoop.eu, available at www.i-scoop.eu/digital-transformation; B Bosworth, 'The Three P's of Digital Transformation' *Forbes* (26 April 2018), available at www.forbes.com/sites/forbestechcouncil/2018/04/26/the-three-ps-of-digital-transformation/#440d7cd76f00.

or 'revolution'. And multiple emerging technologies, such as robots/automation, artificial intelligence, machine learning, the Internet of Things, nanotechnologies, as well as blockchain, mean that such revolution has become an ongoing feature of our economic and social life.

A particularly significant effect of these global digital technologies has been to disrupt the 'old world' of centralised, hierarchical organisations. Technology is currently introducing and driving a shift in the practices and thinking of our society.[9] In particular, the limitations of a centralised, hierarchical and 'proceduralised' world are becoming more apparent.[10] Most obviously, such organisations are slow to adapt to a fast-changing reality and are losing public trust. New digital technologies are driving the emergence of 'flatter', more decentralised forms of social organisation. This change can be felt across society, but particularly in a business context.

The implications for regulators and other policymakers seem apparent. A tension or 'disconnect' is emerging between traditional regulatory models and contemporary business organisations. It, therefore, seems appropriate to deepen our understanding of these new organisational forms as a precondition to designing new regulatory models more fitting to the realities of a digital age.

By way of an example of this disruption, consider platforms. An important adaptation to the digital transformation has been the emergence of 'platform' business models.[11] This term is usually associated with different types of tech companies, ie, companies that operate a social platform (Facebook, Instagram), an exchange platform (Amazon, Airbnb, Uber), a content platform (YouTube, Medium, Netflix), a software' platform (GE's Predix), or even a blockchain platform for smart contracts (Ethereum, EOS). The emergence of these new platforms and services has been one of the significant economic and business developments of the last two decades.[12]

In each of the above examples, the platform creates value by facilitating exchanges between two different but interdependent groups (eg, groups of friends (Facebook, Instagram), content providers and consumers (YouTube, Medium, Netflix) or service providers and users (Amazon, Airbnb, Uber). The platforms leverage networked digital technologies to promote economic exchange, the transfer of information or to connect people. The platform facilitates interactions

[9] S Taut, 'Why Culture Change is Essential for Digital Transformation' *Digitalist* (9 January 2017), available at www.digitalistmag.com/future-of-work/2017/01/09/culture-change-is-essential-for-digital-transformation-04824251.

[10] C Dixon, 'Why Decentralization Matters' *Medium: One Zero* (19 February 2018), available at medium.com/s/story/why-decentralization-matters-5e3f79f7638e; EPM Vermeulen, 'Blockchain Platforms Will Make Us Happier' *Medium: Hackernoon* (21 January 2018), available at hackernoon.com/blockchain-platforms-will-make-us-happier-8e460eb2ce74.

[11] J Herrman, 'Platform Companies Are Becoming More Powerful: But What Exactly Do They Want?' *New York Times: Sunday Magazine* (25 March 2017) 1; N Srnicek, *Platform Capitalism* (Cambridge, Polity Press, 2017).

[12] 'Fuel of the Future: Data is Giving Rise to a New Economy' *The Economist* (6 May 2017), available at www.economist.com/briefing/2017/05/06/data-is-giving-rise-to-a-new-economy.

between creators and extractors of value. It then generates profit for itself, ie, the owner-shareholders of the platform.[13]

The popularity of the platform business model has grown in recent years as interconnected technologies – the Internet, code-based algorithms, and PCs and smartphones – have proliferated. These technologies have advanced the platform business model by allowing the fast, large-scale exchange of products and information utilising decentralised networks. This creates a global ecosystem that encourages registered users and content consumers to add more value to the platform by repeatedly creating more content, which will, in turn, attract additional content creators and consumers (ie, platforms benefit enormously from 'network effects').[14] Such platforms are powered by algorithms or predefined formulas used to 'matchmake' individuals or consumers with service providers/products.

Crucially, the adoption of the platform model now extends well beyond the technology sector. Many non-technology firms can see the benefits of reorganising as platforms. Traditional retailers, for example, are shifting their distribution channels for selling products from 'stores' to online platforms.[15]

The problem, however, is that the most prominent platforms – companies like Amazon, Apple, Facebook and Google – promised a more open, decentralised and less formal style of business organisation, but have, in recent years, disappointed expectations. A youthful, disruptive image was a big factor in their early growth and success. Compared to the corporate giants of an industrial age, the new tech firms were fresh and different. However, as these firms scaled into some of the largest businesses in history, they have become shrouded in controversy.[16] The anti-corporate backlash against the traditional corporate giants has extended to the technology sector (so-called 'techlash').[17]

In part, this is because, as platforms scale – and significantly when they 'go global' – they came to rely on hierarchical organisational structures associated with corporations. Furthermore, to sustain their continued growth, many technology firms went public, exposing them to the short-term (quarterly) financial

[13] C Codagnone and B Martens, 'Scoping the Sharing Economy: Origins, Definitions, Impact and Regulatory Issues' (2016) Institute for Prospective Technological Studies Digital Economy, Working Paper 2016/01, 1.

[14] Price Waterhouse Coopers, 'The Sharing Economy', available at www.pwc.fr/fr/assets/files/pdf/2015/05/pwc_etude_sharing_economy.pdf.

[15] D Rigby, 'The Future of Shopping' *Harvard Business Review* (December 2011), available at hbr.org/2011/12/the-future-of-shopping; M Walsh, 'The Future of E-Commerce: Bricks and Mortar' *The Guardian* (30 January 2016), available at www.theguardian.com/business/2016/jan/30/future-of-e-commerce-bricks-and-mortar.

[16] See, eg, S Galloway, *The Four: The Hidden DNA of Amazon, Apple, Facebook, and Google* (New York, Penguin, 2018); S Zuboff, *Surveillance Capitalism: The Fight for a Human Future at the New Frontier of Power* (Cambridge, MA, Harvard University Press, 2018).

[17] See, eg, J Doward, 'The Big Tech Backlash' *The Guardian* (28 January 2018), available at www.theguardian.com/technology/2018/jan/28/tech-backlash-facebook-google-fake-news-business-monopoly-regulation; K Paul, 'A Brutal Year: How the 'Techlash' Caught up with Facebook, Google and Amazon' *The Guardian* (28 December 2019), available at www.theguardian.com/technology/2019/dec/28/tech-industry-year-in-review-facebook-google-amazon.

pressures associated with a publicly listed corporation. Platforms have, therefore, tended to become more centralised and more 'corporate' and have experienced the same kind of difficulties associated with incumbent corporations.[18] They have struggled to maintain their initial promise, and platforms that were once disruptive have lost much of their initial appeal. And it is hard to ignore the problems created by platforms. There are too many recent examples of well-known platforms 'forgetting' the importance of improving people's lives and instead focusing on the aggressive advancement of their own narrow interests.

However, despite these difficulties, we should also recognise that there is more to platform companies than just using new technologies to facilitate transactions, exchange information, or to connect people. There is another valuable lesson to be learned from the emergence and success of this type of company. At their best – typically in an earlier phase of the corporate lifecycle – what the most successful of these companies were also able to do is organize their 'internal' operations to facilitate collaboration amongst multiple stakeholders to deliver constant innovation in the functionality of the platform and related products and services.[19] These various stakeholders include but are not limited to, managers, employees and investors, but also (and crucially) consumers, developers, content creators, other companies (both large and small), non-profits, educational institutions, governments, etc.[20] Such companies were able to leverage stakeholders' input and feedback to improve the user experience and engagement with the platform and its products, services, and other solutions.[21] In other research, we refer to this as an 'ecosystem' model of organisation and governance.[22] Such ecosystems are characterised by the following features:

- Leveraging the unique characteristics of software technologies (eg, low marginal costs) to deliver a powerful, frictionless experience to end users.
- Adopting a flatter, fluid and more inclusive style of organisation built around networks of unbundled, high-performance, creative teams in which job roles and functions are evolving dynamically in response to the evolving business needs of the firm.
- Embracing a more open, transparent approach to communication and information management relies on new computer-mediated communications, such as social media.

[18] See generally M Fenwick and EPM Vermeulen, 'The End of the Corporation' (2019) European Corporate Governance Institute – Law Working Paper, available at ssrn.com/abstract=3472601.

[19] NB Hack, 'Improving Stakeholder Engagement Increases Productivity, Profit and Sustainability' *Huffington Post* (30 May 2019), available at www.huffingtonpost.com/nadine-b-hack/stakeholder-engagement_b_1556070.html.

[20] J Fritz, 'What is a Stakeholder for a Non-Profit?' *The Balance* (1 March 2017), available at www.thebalancesmb.com/stakeholder-2502118.

[21] Deloitte, *The Digital Workplace: Think, Share, Do*, available at www2.deloitte.com/content/dam/Deloitte/mx/Documents/human-capital/The_digital_workplace.pdf.

[22] See generally M Fenwick and EPM Vermeulen, 'The New Firm' (2015) 16 *European Business Organization Law Review* 595.

- Implementing a new style of digital leadership that focuses on creating an environment that facilitates creativity rather than an exclusive focus on supervising compliance or managing legal risk.
- Utilising open collaboration with all stakeholders, especially multiple external partners, to feed the requirement of continually innovating – what we would term partnering-for-innovation.

This is another crucial lesson to be taken from many technology firms – many of these companies disrupted existing business models by eliminating and replacing traditional intermediaries. These companies facilitated more direct 'peer-to-peer' transactions between service providers/creators/producers, on the one hand, and the consumers, on the other.

In this type of organisation, governance is less about establishing hierarchy and asserting control. Instead, the focus is on creating a flat, open and inclusive organisational environment that leverages the talents of all stakeholders in that company's network.[23] As such, new style firms built around the idea of delivering constant innovation via an open and inclusive process of collaboration and co-creation. By organising for innovation in this way, such firms break from the clearly defined, fixed hierarchies, static roles and authorised procedures of traditional business organisations.[24]

Of course, not all firms maintain this approach as they scale. However, it does point to a different way of organising and operating a business that many people find attractive. It is against the background of these changes that blockchain and related technologies, such as smart contracts, should be understood.

To understand blockchain, it makes sense to first consider the Internet.[25] The Internet enabled a free, fast and global exchange of information and ideas. The blockchain adds another dimension by making it possible to transfer and exchange value and assets without the involvement of traditional (centralised and authoritative) intermediaries. Blockchain technology achieves this by storing personal and other information in a decentralised, accessible and secure online environment. Stated simply, a blockchain is a shared and distributed digital ledger or database that maintains a continuously growing list of blocks.[26] A block can contain a record of transactions involving digital assets but could also include facts or other

[23] GF Corporaal and V Lehdonvirta, 'Platform Sourcing: How Fortune 500 Firms Are Adopting Online Freelancing' (August 2017) *Oxford Internet Institute*, available at www.oii.ox.ac.uk/publications/platform-sourcing.pdf; M Janakiraman, 'Inclusive Leadership – Critical for Competitive Advantage' *Mercer: Insights*, available at mobilityexchange.mercer.com/Insights/article/Inclusive-Leadership-Critical-for-Competitive-Advantage.

[24] M Coletti, P Landoni and R Cagliano, 'Governance of Small Consortia for Innovation: A Multiple-Case Study Analysis' (2018) 1 *International Journal of Competitiveness* 238.

[25] See generally N Mehta, A Agashe and P Detroja, *Blockchain Bubble or Revolution: The Present and Future of Blockchain and Cryptocurrencies* (Seattle, Paravane Ventures, 2019).

[26] EPM Vermeulen, '3 Reasons Why the Blockchain Revolution is (Finally) Becoming a Reality' *Medium: Startup Grind* (5 May 2017), available at medium.com/startup-grind/3-reasons-why-the-blockchain-revolution-is-finally-becoming-a-reality-63bdd90c89e2.

information. Once the record is verified and validated, a block is added to the chain with previous records in linear and chronological order.

What makes the blockchain such a novel technology is that the ledger or database is distributed to a countless number of participants ('nodes') around the world in public peer-to-peer networks (similar to the Internet) or private (or 'permissioned') peer-to-peer networks (similar to an intranet).[27] It is this decentralised character of the blockchain that makes it so potentially disruptive. Participants hosting a copy of the blockchain can be individuals or organisations (and even things). The only condition is that they have a smartphone or Internet connection. Everybody with a smartphone can create a real digital ID and interact with other people in the blockchain network.

Blockchain technology thus enables and facilitates access to finance, insurance services, stock markets, etc. In this respect, it has the potential to promote financial inclusion and end the social exclusion surrounding the provision of financial services. Peer-to-peer transactions are possible because the technology uses a distributed consensus model where the network nodes verify, validate and audit transactions before and after they are executed. This is often safer than a traditional model in which transactions can only be performed by or through a third-party (and trusted) intermediary, such as a bank, judiciary or notary.

At the heart of the blockchain technology, therefore, is a consensus mechanism. A consensus mechanism enables everyone on the network to agree, or reach a consensus, on a shared computational record. In the Bitcoin network, for example, the shared computational record is the creation of a universally accepted list of digital currency transactions between users. This facilitates a traceable record, or ledger, of individual holders.

Network connectivity is vital because it allows multiple identical copies of the blockchain to be available simultaneously across the network. This makes it practically impossible to alter or erase information in the blockchain. The use of cryptographic hashes makes tampering with blockchain records even more difficult, if not impossible. Cryptographic hashes comprise complex algorithms. The result of this combination of technologies is that even a minuscule change to the blockchain will result in a different hash value, making manipulation instantly and readily detectable by other participants.

Digital signatures help establish the identity and authenticity of the parties involved in the transaction. These security measures make blockchain validation technologies more transparent and less prone to error and corruption. Even if they are not 100% secure, they are indeed more reliable than existing methods of verifying and validating transactions via third-party intermediaries.[28]

[27] S Gupta, 'Blockchain: The Next Big Revolution' *Medium: Blockchain Musings* (3 July 2017), available at medium.com/blockchain-musings/blockchain-the-next-big-revolution-dabb748d33fa.

[28] M White, J Killmeyer and B Chew, 'Will Blockchain Transform the Public Sector?' *Deloitte Insights* (11 September 2017), available at www2.deloitte.com/insights/us/en/industry/public-sector/understanding-basics-of-blockchain-in-government.html.

In short, blockchain technology creates an independent and transparent platform for establishing truth and building trust. Intermediaries, bureaucracy and old-fashioned procedures are replaced by code, connectivity and the crowd. The technology increases openness and speed, while at the same time significantly reducing costs.

But perhaps the most significant feature of blockchain is that it is so adaptable. There are multiple possible applications relevant to a business context. Most obviously, blockchain can be used to provide new methods of processing digital transactions (ie, e-commerce or financial services). But blockchain can also be used for cryptocurrencies (eg, Bitcoin), records management (eg, real estate, corporate or medical records), 'evoting' and identity management (IAM). It is for this reason that blockchain technology has been mentioned as one of the most significant disruptive technological innovations since the emergence of the Internet.[29]

The use cases of blockchain expand when combined with so-called smart contracts. In this context, a smart contract refers to a computer program code or protocol that automates the verification, execution, and enforcement of certain terms and conditions of a contractual arrangement.[30] This term was first introduced by Nick Szabo, a computer scientist and legal theorist, in 1994.[31] A smart contract is a computer program code that enables the verification, execution and enforcement of specific terms and conditions of a contractual arrangement. An often-cited example is the purchase of music through Apple's iTunes platform. A computer code ensures that the purchaser can only listen to the music file on a limited number of Apple devices.

A smart contract could also be an essential part of, for instance, a car loan. If the borrower misses a payment (tracked via a blockchain-like technology), the contract will not allow the use and operation of the car (enforced via networked technologies that disable the car automatically, rather than a 'repo man' physically depriving a driver of access to their car).[32] Such smart contracts will become more prevalent in the growing world of the Internet of Things. As more devices are connected to each other, the more smart contracts will be used to execute and enforce legal transactions.

Nevertheless, many still consider blockchain and smart contracts to be a fad or hype.[33] According to this more sceptical view, the hype has been fuelled by

[29] M Hiesboeck, 'Blockchain is the Most Disruptive Invention Since the Internet Itself: Not Just in Finance' *Digital Doughnut* (6 April 2016), available at www.digitaldoughnut.com/articles/2016/april/blockchain-is-the-most-disruptive-invention-since.

[30] TI Kiviat 'Beyond Bitcoin: Issues in Regulating Blockchain Transactions' (2015) 65 *Duke Law Journal* 568.

[31] B Ryder, 'Not-So-Clever Contracts' *The Economist* (30 July 2016), available at www.economist.com/business/2016/07/28/not-so-clever-contracts.

[32] F Küster, 'What Are Smart Contracts in Blockchain Technology' *Captain Altcoin* (14 July 2017), available at captainaltcoin.com/blockchain-smart-contracts.

[33] G Volpicelli, 'Does Blockchain Offer Hype or Hope?' *The Guardian* (10 March 2018), available at www.theguardian.com/technology/2018/mar/10/blockchain-music-imogen-heap-provenance-finance-voting-amir-taaki.

tech firms, particularly in the area of cryptocurrency. Such firms often have over-promised and under-delivered, feeding doubts about the underlying technology of blockchain.

For sure, smart contracts are still a young and developing technology and challenges do remain before they can be deployed on a large scale. Blockchains still have significant technical, operational and scaling shortcomings.[34] Considering the perspective of mathematicians on these issues is interesting. They will often point to the fact that there is still a lack of complete decentralisation in most current applications of blockchain. For instance, the traditional mechanism for validating and verifying a new block of transactions – eg, Bitcoin's proof of work protocol – has led to 'mining pools' as a result of economies of scale and unbalanced reward structures.[35] Also, the anonymity in blockchain organisations means that they are prone to Sybil attacks or 51% attacks. There are also many examples in which the anonymity (and autonomy) has led to hacks. Remember that in a truly decentralised system, the code is the law. This means that any mistakes (stolen/lost passwords, programming bugs, etc) are permanent and irrevocable.

Another important challenge is cybersecurity; supporters of blockchain claim that it is secure by design, but the technology hasn't been adopted widely enough yet for it to be severely tested.[36] Several hacking attacks against digital currencies in recent years underscore such security concerns. Moreover, the use of cryptocurrencies by criminal organisations has damaged the credibility of the underlying technology.

And then there are the transaction costs of shifting to the new technology, which is continually evolving, and which are also high. Not to mention the many technical challenges involved in integrating blockchain databases with existing systems. Recall the car loan contract example discussed above and the need for a sophisticated and reliable interface between the ledger recording repayments and the car software systems that, under certain circumstances (non-payment) will shut down the vehicle.

Finally, there is a great deal of regulatory uncertainty surrounding blockchain and smart contracts, especially in the financial services sector. Legal frameworks globally will have to change to adapt to the growing use of this type of new technology.

Nevertheless, there are signs that we are close to a tipping point regarding the adoption of blockchain and its impact. There is a widespread proliferation of

[34] See, eg P Kasireddy, 'Blockchains Don't Scale. Not Today, at least, But There's Hope' *Medium: Hackernoon* (23 August 2017), available at hackernoon.com/blockchains-dont-scale-not-today-at-least-but-there-s-hope-2cb43946551a; N Singh, 'Every Disadvantage Has Its Advantage: Reviewing Blockchain' *Medium: Hackernoon* (25 February 2018), available at hackernoon.com/every-disadvantage-has-its-advantage-reviewing-blockchain-1965e3462ba4; N Bauerle, 'What Are Blockchain's Issues and Limitations?' *Coindesk*, available at www.coindesk.com/information/blockchains-issues-limitations.

[35] EPM Vermeulen, 'Is There a Future for Blockchain?' *Medium: Hackernoon* (13 May 2018), available at hackernoon.com/is-there-a-future-for-blockchain-dbc86f205d6f.

[36] N Lohade, 'Dubai Aims to Be a City Built on Blockchain' *Wall Street Journal* (24 April 2017), available at www.wsj.com/articles/dubai-aims-to-be-a-city-built-on-blockchain-1493086080.

blockchain applications and initiatives that are considering blockchain. The fact that so many 'old world' organisations are exploring possible uses of blockchains and smart contracts suggests that it not all hype.[37]

A problem with 'old world' centralised, hierarchical organisations is that decision-making processes can become slow, cumbersome and costly.[38] In a fast-paced, consumer-driven economy, this can become a problem for incumbents.[39] The experience with platforms shows how peer-to-peer technologies might deliver a more satisfying consumer experience than traditional firms. This goes beyond the convenience of Wikipedia, Uber or Airbnb when compared to the products or services of traditional encyclopaedia publishers, taxi companies or hotel operators. In a legal context, for instance, eCourt, an online private court, aims to replace traditional legal proceedings.[40] Despite the uncertainties of such new systems, many people are attracted by the speed, convenience and user-friendliness of such decentralised systems.[41] The values of a digital age are pushing consumers towards the more agile solutions offered by younger, flatter organisations that embrace decentralisation.

A similar set of issues affect potential employees as they consider whether to work for old or new-style organisations. The younger Millennial generation view centralisation as a threat to personal autonomy, choice and happiness.[42] An overly proceduralised society drags people down, kills creativity and leads to exhaustion and burn-out. The younger generation intuitively understands that there is little room for manoeuvre in a highly centralised world and find that world frustrating and unsatisfactory. Moreover, hierarchies – which have never been particularly attractive to the younger generation – become even more bothersome amongst a generation losing trust in traditional organisations.[43] As such, a decentralised organisational culture built around blockchain and related technologies potentially creates more opportunities for everyone for personal expression, fulfilment, and – ultimately – happiness. There is greater recognition that hierarchical structures kill open and honest discussion, leading to either indifference, apathy or

[37] G Hileman and M Rauchs, 'Global Blockchain Benchmarking Study' (2017) Cambridge Centre for Alternative Finance, available at www.ey.com/Publication/vwLUAssets/ey-global-blockchain-benchmarking-study-2017/$File/ey-global-blockchain-benchmarking-study-2017.pdf.

[38] TW Malone, 'Bringing the Market Inside' *Harvard Business Review* (April 2004), available at hbr.org/2004/04/bringing-the-market-inside.

[39] M Jaconi, 'The 'On-Demand Economy' Is Revolutionizing Consumer Behavior' *Business Insider* (13 July 2014), available at www.businessinsider.com/the-on-demand-economy-2014-7.

[40] P Causton, 'The E-Court Service – a Vision of the Future' The Law Society (29 January 2015), available at www.lawsociety.org.uk/communities/solicitor-judges-division/articles/e-court-service.

[41] EPM Vermeulen, 'How to Organize Now for Success Tomorrow … Winning Companies Embrace a "Tech-driven" Corporate Culture' *Medium: Best Company* (20 February 2017), available at medium.com/bestcompany/how-to-organize-now-for-success-tomorrow-winning-companies-embrace-a-tech-driven-corporate-e3dd08c9e8f.

[42] M Burke, 'An Uncertain Future: Along with Exciting New Possibilities, Millennials Face a Whole Different Set of Obstacles' (2017) 54, *F&D* 4.

[43] See generally Pew Research Center, 'Millennials in Adulthood: Detached from Institutions, Networked with Friends', available at assets.pewresearch.org/wp-content/uploads/sites/3/2014/03/2014-03-07_generations-report-version-for-web.pdf.

exhaustion. Plus, hierarchies seem to go hand in hand with formal procedures. An over-reliance on procedure – especially procedures designed and imposed from above – takes the joy out of any activity.

The idea that personal happiness, freedom and expression can better thrive in a more decentralised world seems to have taken hold. Therefore, many people are intrigued and captured by blockchain platforms.

III. Disruptive Use Cases

The emergence of technology-driven disruption across all sectors of the economy is without precedent in the history of modern capitalism. In the past, new competitors were essentially forced to adopt the same business models and organisational and governance structures as incumbents (albeit on a smaller scale). This was extremely difficult, given the additional resources and other advantages (eg, a network of established connections and know-how) possessed by incumbents. New companies faced enormous challenges in being competitive under such conditions. The game was rigged against anyone looking to challenge the status quo.

Things are different now. Technology has facilitated a different sort of competition by a different type of firm. The structural benefits of large and closed organisations are significantly reduced as a direct consequence of the new possibilities created by digitisation.

Having situated the emergence of blockchain in the context of more general historical transformation in the organisation and operation of business, let's consider some recent real-world developments in which blockchain and smart contracts are deployed to offer something disruptive. The examples we discuss here are currently small-scale deployments of the technologies. Still, they represent an attempt to offer a different more decentralised alternative future for business and finance and are, therefore, of interest.

A. Reimagining the Firm: Decentralised Autonomous Organisations

Platform companies successfully decentralised the customer experience even if, ultimately, they have disappointed many of those who hoped they might transform the economy, more generally. However, the vision of a more decentralised future has inspired the emergence of the decentralised autonomous organisation (DAO).[44] DAOs are organisations that exist only in code, specifically smart

[44] See, eg WA Kaal, 'Decentralized Autonomous Organizations: Internal Governance and External Legal Design' (2020) University of St Thomas (Minnesota) Legal Studies Research Paper No 20-14,

contracts operating on a blockchain. DAOs are at the forefront of contemporary developments in decentralisation, as they operate without the traditional hierarchy and management layers associated with a centralised business organisation. Instead, a DAO runs on rules that are encoded in smart contracts.

The basic concept of a decentralised organisation can be traced back to 2013, when Daniel Larimer, CTO of EOS, published an article on cryptocurrencies. He suggested that a cryptocurrency could be thought of as equivalent to shares in a decentralised autonomous corporation (DAC) and the source code operates as the equivalent of the by-laws or Articles of Association. The goal is to make profits for the shareholders by offering some products or services to the market.[45] Vitalik Buterin – founder of the dominant smart contract platform, Ethereum – then picked up on this idea with three blog posts on DACs in *Bitcoin Magazine*.[46]

The first high-profile, real-world deployment of this DAC concept was by Christoph Jentzsch, the co-founder of Internet of Things company, Slock.it, in May 2016.[47] The idea was to set up a venture investment fund for the crypto space that did not use a conventional hierarchical corporate structures. Rather, it was built on the blockchain with smart contracts.[48] As such, it was a novel attempt to set up a corporate-type organisation without using a conventional corporate legal form. The underlying rationale was the belief that the crowd would make better investment decisions. The DAO was built on smart contracts programmed in Solidity and ran on the Ethereum's Virtual Machine (EVM). The code was open source with a democratised governance structure that was entirely on-chain, removing structures – management layers – that are traditionally used by principals in agency relationships to maintain control.[49]

More than 10,000 individuals contributed to the DAO's initial coin offering, raising in total around US$150 million. Funders obtained DAO tokens, which allowed them to vote on business decisions, notably which firms to finance and

available at papers.ssrn.com/sol3/papers.cfm?abstract_id=3652481; R Morrison, NCHL Mazey and SC Wingreen, 'The DAO Controversy: The Case for a New Species of Corporate Governance' (2020) 3 *Frontiers in Blockchain* 25.

[45] D Larimer, 'The Hidden Costs of Bitcoin' LTB Network (7 September 2013), available at letstalkbitcoin.com/is-bitcoin-overpaying-for-false-security.

[46] V Buterin, 'Bootstrapping A Decentralized Autonomous Corporation' *Bitcoin Magazine* (20 September 2013), available at bitcoinmagazine.com/articles/bootstrapping-a-decentralized-autonomous-corporation-part-i-1379644274.

[47] 'DAO Reflections and Slock.it with Christoph Jentzsch' *Software Engineering Daily* (23 March 2018), available at softwareengineeringdaily.com/2018/03/23/dao-reflections-and-slock-it-with-christoph-jentzsch; C Jentzsch, 'Christoph Jentzsch (TEDx Talks)' YouTube (9 January 2017), available at www.youtube.com/watch?v=EJrPW3254wg; C Jentzsch, 'The History of the DAO and Lessons Learned' *Slock.IT Blog* (25 August 2016), available at blog.slock.it/the-history-of-the-dao-and-lessons-learned-d06740f8cfa5.

[48] N Popper, 'A Venture Fund with Plenty of Virtual Capital, but No Capitalist' *New York Times* (21 May 2016), available at www.nytimes.com/2016/05/22/business/dealbook/crypto-ether-bitcoin-currency.html.

[49] C Jentzsch, 'Blessing and a Curse': The DAO's Developers on Blockchain in 2016' *CoinDesk* (27 December 2016), available at www.coindesk.com/blessing-and-a-curse-the-daos-developers-on-blockchain-in-2016.

other issues related to the governance of the company. This structure gave DAO members direct and real-time control over the allocation of contributed funds. DAO tokens were fully transferable on peer-to-peer exchanges, ie, a secondary market, similar to shares in a traditional listed corporation.

In this way, the governance of the DAO was not only automated but devoid of any hierarchy – it was completely decentralised by design. The DAO didn't have any directors, managers or employees, ie, the traditional corporate structures that mitigate agency risks. Moreover, the DAO didn't have a physical address or headquarters – it existed as open-source code. In this respect, the blockchain-based smart contract mimicked the role of Articles of Association or by-laws in traditional corporations. But, since the code of the DAO was open source, the token holders would request and vote on any change made to the code. And the openly readable ledger meant anyone could check the integrity of decisions and transactions, creating a high degree of transparency and accountability.

To be sure, flaws in the DAO code made it possible for hackers to transfer one-third of the total contributed funds to a subsidiary account. And these technological limitations meant the premature end of the experiment. Moreover, various legal issues also arose around the DAO. For example, the original DAO claimed to be a crowdfunding contract and made unregistered offers and sales of DAO tokens in exchange for Ether. However, the SEC launched an investigation and determined that, although the DAO claimed to be a crowdfunding contract, it did not meet the SEC's requirements for a crowdfunding exemption from securities laws.[50] Other legal risks raised by the DAO include applicable law (what law applies to an organisation that is not incorporated anywhere and has no office or representatives?), the liability of participants (is a DAO a partnership?), and third-party contractual liability.[51]

And yet, this experience was not the end of DAOs or the vision of a radically different style of business organisation and governance. As described in the previous section, the trend towards flatter, more open organisations is a feature of the most innovative businesses today, and, against this background, the prospects of DAO-like organisations remained attractive to many actors in the blockchain and crypto space. In January 2017, Jentzsch compared the development of decentralised business organisations with the development of planes. He continued to believe that the desire to build flat, unmediated and fully democratised companies could not be halted by some initial setbacks.[52] He announced his next project: a non-profit, charitable decentralised autonomous organisation.

DAO communities have proliferated in the aftermath of the original DAO hack and continue to innovate. Two trends can be identified. One has been to set up DAOs as fully legal companies and the second trend has been to persist with the original, extra-legal vision of the DAO. Here, we briefly consider each of these trends.

[50] Kaal, 'Decentralized Autonomous Organizations' (2020) 23.

[51] See generally M Finck, *Blockchain Regulation and Governance in Europe* (Cambridge, Cambridge University Press, 2018).

[52] Vermeulen, 'How to Organize Now for Success Tomorrow' (2017).

Overcoming legal risk has led to several DAO-related initiatives.[53] Of particular interest are so-called limited liability DAOs. Limited liability DAOs incorporate as a limited liability company (a so-called 'legal wrapper') to maintain control over membership and mitigate legal risk while retaining the 'on-chain' governance structures of the first generation DAO.[54]

The first limited liability DAO, Open Esquire, was organised in New York. This was developed as a hybrid organisation combining the advantages of being a fully compliant legal company with the 'private ordering benefits of Ethereum'.[55] In 2018, in order to incentivise such a business form, the US state of Vermont added a Blockchain-based Limited Liability Companies provision to state law. The second limited liability DAO, dOrg, launched in Vermont in June 2019.

Perhaps the most high-profile example of this type of second-generation DAO is the OpenLaw project. In September 2019, OpenLaw created the OpenLaw DAO, which was also set up as a traditional legal entity.[56] The LAO was established as a limited liability entity organised in Delaware in full compliance with company and securities laws. Again, smart contracts were used to handle governance mechanisms for voting and fund allocation. An Open Law protocol was created for entity formation and member agreements. The LAO thus provided a legal structure to enable members to give grants, invest in blockchain-based projects in exchange for tokenised stock or utility tokens. One significant – and possibly unfortunate – consequence of the legal wrapper is that the LAO is only available to accredited investors, ie, investors who met various threshold financial and other requirements under US Federal securities laws.[57]

The LAO operates as an investment fund – any Ethereum-based project can submit an application to pitch their company to the LAO members. If a member is interested in the project, they can put the project up for consideration by all members. If approved by a majority vote, the project will become a LAO company that will receive funding in the form of a convertible note or seed-stage-type investment.

Several similar schemes have followed. For example, MetaCartel Ventures is a DAO operating as a venture capital fund.[58] The stated aim of these initatives is to transform the commercial world by offering an alternative decision-making model for the governance of firms pooling and distributing capital for early-stage start-ups in the blockchain space.

[53] See, eg C Kim, 'New Interest in DAOs Prompts Old Question: Are They Legal?' Coindesk (29 September 2019), available at www.coindesk.com/new-interest-in-daos-prompts-old-question-are-they-legal.

[54] In addition to the developments discussed here, similar initiatives have occurred in Switzerland, see Kaal (n 44) 44–47.

[55] Kaal (n 44) 40.

[56] The LAO, 'The LAO: A For-Profit, Limited Liability Autonomous Organization' *Medium: Open Law* (2019), available at medium.com/openlawofficial/the-lao-a-for-profit-limited-liability-autonomous-organization-9eae89c9669c.

[57] On accredited investors and private equity markets, see M Fenwick and EPM Vermeulen, 'New Models of Intelligent Investing for the Post-Crisis Economy' (July–August 2020) *Ars Aequi* 708.

[58] G Shapiro, P 'Pet3rpan' and A Soleimani, MetaCartel Ventures White Paper, Version 1.0 (2019), available at github.com/metacartel/MCV/blob/master/Whitepaper.pdf.

The second recent trend for DAOs is to deploy them for various non-investment fund purposes, without the 'legal wrapper'. This can be seen as the continuation of the original, pure form of DAO.

For example, Metaclan is a gaming collective – 'a crypto-native e-sports DAO'.[59] The self-stated goal of Metaclan is to drive the adoption of blockchain-based gaming by 'showcasing the Play2Earn mechanics of various games in the form of quests'.[60] Each quest is created in partnership with gaming studios to reward new gamers and Metaclan members with cryptocurrency and NFT rewards. Metalan's first such quest was built in partnership with Axie Infinity, a Pokémon-like game with collectible monsters that can be created, battled and traded in an open market. Metaclan features a cryptocurrency and bank called the War Chest, which members access to high-quality items, go on raids, and deposit the spoils back in the War Chest.

Metaclan is built on the open-source code of Moloch, a development of the Ethereum blockchain that drives many of the decentralised games in this space. In Moloch, as with other funding-based models, members with shares can propose funding for tasks or ventures, and the community can vote on whether or not to allocate funds from a guild bank. If a member disagrees with the choices of the crowd, they retain the option of exit – so-called rage quitting. The funding for Metaclan was provided by another Moloch-based DAO, Metacartel, which is working on various consumer apps built on Ethereum.[61]

The result of these smart contract-driven developments is that new models of what it means to be a company are emerging. For sure, these technologies and initiatives are at an early stage. However, the business landscape is greatly enriched by these models and, given the increased anti-corporate mood, one should not dismiss their potential to influence the mainstream. Finally, they are further evidence of the contemporary, technology-driven trend towards flatter, more decentralised organisations.

B. Reimagining Financial Services: Decentralised Finance

The second area where smart contracts are driving more decentralised organisational forms and business models is DeFi – or decentralised finance.[62] DeFi has

[59] 'Introducing MetaClan' *Medium: MetaClan* (10 February 2020), available at medium.com/metaclan/introducing-metaclan-4d9e24b68aba.

[60] 'MetaClan Rises' *Medium: MetaClan* (27 April 2020), available at medium.com/metaclan/metaclan-rises-14cf2dad1b79.

[61] See Shapiro, 'Pet3rpan' and Soleimani (2019).

[62] For an introduction, see, eg Bitkom, *Decentralized Finance (DeFi): A New Fintech Revolution?* (Berlin, Federal Association for Information Technology, Telecommunications and New Media eV, 2020); Y Chen and C Bellavitis 'Blockchain Disruption and Decentralized Finance: The Rise of Decentralized Business Models' (2020) 13 *Journal of Business Venturing Insights* 151, available at www.researchgate.net/publication/337111343_Blockchain_Disruption_and_Decentralized_Finance_The_Rise_of_Decentralized_Business_Models; Financial Stability Board, *Decentralised Financial*

become a trending topic in the blockchain space since early 2019. In contrast to the decentralisation of money through Bitcoin, DeFi opts for a broader and more ambitious approach of decentralising traditional financial services across the board. The core of these initiatives is to open conventional financial services to everyone, by establishing a permissionless financial service ecosystem built on blockchain and smart contract infrastructure. As such, DeFi is an ambitious attempt to decentralise traditional financial use cases such as lending, investment, wealth management, payment and insurance.

DeFi is based on consumer-facing decentralised applications (so-called dApps). By running these dApps on a blockchain, DeFi creates a peer-to-peer financial network. dApps are built with multiple smart contracts (which function like Lego building blocks). More specifically, smart contracts run the back end of the application, notably the underlying business operations. However, not everything in the dApp runs on smart contracts. The front end – the user interface – still needs to be coded in some other language. As such, a dApp requires more functionality, which can't exclusively be done using smart contracts.

Although the DeFi movement is technology-neutral, it has emerged on blockchain platforms because of the easily programmable character of smart contracts and a large developer base. Today, most DeFi projects are being built on Ethereum, making it the default blockchain for many dApps. While it is hard to predict which protocols and platforms will get the most attention in the medium-to-long term, the flexibility and the enthusiastic developer base give Ethereum an advantage. DeFi projects now account for a significant slice of Ethereum activity.

Some examples of dApp use cases that illustrate the flexibility of this model, as well as the vitality of the DeFi space, include:

- DeFi crypto borrowing and lending tools facilitating peer-to-peer transactions outside the traditional financial system.[63]
- DeFi asset management tools and aggregators. These are tools designed to improve the user experience of finance by aggregating information from multiple sources and executing different transactions (payments, lending, borrowing, etc) across various platforms from a single dApp.[64]
- DeFi insurance tools. Tools for hedging smart contract risk in which members decide on the validity of claims, and every decision is recorded on a blockchain.[65]

Technologies: Report on Financial Stability, Regulatory and Governance Implications (Basel, Financial Stability Board, 2019); J John and L Lundy-Bryan, *Mapping Decentralized Finance* (London, Outlier Ventures, 2020); A Popescu, 'Decentralized Finance: The Lego of Finance' 7 *Social Sciences and Education Research Review* 314; F Schar, 'De-Centralized Finance: On Blockchain and Smart Contract-based Financial Markets' (2020), available at www.researchgate.net/publication/340061422.

[63] See, eg R Mitra, 'DeFi Use Cases: The Best Examples of Decentralised Finance' *Blockgeeks* (2020), available at blockgeeks.com/guides/defi-use-cases-the-best-examples-of-decentralised-finance.

[64] See, eg, 'Aggregration Theory Applied to DeFi' *Deribit Insights* (9 July 2020), available at insights.deribit.com/market-research/aggregation-theory-applied-to-defi.

[65] See, eg, H Karp and R Melbardis, Nexus Mutual White Paper, available at nexusmutual.io/assets/docs/nmx_white_paperv2_3.pdf.

- DeFi derivatives.[66] In the DeFi space, these are smart contracts that are linked to Bitcoin and major altcoins.
- DeFi oracle tools. Smart contracts cannot read off-chain data, so if parties need the price of Bitcoin or gold, for example, to perform the contract, it cannot be done from inside the smart contract. Oracles are trusted third parties that use different methods and tools to add that information to the smart contract (and create mechanisms for contractual parties to dispute it).[67]
- DeFi governance tools. These are firms focused on providing tools for more transparent and inclusive management and governance of DeFi firms, explicitly facilitating the transition to decentralised autonomous organisation.[68]
- DeFi platform tools. These are firms looking to rival Ethereum by offering multiple services, including a development and blockchain platform for deploying smart contracts and developing dApps.[69]

Advocates of DeFi point to several advantages over traditional financial service providers. From a user perspective, DeFi offers so-called censorship-resistant finance. This idea – which is frequently mentioned in the DeFi discussion – refers to the fact that while traditional financial institutions are in the hands of intermediaries, blockchain / smart contract / dApp-based DeFi is not owned by a single entity. As such, it is virtually impossible to tamper with (or censor) it. This non-custodial aspect means that individuals can interact with others without having to place trust in third parties (ie, incumbent financial service providers). As such, DeFi offers opportunities to access services that previously might have been limited or, at least, heavily regulated and controlled. And, given that DeFi operates on the blockchain, there is a much greater degree of transparency and accountability.

From a developer-founder perspective, anyone can build dApps using readily available software and other technologies. Since the technology is modular and coding in Solidity (the language of Ethereum) is relative easy (it is influenced by JavaScript, C++ and Python), it is possible to create something innovative, thus reducing the barriers to entry for new players.[70] The ease of integration with other protocols and between dApps is also unparalleled. This promise of better integration distinguishes the DeFi ecosystem from more traditional financial services, but also first-generation fintech firms, which have typically developed their organisation and services in siloes.

[66] See Mitra, 'DeFi Use Cases' (2020).

[67] See, eg Tellor Core, 'Tellor 101' *Medium* (27 November 2019), available at medium.com/tellor/tellor-101-28ba5fe4cc7a.

[68] See, eg W Foxley 'DeFi Lender Aaave Rolls out Governance Token on Path to Decentralization' *Coindesk* (29 July 2020), available at www.coindesk.com/defi-lender-aave-rolls-out-governance-token-on-path-to-decentralization.

[69] See, eg L Kelly, S Rothrie and P de Havilland, 'Who's Afraid of Ethereum: The Top 12 Smart Contract Platforms' *Crypto Briefing* (7 June 2020), available at cryptobriefing.com/whos-afraid-ethereum-top-12-smart-contract-platforms.

[70] See generally J Chriest, 'From Javascript to Solidity: A Beginners Dip into Solidity' *Medium: Coinmonks* (4 July 2018), available at medium.com/coinmonks/from-javascript-to-solidity-12317e8965de.

Finally, from a societal perspective, advocates believe that using blockchain technologies and smart contracts can create a financial system that is fairer and more inclusive and can make a contribution to a more sustainable model of social and economic development.[71]

Of course, there are critical voices and sceptics. In particular, there are concerns about the usability of DeFi and, as a consequence, the potential for dApps to scale beyond the current niche market. It is often suggested, even by leading figures in the DeFi movement, that there is a difficult trade-off to be made between decentralisation and usability. For example, the onboarding of new clients is demanding without an emphasis on usability. Yet, this may require some compromises to make a dApp appealing. This is a familiar dilemma for innovators – how to bridge traditional expectations with new technologies? But, the choices in the context of DeFi seem particularly difficult given the risks, on the one hand, and the ideological and technological commitment to decentralisation, on the other.

From a DeFi operator perspective, the biggest issue remains building and maintaining consumer trust. Users may well be convinced that smart contracts execute as programmed. However, they are still programmed by humans who are (inevitably) prone to mistakes. Moreover, gaining trust in a technology that embodies and aspires to trustlessness is clearly challenging for designers of these applications. Consumers often perceive trust differently, and any decision to trust is based on a diverse range of complex factors.

Research on user adoption of DeFi has highlighted how participants need to fundamentally believe in the viability of the crypto ecosystem to adopt dApps.[72] Also, a complex set of questions and trust attributes have been articulated by participants in the ecosystem. For example, reputation (ie, how long has the dApp been in operation and is it adequately insured and audited?); social proof (ie, what is the volume of trade and is the dApp backed by reputable companies?); transparency (ie, is the dApp non-custodial and is the code open source?); and, user proof (ie, has the user tried it and did the product work as promised in frictionless way?).

Finally, there are also concerns from some economists that a more decentralised financial system creates more systemic risks.[73]

Nevertheless, despite these more critical voices, the DeFi ecosystem expanded significantly post-2019. A common way to measure the growth of DeFi is to look at the amount of locked funds. Locked funds are the funds that consumers have trusted into smart contracts operating in DeFi dApps. An increasing amount of funds locked in DeFi over time represents growing confidence among users

[71] B Wigley and N Cary, *The Future is Decentralised* (New York, UN Development Programme, 2020).

[72] See Consensys (2020) Defi User Research Report, available at pages.consensys.net/codefi-def-user-research-report.

[73] D Perez, A Gervais and D Harz, 'The De-Centralized Financial Crisis: Attacking DeFi' *Researchgate* (2020), available at www.researchgate.net/publication/339374442.

to place their money in the hands of smart contracts to interact with these new financial tools. Significantly, DeFi gained headlines on 6 February 2020 when the US$ 1 billion of locked in funds was passed, and this figure has continued to rise.[74]

IV. Conclusion

This chapter is a preliminary attempt to locate the emergence of blockchain and smart contracts in a broader narrative of a historical trend towards more decentralised business forms. The first part of the chapter described this trend and the second part focused on some marginal – but nevertheless significant – contemporary deployments of smart contracts as further evidence in support of this trend. Clearly, fully-fledged decentralisation doesn't exist yet. But a trend towards more decentralisation and disintermediation in our economy, culture and society seems evident.

Nevertheless, big claims about a blockchain revolution should be treated with caution. These are still young technologies and finding the best application remains a challenge. And, as evidenced by other new technologies (eg, autonomous cars), 90 per cent of the work may be needed for the last 10 per cent of performance. Remarkable advances have been made in blockchain over recent years, even if the optimism of 2016/17 has dimmed somewhat. And achieving this final 10 per cent and bringing the technologies to the mainstream may require a different approach from what has previously been pursued. Nevertheless, as the big claims about smart contracts and blockchain fade away, local solutions to specific problems may usher in a more modest, but still far-reaching, transformation.

[74] E Muzzy, D Sui and B Gheorghe, 'The Q2 2020 DeFi Report: An Analysis of Ethereum's Decentralized Financial Ecosystem in Quarter 2 2020' (2020), available at f.hubspotusercontent10.net/hubfs/4795067/ConsenSys%20Q2%202020%20DeFi%20Report.pdf.

9

The Uncertain Future of Smart Contracts

MARCELO CORRALES COMPAGNUCCI,
MARK FENWICK AND STEFAN WRBKA

I. Introduction

In the context of the exponential growth of new technologies, any attempt to think about the future becomes enormously challenging. The conventional modern hope that we might learn from past experience and, by doing so, anticipate or otherwise predict future trends has faded due to the cognitive and normative uncertainties that surround today's technology.[1] As such, 'prediction' becomes much harder in an era of fast-paced, technology-driven economic, social and cultural changes. Things move so quickly, often in unknowable directions, leaving us incapable of even grasping the present, let alone identifying a trajectory that can form the basis for any reliable predictions about where we might be going.[2] In thinking about an indeterminate present and undecidable future, we need to combine imagination (everyone is now in the business of science fiction) with the realisation that our predictions are very likely to be proven wrong. Navigating the future is an exercise in managing various types and degrees of uncertainty.

Nevertheless, ongoing efforts to deepen our understanding of new technologies and their legal, social and cultural meaning remain significant. Writing about the future is less an exercise in genuine anticipation and more of a call for action. Not so much 'this is what I think will happen' and more 'this is what I want to happen'. Giving people the resources and capacities to discuss, construct and defend credible visions of possible futures becomes crucial.

By way of a conclusion, we, therefore, first review some of the ongoing uncertainties surrounding smart contracts and suggest that greater experimentation in regulatory design represents one legitimate response to these uncertainties. And,

[1] See, eg N Luhmann, *Observations on Modernity* (Paolo Alto CA, Stanford University Press, 1992) 44–62.

[2] S Arbesman, *Overcomplicated: Technology at the Limits of Comprehension* (New York, Portfolio, 2017) for an account of how technology is increasingly beyond the understanding of those individuals most familiar with its structure and operation.

since the future of smart contracts is so closely connected with the future of blockchain, we end with some reflections on the uncertain future of distributed ledger technologies, more generally.

II. The Future of Smart Contracts

Many uncertainties still surround smart contracts. Here, we focus on legal uncertainty by way of illustration, although ongoing technological uncertainties should also be noted, specifically security issues, digital signature issues, the lack of common technical standards, and the question of whether open-source or proprietary technologies are the best way forward.

As documented by several authors in this volume, the legal system looks to traditional legal requirements to determine whether a smart contract is enforceable. It seems clear that these requirements can be satisfied in the case of many smart contracts. Although some types of contract need to be in writing, most agreements do not need to take any specific form (eg, a formal, written agreement) to be legally enforceable. Thus, many code-based agreements are valid, subject to general contractual rules. However, the widespread adoption of smart contracts still faces several legal difficulties. Below we briefly describe five uncertainties that have been identified in earlier chapters.

A. Understanding Coded Terms

If a contract is partly expressed in code, then the understanding of that code by the parties becomes relevant. Parties to an agreement (particularly non-experts, such as consumers) may not be bound by those terms which they do not understand or there may not be sufficient mutual understanding of the terms of the agreement to form a contract at all. This seems to be a particularly pressing concern in the context of B2C deployment of smart contracts.

A key challenge in the widespread adoption of smart contracts, therefore, is that parties may need to rely on a third party to either capture the parties' agreement in code or confirm that code written by a third party is accurate. This can be compared to the hiring of a lawyer to explain the legalese of paper-based contracts. A more sceptical view would be to argue that whereas non-lawyers can typically understand key provisions, especially those setting forth business terms, a non-programmer would not understand any aspect of even a simple smart contract. Consequently, parties relying on smart contracts may need to draft a separate term sheet stating how and what the smart contract should do, which could be provided to the programmer. The parties may also want written representations from the programmer that the code will perform as stated. In the absence of widely used templates, the parties would need to enter into a separate written agreement with the smart contract programmer.

B. Off-Chain Resources

Many smart contracts require information that is not stored on the blockchain itself – so-called off-chain resources. For example, imagine an insurance contract that pays out if a flight is delayed by more than two hours and that information is not on the blockchain. In such a case, the parties will need a so-called oracle. Oracles are trusted third parties that gather off-chain information and then 'push' that information to the blockchain. In the previous example, the oracle would monitor flight delays, add information about any such delay to the blockchain, and the contract would then automatically pay out. Oracles are a solution to utilising off-chain resources, but this process adds another party with whom the parties may need to contract. This can detract from the benefits of smart contracts and creates additional risks. For example, an oracle might experience a system flaw and be unable to push out the necessary information, provide erroneous data, or simply go out of business. Smart contracts will need to account for and mitigate these additional risks.

C. Amending Automated Agreements

One of the advantages of code-only smart contracts is their ability to automatically execute transactions without the need for human intervention. However, this automation, and the fact that smart contracts cannot easily be amended or terminated unless the parties incorporate such capabilities during the creation of the smart contract, creates further challenges. For example, with ordinary language contracts, a party can excuse a breach simply by not enforcing penalties. If an essential or longstanding customer is late with a payment, for example, the counterparty can (rationally) decide that preserving the relationship is more important than any available termination right. However, if there is a smart contract, the option not to enforce the agreement may not exist. A late payment, for example, might result in the automatic payment of a penalty charge from the customer's account or the termination of a customer's usage of an Internet of Things-connected device. The automated character of smart contracts might not align with the more flexible way many businesses operate in the real world and integrating such flexibility would create technical challenges and a reduction in the benefits of smart contracts.

D. Collateral Legal Issues

Smart contracts inevitably raise complex legal issues in related fields of information law, most obviously data protection and privacy, as discussed in this volume. Moreover, given the diverse range of use cases of smart contracts in areas like company law (eg, decentralised autonomous organisations) and financial law (decentralised finance), these collateral legal effects are further complicated, raising the need for greater coordination and harmonisation between fields of law that might in the past have operated more independently. In addition, the transaction costs of designing smart contracts are significantly increased by the need to incorporate more fields of law.

E. Electronic Agents

As artificial intelligence develops, questions will inevitably arise about the legal capacities of electronic agents. The laws of most jurisdictions do not yet explicitly address electronic agents, ie, can a contract be formed through the interaction of electronic agents, on the presumption that natural persons intended to create a legally binding contract? A second possible use case would involve interactions between an electronic agent and a natural person. Designing rules that might allow electronic agents to be involved in transactions without revoking the legal validity also raises several issues.

In short, smart contracts have enormous potential to revolutionise contracting, particularly in commercial settings, and current contract law seems robust enough to deal with many of the issues surrounding the enforceability of such agreements. However, there are still some important legal issues that need to be resolved.

Writing in the 1980s, Gunther Teubner famously identified a 'regulatory trilemma' facing all regulators in the context of late capitalism. Broadly speaking, Teubner argued that any regulatory intervention faces three types of risk:[3] the risk of the regulatory action not working (ie, the regulation misses the target or is otherwise ineffective); the risk of breaking the thing it seeks to regulate (ie the regulation removes any incentive to engage in the activity that is being regulated); and the risk of undermining the law (ie, the regulation undermines the doctrinal integrity of the law and legal system, more generally). The 'trilemma' that Teubner described can be reformulated as a question: How can we ensure that any regulatory intervention is effective, responsive *and* legally coherent?

This seems to be a particularly pressing problem in the context of smart contracts. It is important that any regulatory action is effective – that consumer interests are adequately protected. Moreover, it is important that regulation is not overly burdensome and kills innovation, leading to the non-usage of smart contracts and a possible an exodus of start-ups and talent to other jurisdictions that offer a friendlier regulatory environment. Finally, regulation needs to be consistent with other features of the legal system and the existing capacities, know-how, and experience of regulators.

In tackling these issues, one possible approach is greater experimentation in regulatory design. In an age of constant, complex and disruptive technological innovation, such as smart contracts, knowing what, when and how to structure

[3] G Teubner, *Dilemmas of Law in the Welfare State* (London, De Gruyter, 1986).

regulatory interventions has become much more difficult.[4] Regulators can find themselves in a situation where they believe they must opt for either reckless action (regulation without sufficient information) or paralysis (doing nothing). Inevitably in such cases, caution tends to triumph over risk. But such caution merely functions to reinforce the status quo. The result is that new technologies may struggle to reach the market in a timely or efficient manner.

One response to this predicament that has been explored in many jurisdictions over the last decade is to recognise the need for greater policy experimentation.[5] For example, in April 2016, the UK Financial Conduct Authority (FCA) announced the introduction of a so-called regulatory sandbox. This scheme allowed both start-ups and established financial service providers to roll out and test new ideas, products and business models in the area of Fintech (ie, new technologies, many of which are blockchain-based, aimed at making financial services, ranging from online lending to digital currencies).

The aim of the initiative was to create a safe space in which businesses could test innovative products, services, business models and delivery mechanisms without immediately incurring all the normal regulatory consequences of engaging in the activity in question. In practice, this means that relevant rules and regulations do not apply to a particular class of new services, ie, firms apply for an individualised suspension of the standard rules. Within the sandbox, the regulator aims to foster innovation by lowering regulatory barriers and costs for testing disruptive innovative technologies, while ensuring – via a vetting process – that consumers will not be negatively affected. In exchange, the regulator then receives data from the firm allowing better informed regulatory design.

On the other hand, however, one might argue that regulatory sandboxes create a two-tier system of start-ups. Those selected in the sandbox are given an unfair advantage over those that are not. Arguably, the most significant tangible benefits to sandbox firms are the contacts with the regulator and the credibility that the participation in the regulator's sandbox gives them vis-à-vis customers and financiers.

The credibility gains, as well as the lighter regulatory requirements, could undoubtedly prove advantageous. One might also question if regulators have the necessary capacities to determine whether a business concept is innovative. Rather than simply copying the model of corporate innovation accelerators, regulators may instead want to engage in a more open dialogue with all (or at least a broader group) of start-ups that need assistance navigating the complex web of regulatory requirements. This could be achieved through innovation hubs that are essentially schemes set up by competent authorities to enable firms to engage with the

[4] See generally M Fenwick, WA Kaal and EPM Vermeulen, 'Regulation Tomorrow: What Happens When Technology is Faster than the Law' (2018) 6 *American University Business Law Review* 561, 561–63.

[5] ibid.

authorities on Fintech-related issues and seek clarification on licensing and regulatory requirements.

The regulatory sandbox model has proved attractive, with many other jurisdictions adopting such an approach.[6] As different countries compete to attract innovative start-ups, the issue of the regulatory environment becomes an increasingly important consideration. After all, the regulatory situation will be a crucial consideration for any firm when deciding its home base. In a technology-driven, global economy, those jurisdictions that fail to engage with new technologies or adopt rules and regulations attractive to founder-innovators risk being left behind.

A key element of such regulatory experimentation is a recognition that incumbent companies, start-ups, governments and other stakeholders, including consumers, must work together in partnership to ensure that vital interests are protected while facilitating innovation. Regulators must acknowledge the informational asymmetries that exist between the public and private sectors and build new collaborative relationships with actors in the private sector to close this gap. There needs to greater outsourcing of legal work and cooperation with public–private partnering to create new technologies, such as blockchain.

Of course, national governments and other regulators must set smart boundaries for the risk they are willing to take that are agreed with regulated entities. However, within these boundaries, they must allow and encourage freedom and innovation. This does not mean that within these boundaries, a free-for-all should be tolerated. Instead, within carefully negotiated limits, it is all about building and maintaining trust amongst all participants via constant dialogue and sharing of information. In this respect, trust must be earned from all the stakeholders involved and affected by new technologies.

As such, community-driven regulatory design is a version of policy experimentation. The crucial factor here is the changing context. In the context of the digital revolution and the new pressures it has created, there is a unique degree of openness and visibility both within society in general and within the emerging ecosystems. A check on regulatory capture is the new visibility that digital technologies have created and the dependency that open ecosystems have on remaining committed to the values of a free, open digital culture. If the check on power is visibility, transparency and the demand for authenticity, then the key to ensuring these values are maintained are those infrastructures that facilitate speech, such as social media.

In the context of smart contracts, there is evidence of some regulatory innovation. In 2017, the US state of Arizona, for example, passed legislation allowing the use of smart contracts in commercial transactions and precluding a contract from being denied legal effect because a contract contains a smart contract term.[7]

[6] See M Fenwick, S Van Uytsel and Ying B (eds), *Regulating Fintech in Asia: Global Context, Local Perspectives* (Singapore, Springer, 2020).

[7] SH Kimpel and C Adcock, 'The State of Smart Contract Legislation' Hunton Andrews Kurth (5 September 2018), available at www.blockchainlegalresource.com/2018/09/state-smart-contract-legislation/#:~:text=Arizona%20led%20the%20way%20in,contains%20a%20smart%20contract%20term.

Several other states followed, including California, New York and Texas.[8] In 2018, the US state of Vermont added a Blockchain-Based Limited Liability Companies provision to its law, allowing the creation of a smart contract-driven decentralised autonomous organisation.[9] A similar development has occurred in Switzerland.[10] A final example of such experimentation, the Channel Island of Guernsey introduced legal provisions that allowed the formation of a contract through the interaction of electronic agents.[11]

III. The Future of Blockchain

Advocates of blockchain believe that decentralised ledger technologies can address some of the most pressing problems of a digital age. Most obviously, the massive concentration of economic power in large technology companies such as Amazon, Apple, Facebook, Google, etc. Advocates think that this and other problems are best addressed with more and better technologies, rather than through more regulation or state intervention. And, in the most potent version of this story, the claim is that blockchain have the potential to transform capitalism and herald in a more sustainable, egalitarian and decentralised future.[12]

It is easy to be sceptical in the face of the idealism surrounding blockchain and related technologies, such as smart contracts. After all, this narrative cuts against our experience of previous disruptive technologies.[13] New technologies often start in the hands of the dreamers motivated by the dream to make the world better (the Apple of Steve Wozniak). But such an idealistic spirit rarely lasts, and successful technologies ultimately end up in the hands of corporations driven by the desire to maximise profits, market share and return on investment (the Apple of Steve Jobs). According to this view, the digital revolution is just another chapter in a much longer history of the failure to make technology work for all. Besides, the technology giants of a digital age are now amongst the largest

[8] C Adcock, 'An Update on Smart Contract Legislation' *The National Law Review* (15 April 2020), available at www.natlawreview.com/article/update-state-smart-contract-legislation#:~:text=Several%20states%20have%20passed%20or,permitting%20the%20use%20of%20related.

[9] See, eg WA Kaal, 'Decentralized Autonomous Organizations: Internal Governance and External Legal Design' (2020) *University of St Thomas (Minnesota) Legal Studies Research Paper No 20-14*, 41–44, available at papers.ssrn.com/sol3/papers.cfm?abstract_id=3652481.

[10] ibid 47.

[11] B Rees, 'Innovative New Law Opens Up Guernsey to Artificial Intelligence' Ogier (18 July 2019), available at www.ogier.com/publications/innovative-new-law-opens-guernsey-up-to-ai#:~:text=The%20newly%20enacted%20Electronic%20Transactions,for%20future%20development%20in%20many.

[12] See, eg D Tapscott and S Tapscott, *Blockchain Revolution: How the Technology Behind Bitcoin is Changing Money Business, and the World* (New York, Portfolio, 2016).

[13] See, eg C Perez, *Technological Revolutions & Financial Capital: The Dynamics of Bubbles and Golden Ages* (Cheltenham, Edward Elgar, 2002); T Wu, *The Master Switch: The Rise and Fall of Information Empires* (New York, Vintage, 2010).

companies that have ever existed and there is an ever-increasing inequality in wealth distribution.[14]

So, everything we know about the history of technology should make us treat claims about the transformative potential of blockchain and smart contracts with some caution – the potential of distributed ledgers can be difficult to see through all the hyperbole that surrounds the Blockchain Revolution.[15]

It is unfortunate, for instance, that blockchain technology attracted opportunists keen to make a quick profit. The result? A series of ICO scams and other scandals between 2017 and 2019 that discredited the technology in many people's eyes before it had any real-world impact on peoples' everyday lives. But, once the blockchain hype has faded, and the opportunists moved on to the next big thing, will these technologies be able to deliver? Or, are the sceptics right when they suggest that this is just the latest example of another technology-driven bubble? What is the future of blockchain?

In answering these questions, it is helpful to consider our recent experience of digital technologies and the currently dominant technology firms. The Internet today comprises two connected but distinct layers. Firstly, there are a series of open-source protocols, such as HTTP, GPS, IMAP, POP, SMPT, etc, that first allowed computers to communicate with one another across global networks and which still provide the basic infrastructure of the system. The essential characteristic of such protocols is that no one owns them, and anyone can use them free of charge. There is no licence fee involved in using HTTP to set up a web page, or in using SMTP to send an email, or GPS to identify a location.

Secondly, there is the web-based layer, which emerged later, and which sits on top of the protocols providing various services. Think Amazon, Facebook, Google, Twitter. This layer is operated by profit-seeking businesses that – in contrast to the authors of the protocols – have sought to maintain tight control over services and operations. As such, the history of the Internet can be told as a story of a shift in power from the open protocol idealism of the early years to the closed, centralised, corporations that dominate today.[16]

Many of the companies operating on this second layer provide a coordination function between two or more groups of users. This business model is usually described as a platform.[17] Some platforms facilitate connections between the buyer and seller of goods (eBay, Amazon, Alibaba); some facilitate connections between those wanting a service and those willing to provide it (Uber, Airbnb). Others

[14] See generally S Galloway, *The Four: The Hidden DNA of Amazon, Apple, Facebook, and Google* (New York, Penguin, 2018).

[15] Tapscott and Tapscott, *Blockchain Revolution* (2016).

[16] W Craig, '15 Biggest Internet Controversies of the Past Decade' *FX Blog* (2018), available at www.webfx.com/blog/web-design/15-biggest-internet-controversies-of-the-past-decade.

[17] See generally GG Parker, MW Van Alsyne and SP Choudry, *Platform Revolution: How Networked Markets are Transforming the Economy and How to Make them Work for You* (New York, Norton, 2016); A Moazed and NJ Johnson, *Modern Monopolies: What it Takes to Dominate the Twenty First Century Economy* (London, St Martin's Press, 2016).

simply facilitate connections (information exchange) between friends (Facebook), content creators and consumers (You Tube, Medium, Netflix), or app developers and users (Google, Apple). However, what is common to all platforms is that they coordinate connections between two groups: the creators and the extractors of value. The platform then generates a profit from making these connections, either by taking a commission or through the sale of advertising.

The emergence of platforms is an important event because they have become a common feature of everyday life within such a short period. To illustrate this, consider that it took the radio 38 years to reach 50 million users. It took television 13 years to achieve the same degree of market penetration. But Facebook took only two years to gain the same number of users. Now, it has an active user base of over two billion.[18] As of the summer of 2020, five of the world's six most valuable firms were built around a platform or, at least, have a platform as a core element of their business.[19]

What is also clear, however, is that as platforms have scaled, they have struggled to maintain their initial promise. Platforms that were once disruptive have lost much of their initial appeal. In 1998, Google was founded as an exciting young company with a unique motto: 'Don't Be Evil'. Over two decades later, many people now believe that this slogan is, at best, an afterthought. It is indeed hard to ignore the problems experienced and created by platforms – there are too many examples of well-known platforms abusing their position.[20]

If we accept this version of the digital transformation, how should we respond? Again, there are competing views. Some claim that our only hope is to resort to the Leviathan (the nation-state or regional organisations, such as the EU) to rein in these corporate giants through more and better regulation.[21] Think anti-trust laws, data protection laws, or laws controlling online speech. According to this line of thinking, we cannot fix the problems with more technology.

Advocates of the blockchain, however, take a different view. These are not problems that can easily be tackled by smarter regulation. The power and reach of the Internet giants are just too great for any law to be meaningful or useful. The size of many platforms makes them mainly immune to state action, as a result of the massive information asymmetries that now exist between public and private actors.[22] Instead, advocates of distributed ledgers emphasise the importance of

[18] T Aeppel, '50 Million Users' *Wall Street Journal* (20 March 2015), available at blogs.wsj.com/economics/2015/03/20/50-million-users-the-making-of-an-angry-birds-internet-meme.

[19] DB Yofie, A Gawer and M Cusumano, 'A Study of 250 Platforms Reveals Why Most Fail' *Harvard Business Review* (May 2019), available at hbr.org/2019/05/a-study-of-more-than-250-platforms-reveals-why-most-fail.

[20] Galloway, *The Four* (2018).

[21] ibid.

[22] See generally M Fenwick, JA McCahery and EPM Vermeulen, 'The End of "Corporate" Governance: Hello "Platform" Governance' (2018) 20 *European Business Organization Law Review* 171; M Fenwick and EPM Vermeulen, 'A Sustainable Platform Economy & the Future of Corporate Governance' (2019) European Corporate Governance Institute Law Working Paper No 441/2019, available at doi.org/10.2139/ssrn.3331508.

technology-based alternatives to provide us with the direction to build something different. This is a view that needs to be taken seriously, and it is in this context that we need to think about the emergence of distributed ledger technologies, such as blockchain, and smart contracts.

The essential claim of the advocates of the technologies is that distributed ledger technologies can bring about a transformation to a better world. To understand why and how it is helpful to go back to the origins of blockchain and the Bitcoin whitepaper by Satoshi Nakamoto.[23] In this first statement, Nakamoto proposed a system for a digital currency that did not require a centralised, trusted authority to verify transactions.

Two key elements characterise the general approach. Firstly, a database is distributed across many computers, with no single authority controlling and verifying the authenticity of the data. Secondly, the work of maintaining the database – what we now refer to as 'mining' – is rewarded with small payments, in the form of tokens. If you use a part of your computer's power to maintain the integrity of the database, you receive a reward in the form of tokens that can then be used to 'buy' services or sold to third parties. These tokens grow increasingly difficult to earn over time, ensuring enough scarcity in the system. If you helped at the beginning (and helped the database to develop), you would receive a larger reward, thus incentivising early adoption.

Advocates believe that this combination of features is game-changing.[24] They provide a way of agreeing on the contents of a database without anyone being in charge of, owning or otherwise controlling that database. Moreover, they create a mechanism for rewarding people that made the database more valuable, but – crucially – without those people being paid by the owner-controller of that database or owning shares in the corporation that controls the database. Nakamoto provided a new model for supporting open protocols that was not available when the first tech giants emerged.

How then might this technology have the potential to transform capitalism, and how is it connected to the protocol layer of the Internet described above? A comparison with Airbnb can be used to illustrate the possibilities of a distributed ledger model. A new open protocol could be created that contains a request: 'I would like a room in PLACE between DATES'. A decentralised blockchain database might then record the data of all users, such as personal information, past trips, credit card details, preferences and user and host rankings. The protocol for transmitting this request out onto the Internet would be completely open. Anyone (individuals, private companies, public authorities) who wanted to develop an app for responding to such requests would then be free to do so.

[23] S Nakamoto, 'Bitcoin: A Peer-to-Peer Electronic Cash System' (2008), available atbitcoin.org/bitcoin.pdf.

[24] S Johnson, 'Beyond the Bitcoin Bubble' *New York Times Magazine* (16 January 2018), available at www.nytimes.com/2018/01/16/magazine/beyond-the-bitcoin-bubble.html.

In this model, when you transmit your bid, you would not need to commit to a single provider (as you do now with Airbnb). Still, you would instead be free to announce your wishes to the world via the secure protocol and wait for competing offers from diverse providers of accommodation, ranging from anyone with a spare room though to large multinational hotel companies.

Tokens would be vital in allowing such a protocol to develop and scale. Early adopters would be rewarded with tokens that they could then use to either buy accommodation services themselves or sell on an exchange for real-world currencies. Moreover, early adopters (app developers, providers of accommodation, etc) would receive a proportionately larger share of tokens for entering and helping to develop the new ecosystem. As the protocol developed, it would then attract outside investors, which would give the token a greater monetary value that, in turn, would encourage more participation, resulting in positive network effects.

Critics might argue that one company or group of companies might monopolise the new protocol, in the same way that the tech giants of today dominate various sectors of the Internet economy. Indeed, fully fledged decentralised blockchain networks do not exist yet. Consider the technical and operational shortcomings of the Bitcoin blockchain. In discussions with mathematicians and other technologists, several weaknesses are identified. For example, Bitcoin's proof of work protocol has led to mining pools because of economies of scale and unbalanced reward structures. The anonymity in the blockchain network means that it is prone to Sybil and 51% attacks.

Still, there are advantages in an open-source plus decentralised database model that makes such a process of 'cartelisation' less likely. For a start, it would not present the same opportunities for abuse and manipulation that you find in the centralised systems of Amazon, Facebook, YouTube, etc. If a particular service provider did something that a user did not like, it would be much easier to switch to an alternative service provider. The user's information would not be retained by the service provider on a centralised database, but a decentralised, open-source database connected to the protocol. As such, open standard would have a disciplining effect on platform operators, as it would facilitate a level of migration (to other providers or simply opting out altogether) that is impossible today with centralised systems.

Tokens might also give a blockchain-based open protocol several advantages. It would provide an infrastructure to reward content creators. This seems preferable to the current situation on many platforms – mostly social media platforms – where most content providers act without compensation or, at least, compensation is tilted towards a minority of creators and it is the platform companies that receive all the economic value of that content via the sale of advertising.

Finally, there are the potential security gains of a decentralised network. Would our personal information or transactions be more secure in a distributed blockchain than behind the elaborate security mechanisms of giant corporations like Google or Facebook? An openly readable ledger means anyone can check the integrity of transactions. The distributed cooperation component implies that 'attackers' must out-compute the entire network (which is practically impossible).

A more decentralised reality has already started to emerge. And, trust in large, centralised corporations has already declined (mainly due to the concentration of power, wealth and information), and distributed ledger technologies, including blockchain, are viewed by many as offering an alternative model. These technologies can create a more level playing field, greater transparency and applications that run precisely as programmed without any possibility of downtime, censorship, fraud or third-party interference. This new relationship with digital technology also makes it possible to have peer-to-peer connections, communications, interactions and transactions. The looser (digital) connections and interactions are faster and more comfortable than the old formal ways of making fixed appointments and ritualised meetings. The Millennial generation, in particular, appears to value this.[25]

Nevertheless, many commentators still consider blockchain-based technologies and smart contracts to be a fad or just hype, at least in terms of the usefulness in real-world settings. According to this more sceptical view, the hype has been fuelled by numerous tech firms, particularly in the area of cryptocurrency and ICOs. Such firms often have over-promised and under-delivered, feeding doubts about the underlying technology of blockchain. And, for sure, challenges do remain. Blockchains still have significant technical, operational and scaling shortcomings. For instance, the traditional mechanism for validating and verifying a new block of transactions – eg, Bitcoin's proof of work protocol – has led to mining pools due to economies of scale and unbalanced reward structures.

There are also security concerns. Recall that in a decentralised system deploying smart contracts, the code really is the law. This means that any weaknesses or mistakes (stolen/lost passwords, programming bugs, etc) are permanent and expose that blockchain to security risks – supporters of blockchain claim that it is secure by design. Still, the technology has not been adopted widely enough yet for it to be severely tested. Several hacking attacks against digital currencies and other blockchain-based systems underscore such security concerns.

Moreover, the use of cryptocurrencies by criminal organisations has damaged the credibility of the underlying technology. And then there are the costs of shifting to the new technology, which is continually evolving, and which are also high – not to mention the many technical challenges involved in integrating blockchain databases with existing systems. Recall the car loan contract example and the need for a sophisticated and reliable interface between the ledger recording repayments and the car software systems that, under certain circumstances (non-payment) will shut down the vehicle. Finally, there is a great deal of regulatory uncertainty surrounding blockchain, especially in the financial services industry.[26]

[25] See generally Pew Research, (2010) 'Millennials: A Portrait of a Generation Next', available at www.pewresearch.org/wp-content/uploads/sites/3/2010/10/millennials-confident-connected-open-to-change.pdf.

[26] P de Filippi and A Wright, *Blockchain and the Law: The Rule of Code* (Cambridge, MA, Harvard University Press, 2018).

Despite these difficulties, however, there is widespread interest in blockchain and business-related initiatives considering blockchain. The fact that so many 'old world' organisations, as well as younger start-ups, are exploring possible uses of blockchain, as well as smart contracts is, at least, suggestive that it is not all just hype and that something interesting is happening. In addition, many projects are exploring more out-of-the-box experiments in decentralisation that utilise blockchain to create a radically different business model or form of business organisation.

We currently live in a fast-developing space between two co-existing worlds: a centralised 'old world' of hierarchical and siloed organisations; and an emerging, flatter, more decentralised world. The centralised world with its hierarchical structures, systems and procedures still prevails, and it appears unlikely that we will say goodbye to such organisations anytime soon. Traditional organisations still enjoy enormous power, and the success of more decentralised systems depends on the capacities and enthusiasm of the parties involved. Nevertheless, a more decentralised world has already started to emerge, much of which is connected with blockchain.

INDEX

www.ingramcontent.com/pod-product-compliance
Lightning Source LLC
Chambersburg PA
CBHW071257180926
51613CB00001B/54
* 9 7 8 1 5 0 9 9 3 7 0 2 8 *